SO-BNI-736

Water damage
noted
TWPP
12-20-19

WHEELS
AND
LOOMS

Twinsburg Library
Twinsburg, Ohio

WHEELS AND LOOMS

Making equipment for spinning and weaving

David Bryant

B.T. Batsford Ltd
London

To Valerie

© David Bryant 1987
First published 1987

All rights reserved. No part of this publication
may be reproduced, in any form or by any means,
without permission from the Publisher

ISBN 0 7134 4828 8

Typeset by Servis Filmsetting Ltd, Manchester
and printed in Great Britain by
The Bath Press Ltd, Bath, Somerset
for the publishers
B.T. Batsford Ltd
4 Fitzhardinge Street
London W1H 0AH

CONTENTS

ACKNOWLEDGMENTS

I should like to express my sincere thanks to all those who offered their help and guidance during the preparation of this book. In particular, Joan Lawler of Tynsell Handspinners for supplying the carding cloth for the design of the handcarders; Helmshore Local History Society owners of the great wheel for permission to measure and photograph this; Alan Mitchell, editor of *Practical Woodworking* for permission to use extracts of a Hebridean spinning wheel article, and Marion Derrick for allowing me to take photographs of this item; Mr Van Riemsdikt, Science Museum, London for permission to take measurements of the Arkwright spinning wheel; Shirley Dawson for allowing me to take measurements of the spinning stool design; Roy Hilton for providing the photograph of the four shaft loom. I also owe special thanks to Gil Osorio for cross checking the manuscript and technical details of the weaving section and offering many valuable comments.

Finally thanks go to my wife for checking the manuscript, offering comments on the spinning section and practical advice, and also for the patience, help and encouragement needed to complete the task.

PREFACE

The origins of this book started off some years ago, sparked by an interest in spinning and weaving, and in particular the design and construction of the equipment for this craft. Initially the reproduction of an antique hoop rimmed spinning wheel was attempted. At the time only an old metalwork lathe was available, and whilst it ran a bit slow for woodturning, with an adapted tool rest a quite passable result was achieved. The shortage of designs soon prompted me to produce my own, expand the range, and advance also into loom design.

This book of designs is divided into two parts, spinning and weaving, and the collection covers a wide range of equipment which over the years has undergone gradual improvement and refinement. They are presented in order of chronological and technological development, from the spinning spindle to the flyer spinning wheel, and from the tabby loom to the foot power loom. There are designs also for the supporting accessories such as carders and warping equipment.

A useful background to the understanding of spinning and weaving equipment is the design evolution aspect, and this is discussed often as an introduction to the constructional details. Also included are some notes on the use of the equipment; these are not in depth, but are sufficient for the beginner, who can then follow up this aspect in specialist publications, if desired. Where there are points of difficulty, or particular techniques in construction, these have been expanded on and discussed in some detail in the appropriate chapter.

With regard to the working drawings, the following notes on the standards and conventions used will be of assistance to the reader. First the drawings are generally metric, with dimensions in millimetres unless otherwise stated (this also applies to the tables). For the benefit of those perhaps not familiar with these, imperial dimensions are given in brackets adjacent to each metric figure. These are in inches (in) unless otherwise stated. The imperial equivalents are more or less exact, depending on the degree of minute correctness necessary. Another symbol used on the drawings which may not be familiar to all is the notation 0; this is the international symbol for diameter. With regard to the parts lists given, where turned items are concerned the dimensions generally include a small allowance for waste on diameter and length. Where straight timber items are involved, no cutting allowances have been added, and the reader may need to make suitable adjustments before ordering the wood.

One of the most satisfying things about building wheels and looms is that it is a craft within a craft. The basic skill of woodwork is needed to construct them, but when finished they lead directly into the textile world of spinning and weaving. Making a spinning wheel, in particular, is not so much a test in woodturning, but more a challenge in the accurate assembly of the machined parts to produce a piece of equipment which will spin a thread. Looms, by contrast, are generally easier to build, being for the most part composed of straight section timber. Many people build wheels and looms for the satisfaction and achievement of making a working product, but the question of cost should not be dismissed. Commercial equipment is available, but the expense may necessitate a compromise on choice. Making your own equipment helps to remove this restriction, and the material cost is much reduced.

Finally, this book is an attempt to fill a much needed gap in spinning wheel and loom design, and a reference book on their construction.

David Bryant Knutsford

1
SPINDLES

INTRODUCTION

Woven materials found on mummies in Egyptian tombs of thousands of years ago show that man knew how to spin the threads for cloth at this time. The earliest known device for doing this is the spinning spindle. It is the very basis, indeed the origin of all spinning, and so it is appropriate in this book of designs of spinning and weaving equipment to begin with this item. Three spindle designs are offered; however, before outlining the details and measurements, let us look at the principle, and at their probable development from the Stone Age.

Prehistoric man, perhaps by experimenting in twisting and extending wool fibres together by hand, found that these would interlock and form a simple thread. No doubt the first trials gave rather rough coarse yarns. Perhaps he collected this up onto a short stick, and then, accidentally dropping it, but still holding the thread end, watched the yarn unravel. Wondering if this twisting of the stick could be used to produce a more even thread than by hand, and investigating further, he discovered that by the addition of a lump of clay, or a small stone, the twig, suspended from the thread at one end, could be made to spin in a more regular manner, sustaining its momentum. This helped to put the twist into the wool fibres as they were drawn down by hand. The device was later called a *spinning spindle* (*Fig. 1.1*), and using it man found that a very acceptable thread could be produced. Our museums have many examples of ancient spindles, and it is from these that the development of the spinning wheel, and more recent industrial mechanisation for yarn production, has since evolved.

Today, handspinners still use the drop spindle, especially for teaching students the principles, and before advancing onto the flyer spinning wheel. Spinning spindles are easy to make, and fig. 1.2

Fig. 1.1 Ancient spinning spindle

shows three that the reader can construct, giving the dimensional information.

SPINDLE 1

Spindle 1 is the simplest to build, consisting of a 10mm (⅜in) diameter wood dowel fixed through an 80mm (3⅛in) diameter wood disc. The latter is woodturned on a mandrel fixed to the lathe headstock (*Fig. 1.3*). To mount the wood disc on the mandrel, it is pre-drilled to the dowel size using a flat auger. A slightly undersize drill is ideal for this purpose, so that when the disc is pushed onto the

Fig. 1.2 Spinning spindle dimensions

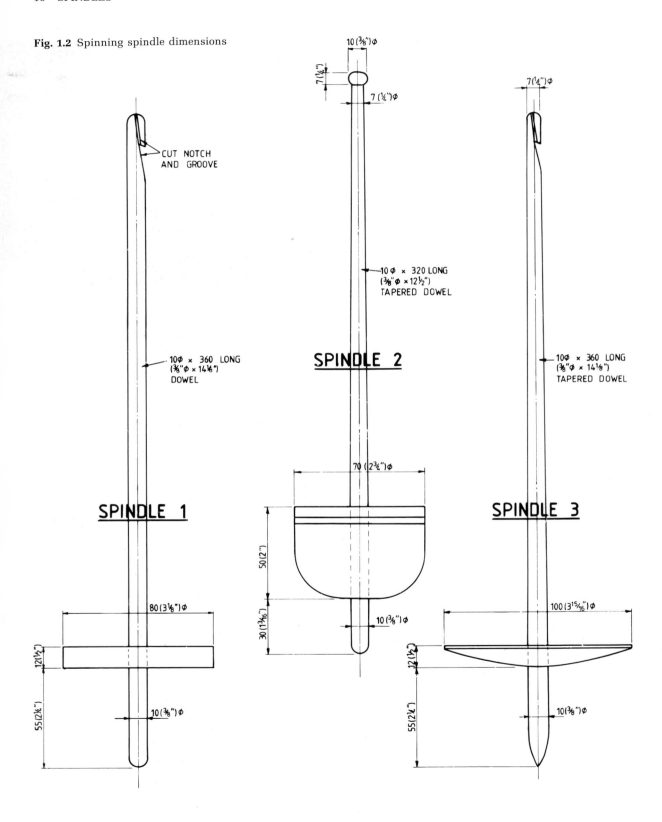

spindle it is a tight fit, no gluing being necessary. An undersize drill can be made by grinding down slightly the edges of the auger.

If no woodturning facilities are available, you can still produce an acceptable result, using a disc sander in conjunction with a disc jig, as show in Fig. 1.4. The jig consists of a small flat board with a 10mm (⅜in) diameter peg set into it, and having an adjustable edge strip fixed underneath it. The edge strip has two coarse and two fine adjustment screws. In use the wood disc to be made is pre-drilled, and cut roughly to size using a coping saw. It is then placed over the peg jig, and this arrangement is held on the sanding table and against the edge of it. The wood disc is then slowly rotated against the sander, to clean up the rim. The distance between the peg and the sanding disc is equal to the radius of the disc you wish to make. Before pushing the disc onto the spindle, note that, to finish, the latter requires a notch cut at the end to which to secure the thread. The spindle is now complete and ready for use.

SPINDLES 2 AND 3

Spindles 2 and 3 are more refined examples requiring proper woodturning facilities. Spindle 2 is intended for heavier threads, and spindle 3 is a more artistic version of spindle 1.

SPINDLE SPINNING

Of all the natural fibres, sheep's wool is the least difficult to learn with, and it is suggested that a beginner sticks to this initially. You can spin straight from the fleece, but normally a teasing and carding process is carried out which cleans and dresses the fibres so that they all lie in the same direction. A design for handcarders is given in Chapter 2 along with a description on how to use them. The end result is the production of a number of wool rolags (fleecy cardings) ready for use with the spinning spindle.

Spinning a thread involves two principle actions: drawing out the fibres, and putting in the twist. Tie about 600mm (2ft) of ready-spun wool onto the spindle, and loop it round, as shown in Fig. 1.5, finishing with a half hitch at the upper notched end. Taking the spindle in the left hand, and the carded rolag of wool in the right, pull out a few fibres from the rolag end, and draw them over say 150mm (6in)

Fig. 1.3 Machining a spindle whorl

of the ready-spun yarn on the spindle. Holding the wool fibres tight between the right thumb and fingers, and giving the spindle a clockwise spin with the left hand, the carded wool will now twist over the existing yarn, and continuing, will produce a new length of thread.

With the spindle still spinning, close the left-hand thumb and fingers on the yarn 25–50mm (1–2in) below your right-hand thumb and fingers. Release the latter slightly and slide them up, thus effectively drawing down new wool fibres ready for spinning. Pinch tight again with the right thumb and fingers on the wool, and release the left hand from the threads, thus allowing the spindle to put in the twist to the new yarn. Continue this process of

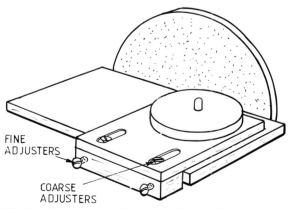

Fig. 1.4 Disc jig for making spindle whorls

Fig. 1.5 Spinning spindle in use

drawing down new fibres and putting in the twist to form thread until the spindle nearly touches the floor. Unhook the yarn from the spindle and wind the new thread onto the shaft above the disc. Reattach this to the spindle end and continue spinning as before.

Your first efforts may be somewhat unprofessional, producing knobbly thick and thin yarn, possibly to the extent of breaking in the latter case. However, persevere with a few more rolags, and in particular appreciate the importance of allowing the twist to enter the rolag in a controlled manner, giving attention to the correct sequence of pinching and releasing the fingers on the fibres. You will gradually improve to form a more even yarn. Spinning, as described above, with the spindle

rotating clockwise (looking down) produces a 'Z' twisted yarn. Spinning with the spindle rotating alternatively anti-clockwise forms an 'S' twisted thread (*Fig. 1.6*).

When a quantity of thread has been spun, it will have built up into a cone shape on the spindle. This can then be gently eased off and placed on a suitable stand, consisting of a dowel fixed into a board. If you are using single ply wool, this can then be wound off onto a niddy noddy to make a skein. If you require a double ply yarn, then a second cone of 'Z' twisted thread will be needed. These two cops of yarn are then combined, using the spindle rotating in the opposite direction (i.e. 'S' twisted). The method is usually to draw the threads from the cops placed behind you, over your shoulder. This can then be drawn off onto the niddy noddy to make a skein of double ply wool.

Fig. 1.6 S and Z twist

2
HAND CARDERS

INTRODUCTION

Before wool from a fleece is spun into a thread, it has
to be teased and carded. Teasing is the separation of
the wool prior to carding, and the removal of thorns,
lumps and debris. This is followed by the carding
operation, which is simply a method of straighten-
ing out the fibres and preparing them into a rolag
ready for spinning. For this a pair of hand carders is
required, as illustrated in Fig. 2.1. Each consists of a
small board, with a square of carding cloth mounted
on it, and a suitable handle so that the carder can be
manipulated. The carding cloth itself consists of a
bed of closely-spaced slightly hooked wires, set into
a tough fabric base. The earliest hand carders
possibly date from around the thirteenth century,
and today they are an essential part of the
handspinning process.

CONSTRUCTION

Hand carders may be either straight backed or
curved backed. The design here is for a pair of
straight backed carders, which are the easiest to
make. The dimensional details are given in Fig. 2.2.
The most important factor to consider when making
them is the hard wear they will experience in use;
thus they need to be strong but light. The board size
is typically 190 × 125mm (7½ × 5in), but it is suggested that __ ~arding cloth is purchased first, so
t___ ese can be tailor-made to suit. (Sources for
ca____.g cloth are given in the list of suppliers.) The
cloth is supplied in various grades, and the backing
is usually a tough vinyl fabric or leather. The
pitching of the hooked wires may also vary. Carding
cloth needs to have a reasonably stiff backing, since
if it is too flexible it tends to bend unduly in use and
will not card properly. The dearest is usually leather
based, but this is not necessarily the most hard
wearing.

Fig. 2.1 Hand carders

The board thickness is typically 10–12mm ($\frac{3}{8}$–$\frac{1}{2}$in),
and the suggested material is a hardwood such as
ash, birch or sycamore. Alternatively a high grade
plywood (e.g. birch faced multiply), not stoutheart,
could be selected. Carders have been made of
softwood, but with this material it is not so easy to
attach the carding cloth without the risk of the wood
splitting. The carding cloth is attached to the boards
along the edges, using staples rather than tacks. To
be effective and to keep the cloth secure the staples
need to be strong and to penetrate well into the
board. On hand carders the cloth is never glued to
the boards as this looses the flexible feel that the
spinner requires.

Bearing in mind the earlier remarks on strength,
the connection between the board and the handle
must be rigid. The design features a screwed and
glued fixture, but equally jointing is sometimes
employed – often a dovetail shaped half joint.

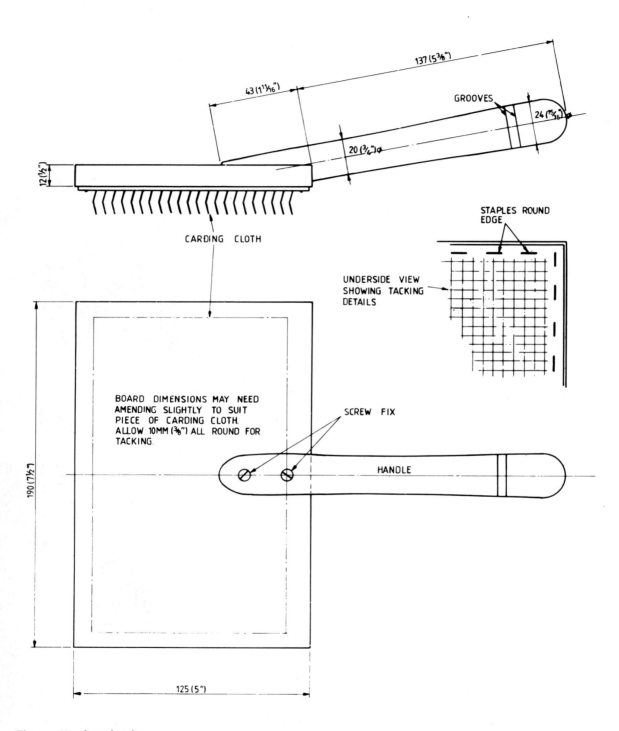

137 (5³⁄₈")

43 (1¹¹⁄₁₆")

GROOVES

24 (¹⁵⁄₁₆")

20 (³⁄₄") dia

12 (½")

CARDING CLOTH

STAPLES ROUND EDGE

UNDERSIDE VIEW
SHOWING TACKING
DETAILS

BOARD DIMENSIONS MAY NEED
AMENDING SLIGHTLY TO SUIT
PIECE OF CARDING CLOTH.
ALLOW 10MM (³⁄₈") ALL ROUND FOR
TACKING.

SCREW FIX

HANDLE

190 (7½")

125 (5")

Fig. 2.2 Hand carder dimensions

FLAT BACKED CARDERS

CURVED BACKED CARDERS

Fig. 2.3 Flat and curved backed hand carders

Jointing is particularly appropriate if construction of curved backed, rather than flat backed, carders is being considered (*Fig. 2.3*). The curved back is a little more difficult to make, but many spinners prefer this style.

CARDING

Carding usually presents no problems, but for beginners the following step-by-step procedure may be of assistance (*Figs. 2.4 to 2.8*). These instructions assume the reader to be right-handed. Before starting, the carders should be identified as left and right.

Step 1 Place the left carder firmly on your lap. Take a quantity of teased wool and spread it evenly over the hooked wires (*Fig. 2.4*).

Step 2 Take the right carder and stroke this across the left carder several times. This is the carding action: it will straighten the fibres and make them fluffy. However, some wool will transfer to the right carder where it is not wanted (*Fig. 2.5*).

Step 3 To transfer the wool on this carder back to the left one, reverse the right carder so that the handles of both are the same way round (*Fig. 2.6*). Make a sweeping action forward with the right carder against the left, this will peel the wool off the right carder. If you examine this action carefully, you will see that the hooks on the left board are effectively digging into the wool on the right one, and those on the latter are tending to release the wool by virtue of the direction in which these wire hooks are facing. Repeat steps 1, 2 and 3 until you are satisfied with the carding, that the fibres are nicely aligned and that the wool is fluffy.

Fig. 2.4 Step 1: spreading wool on carder

Fig. 2.5 Step 2: carding action

Fig. 2.6 Step 3: transferring wool between carders

Fig. 2.7 Step 4: removing wool from left carder

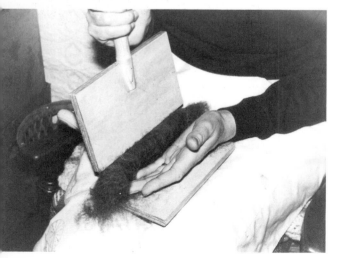

Fig. 2.8 Step 5: forming a rolag

Step 4 To remove the wool from the left carder, keep the carders round the same way as for step 3. Use the right-hand carder to raise the wool gently off the other board. This will give a small fluff of wool clear of the wires (*Fig. 2.7*).

Step 5 The final operation is to make the rolag. To do this place the carded wool on the back of the right board, and gently curl this over to form a roll, or rolag. Use the back of the left carder to assist with this. The rolag is now complete, and ready for spinning into a thread. The fibre alignment is round the rolag, not along its length (*Fig. 2.8*).

3
NIDDY NODDIES

INTRODUCTION

If you have followed the instructions in the first two chapters, you will by now have produced a basic spinning kit, i.e. a spinning spindle and a pair of hand carders. Not doubt too you will have successfully spun and plied a quantity of yarn, and the question will be posed, 'How should this be handled?'. Usually it is not wound into a ball yet, for the wool has first to be washed, and possibly also dyed if this was not done prior to spinning. Instead it is skeined into loose hanks where it is ideal for this purpose. The equipment used for skeining is the niddy noddy, as shown in Fig. 3.2.

CONSTRUCTION

Two designs are given, and the details are as shown in Fig. 3.2. The parts list for these is in Table 1. In design (1) the niddy noddy is hand-held using the centre spar item (2), and the loop length is approximately 2m (6½ft). In design (2) the niddy noddy is held by a handle at the base, and the loop length is rather shorter at 1.5m (5ft). If you prefer different loop lengths, perhaps to suit imperial measurements, the distance between the cross spars can be adjusted accordingly. Design (2), however, is not suited to significant shortening.

Design (1) uses woodturned spars, items (1) and (2), and the dimensions for these parts are given in Fig. 3.3. When assembling these, the cross spars (1) have to be accurately drilled transversely, and on round items this sometimes gives slight problems. A solution is to mount the spar on vee-blocks to hold it at right angles under the drill press whilst being machined (*Fig. 3.1*). Design (2) is rather simpler to make, using square section timber and dowel, and the details are self-explanatory. The cross spars (3) should be pinned as well as glued.

Which design you build is really a matter of personal choice. If you prefer design (1) but do not have turning facilities, this could be adapted along the lines of design (2), but with a 60mm (2⅜in) extension either end over the cross spar positions. Fig. 3.4 shows a niddy noddy in use.

Fig. 3.1 Drilling transverse holes

Table 1: Niddy Noddy Parts List

Item	Description	No. off	Material	Dimension
1	Cross spar (1)	2	Hardwood	32 sq. × 330 long (1¼in sq. × 13in long)
2	Centre spar	1	Hardwood	32 sq. × 490 long (1¼in sq. × 19¼in long)
3	Cross spar (2)	2	Hardwood	12 dia. × 150 long (½in dia. × 6in long)
4	Centre spar	1	Hardwood	22 sq. × 560 long (⅞in sq. × 22in long)

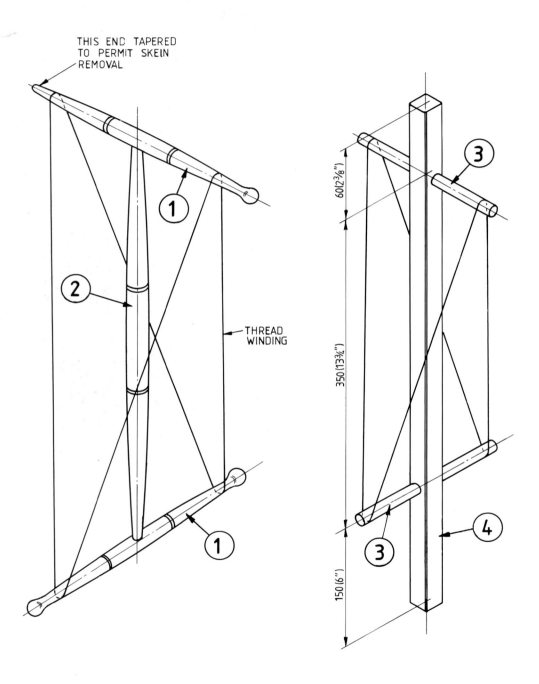

THIS END TAPERED
TO PERMIT SKEIN
REMOVAL

THREAD
WINDING

60(2³⁄₈")

350(13¾")

150(6")

Fig. 3.2 Niddy noddy details

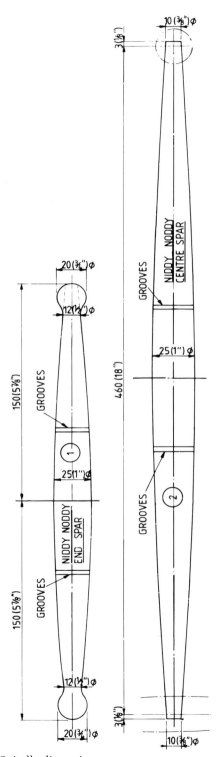

Fig. 3.4 Using a niddy noddy

Fig. 3.3 Spindle dimensions

4
GREAT WHEEL

HISTORY

In order of historical development the next design to be featured is the great wheel, Fig. 4.2, which is thought to have originated from China, and been introduced to this country via India, the Middle East and Europe. The wheels were sometimes known as walking, muckle or spindle wheels, and large numbers were in use for domestic thread production before the Industrial Revolution. At the time, the development was a significant step forward in thread mechanisation from the spinning spindle, and in retrospect can be seen as the logical evolution of this tool. Imagine someone trying to speed up the spinning process by experimenting with the spinning spindle – turning it on its side with the shaft horizontal, and then mounting it in crude bearings so that it spun freely. This would obviously spin quite successfully, as did the drop spindle, if only it could be kept rotating in its new position. Using further ingenuity the inventor then grooved the spindle whorl to turn it into a pulley, and arranged for this to be rotated at speed by a cord driven by a large wheel set horizontally near the spindle. Thus the great wheel came into being; the operator stood next to it, the wheel itself being rotated by the right hand, whilst the left hand spun the thread from the spindle end.

DESIGN

The great wheel design here is a measured drawing of an original on display at Quarry Bank Mill, Styal. The general arrangement is shown in Fig. 4.2, and for the associated parts list see Table 2. It consists of a spindle driven by a large wheel mounted on a gently sloping base, and standing on three legs. It is constructed in oak.

The wheel itself is large, typically measuring 900–1200mm (36–48in) diameter, this one being 1070mm (42in) across. It is of hoop rimmed design, that is it is made from a circumferentially bent wood strip. This is traditional of the period; indeed the style reflects the limitations of the woodturning facilities then available. This was done on primitive pole lathes, primarily suited to spindle turning between centres. Turning large-diameter work, such as a segmented rim construction, whilst not insurmountable, would certainly have presented problems at the time. If you examine the great wheel you will see that only small-diameter spindle turning is necessary. To summarise then, this great wheel design is plain and simple, devoid of aesthetic decoration, and an example of the work horse it was intended to be in the day that it was built.

CONSTRUCTION

Construction can begin with either the wheel itself or the base arrangement; it is usually more practical to begin with the latter, since in this way the assembly progressively reaches its final form. Referring to Fig. 4.2, the base (1) consists of a 220 × 75 × 990mm ($8\frac{3}{4}$ × 3 × 39in) long timber section, and a waney edged log could probably be used to good effect. The legs (2) and (3) require only simple woodturning, and are fitted into drilled holes in the base. (If you have difficulty getting the leg angles correct, Chapter 5 offers some useful tips on this aspect.) Having assembled the base, then make the wheel post (4), which is fitted into a mortice cut out as shown in Fig. 4.1.

The next step is to build the wheel, and whilst the spokes (6) and hub (5) are easy to machine, the rim itself may present a few problems. The latter involves the bending of a long flat strip of wood (or perhaps two shorter ones) to form the wheel circumference, and is done by steaming the wood to make it pliable. As steam bending is a rather specialised art, readers will appreciate a digression at this point to discuss the principles, and some helpful advice on this topic.

WOOD BENDING

To be successful, wood bending requires an understanding of the mechanism, of which there are three important factors.

a Wood will not bend with any ease until made semi-plastic.

b Wood fibres bend much more readily when in compression than in tension.

c Wood selection and section dictate the minimum radius possible.

Firstly, with regard to wood plasticity, it should be noted that kiln or air dried wood, which is normally strong and stiff, can be made semi-plastic by heating it in a steam atmosphere. In this condition it can be made to deform under controlled conditions, and when later dried out the wood will retain its new shape without springing back. Air dried timber is generally easier to bend than kiln dried material.

Steam at atmospheric pressure is suitable, and the usual method is to build a steaming chamber, such as that shown in Fig. 4.3. This consists of a vertical water boiler section, with a horizontal steaming box set across the top. It is best to set this up outdoors and away from buildings, for obvious reasons. Perhaps the coals of a barbeque could be used as the firing medium. Alternatively, and perhaps more practically, you could consider boiling the water using a three kilowatt electric element. Whatever method is used, however, do bear in mind the safety implications of the chosen combination. A pair of heavy duty gloves will also be required to handle the wood in its high temperature state.

With regard to the second issue, the ability of wood to bend more easily in compression than in tension, the following are generalised limits which wood, when plastic, will deform to without fracture or rupture.

Tension 2%   Compression 30%

Table 2: Great Wheel Parts Lists

Item	Description	No. off	Material	Dimensions
1	Base	1	Hardwood	220 × 75 × 990 long (8¾ × 3 × 39in long)
2	Leg (1)	2	Hardwood	48 dia. × 360 long (1⅞in dia. × 14¼in long)
3	Leg (2)	1	Hardwood	48 dia. × 400 long (1⅞in dia. × 15¾in long)
4	Wheel post	1	Hardwood	75 × 50 × 710 long (3 × 2 × 28in long)
5	Hub	1	Hardwood	110 sq. × 110 long (4½in sq. × 4½in long)
6	Spoke	12	Hardwood	28 sq. × 530 long (1⅛in sq. × 21in long)
7	Hoop rim	2	Hardwood	90 × 7 × 1900 long (3½ × ¼ × 75in long)
8	Axle	1	Steel	16 dia. × 200 long (⅝in dia. × 8in long)
9	Spindle post	1	Hardwood	105 × 20 × 700 long (4¼ × ¾ × 27¾in long)
10	Bearing block	2	Hardwood	32 × 25 × 100 long (1¼ × 1 × 4in long)
11	Pulley whorl	1	Hardwood	38 dia. × 9 thick (1½in dia. × ⅜in thick)
12	Spinning spindle	1	Steel	7 dia. × 290 long (¼in dia. × 11½in long)
13	Box	1	Hardwood	50 × 20 × 1250 long total (2 × ¾ × 50 in long)
14	Screw post	2	Hardwood	38 sq. × 240 long (1½in sq. × 9½ in long)
15	Screw bar	1	Hardwood	25 dia. × 300 long (1in dia. × 12in long)
16	Screw bar nut	2	Hardwood	65 sq. × 25 thick (2½in sq. × 1in thick)
17	Drive band	1	Cord	–
18	Nuts/washers/ split pin	–	Steel	M16 Iso (⅝in Whit) nut

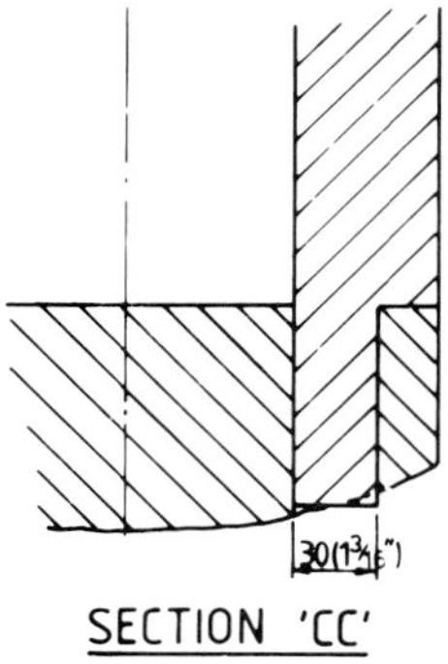

Fig. 4.1 Wheel post fixing detail

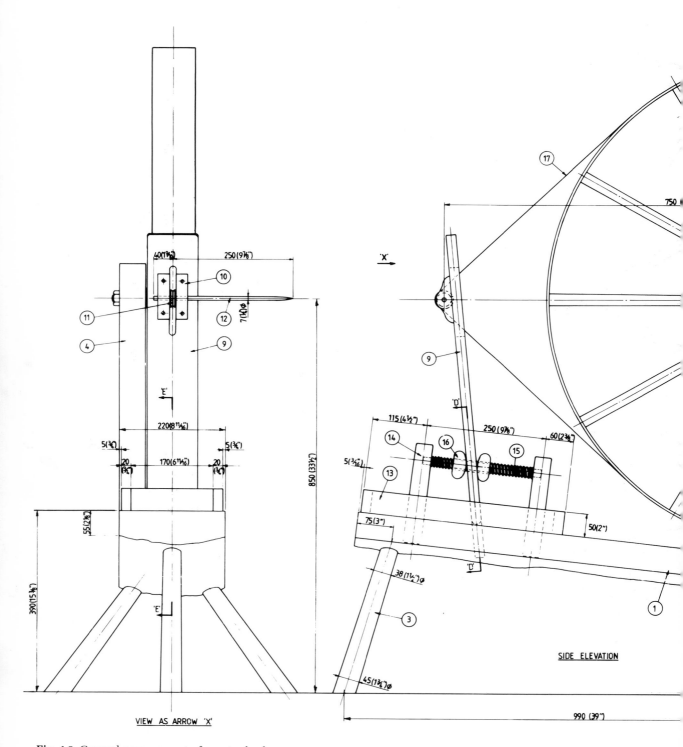

Fig. 4.2 General arrangement of great wheel

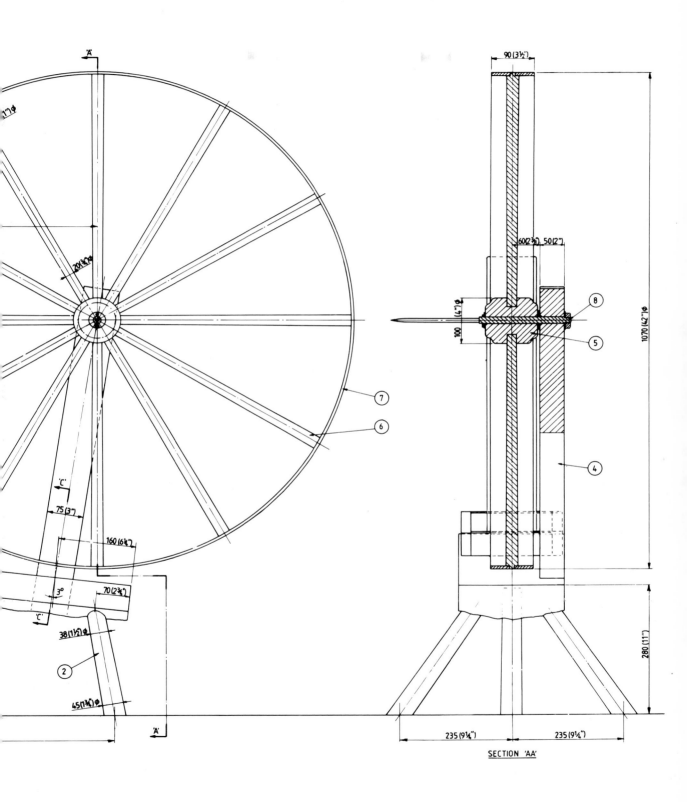

SECTION 'AA'

Thus the art of successful wood bending is to put the wood fibres totally into compression. This is done with the aid of a metal strap, Fig. 4.4. Note that in the unsupported condition the outer wood fibres are in tension, and the inner ones in compression. Thus the danger of splitting is high on the outer surface. In the supported state, however, the strap is in tension, and tends to put all the wood fibres into compression. The risk of fracture is hence very much less when a strap is used.

The third factor governing wood bending is the choice of species: some woods are relatively easy to bend, whilst others are extremely difficult to deform. Table 3 gives the bending properties of a number of common woods. This shows that timbers such as mahogany and teak are difficult to bend, and so we would not consider making the wheel rim of these. On the other hand, woods such as oak and ash would be quite acceptable, and indeed these are a frequent choice.

Rim Bending The rim bending operation is done round a former fixed to a base board. In this case it would be one the shape of the rim's inside radius. It needs to be strong and rigid, bearing in mind the forces which will be exerted on it. The timber to be bent should be free from shakes and knots, and in steaming one hour per 25mm (1in) of thickness should be allowed. Thus for a rim thickness of 7mm (¼in) a steaming time of about 20 minutes would be

Table 3: Wood Bending Properties

Wood	Maximum bending radius for 25mm (1in) thick timber	
	Unsupported	**Supported**
Ash	300 (12in)	64 (2½in)
Beech	330 (13in)	38 (1½in)
Cherry	430 (17in)	51 (2in)
Elm	340 (13½in)	38 (1½in)
Mahogany	910 (36in)	840 (33in)
Oak	330 (13in)	51 (2in)
Teak	890 (35in)	460 (18in)
Yew	420 (16½in)	220 (8½in)

Source: Woodbending handbook, **Forest Products Research Laboratory**

sufficient. In manipulating the bend you should work steadily and swiftly, and have several cramps ready to hold the bent wood to the former. The wood cools rapidly and you have only about a minute or two to complete the operation. If it is not completed at one go, remember it will not go back in the steaming box once bent out of straight! From this aspect it is probably better to tackle the rim bending in two pieces and splice these together. For a rim of only 7mm (¼in) thickness you may not need to use a supporting strap, but if you do it is preferable to make this of stainless steel, as ordinary mild steel tends to stain woods, notably oak. The strap should be the rim width × 1.2mm (18 SWG) thick.

Wheel assembly Assuming the rim has been successfully bent to its circular shape, the remaining wheel parts are then completed. The spokes (6)

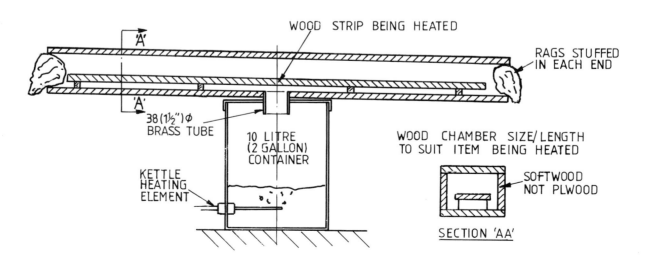

Fig. 4.3 Wood steaming chamber

require only simple spindle turning, and the hub (5) is machined on a 16mm ($\frac{5}{8}$in) diameter mandrel (i.e. axle size) between centres. To finalise the wheel assembly a jig is required to hold the items together whilst being glued. The wheel is too large for a full outer mould to be made, so instead the jig consists of a number of adjustable radial blocks screw fixed to a flat board. Fig. 4.5 shows the arrangement. The rim is placed in position on the spokes and hub. The spokes have spigots either end locating in matching holes in the rim and hub. The adjusting blocks are then moved in to hold the assembly tight, and the rim ends feathered together. In the original wheel, nails or screws instead of spigots were used for holding the spoke ends to the rim. Which you use is a matter of personal choice; the craftsman will probably opt for the spigot method, but if screws are used these should be of brass not steel.

Alignment/Concentricity One of the biggest problems with wheels is making the assembly concentric so that it runs smoothly. Nothing is worse than a wheel which humps up and down, and also wobbles from side to side. A very simple method of checking for wheel concentricity and axial end play is as follows. Referring to Fig. 4.5, a wooden bar is mounted on the wheel axle with a pointer at the end adjacent to the rim. This bar is slowly rotated and, as it moves round, any concentric deviation will be shown up by variation in the radial dimension 'X'. Similarly any axial deviation will be indicted by variation in the dimension 'Y'. Correction can then

be applied by adjustment to the holding blocks, and twisting of the hub. Experiment with this first to get the feel of things before gluing the wheel together.

Spindle The completed wheel is mounted on the wheel post (4) and attention then focused on the construction of the spindle post (9), and screw tension device. These details are given in Fig. 4.7. The spindle post fits into a tapered slot in the base (see section DD and EE). The screw tension arrangement consists of two screw posts (14) between which is fitted a 25mm (1in) diameter wooden screw rod (15) and nuts (16). Further information on cutting wooden screw threads is given in Chapter 6.

The last items to be fitted are the spinning spindle (12), pulley whorl (11), and bearing blocks (10), as shown in Fig. 4.7 section BB. Note that the spindle end is ground to a tapered point, the significance of which is discussed later. Pulley (11) is secured to the spindle using epoxy glue. You might consider fitting brass ferrules in the bearing blocks for smoother running. Finally, add the drive cord to make the wheel fully operational.

Improved features One of the disadvantages of the original design is that the alignment between the wheel and spindle whorl is fairly critical. A way of overcoming this is to replace the fixed wheel post with a woodturned post fitting instead into a tapered hole in the base. This innovation allows the wheel post to be twisted, thus permitting alignment

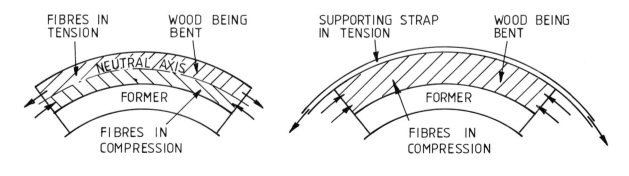

FIBRES IN TENSION   WOOD BEING BENT

NEUTRAL AXIS

FORMER

FIBRES IN COMPRESSION

BENDING WITHOUT SUPPORTING STRAP RISKS TENSILE FAILURE

SUPPORTING STRAP IN TENSION   WOOD BEING BENT

FORMER

FIBRES IN COMPRESSION

BENDING AIDED BY SUPPORTING STRAP

Fig. 4.4 Wood bending former and support straps

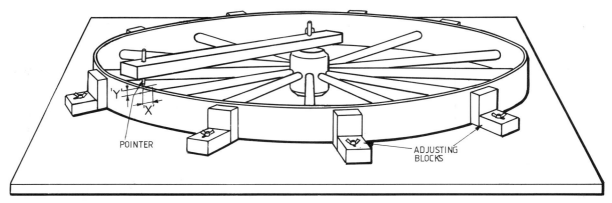

Fig. 4.5 Wheel assembly jig, and method of checking for concentricity and axial displacement errors

to be adjusted. Fig. 4.6 shows a wheel with this feature. Also, an alternative to fixed spindle bearings is to use leather ones. Fig 4.8 shows a wheel fitted with these details.

USING THE GREAT WHEEL

You will recall from Chapter 1 that the spinning spindle has a notch arrangement at the top end, its purpose being to provide a means of securing the thread using a half hitch. The twist was then put in the drawn out wool fibres by giving the spindle a spin. One could imagine this same procedure being applied to the spindle of the great wheel, but the intermittent hitching and unhitching at the spindle end would not be an improvement on the spinning spindle, and it certainly would not speed up the process, which was, after all, the object.

However, the spindle design on the great wheel is subtly different to the spinning spindle, and instead tapers to a point. It is this simple innovation which helps speed up the spinning process. In fact, unlike the drop spindle, where the wool is spun in line with the spindle axis, it is now held at an angle of approximately 45 degrees, as show in Fig. 4.9, the reason for which is explained below.

As an experiment, tape a piece of ready-spun wool onto the spindle near the bearing, and prepare a number of wool rolags following the carding instructions in Chapter 2. Standing beside the wheel, pull out a few wool fibres and overlay them along the end of the ready-spun wool. Hold the wool fibres and yarn together with the left hand approximately 8cm (3in) back before the overlay. Now gently rotate the wheel with the right hand to set the

Fig. 4.6 Woodturned wheel post

spindle spinning, and, holding the yarn at a 45 degree angle to the axis as shown in Fig. 4.9, watch the thread twist towards the spindle point. It will eventually flick off the tip, and in doing so will fall back slightly from the point, only to be picked up again and twisted along to the end.

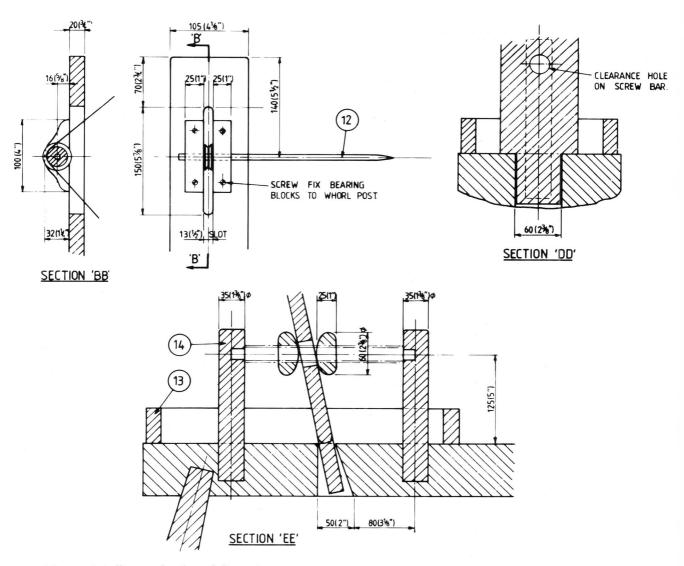

Fig. 4.7 Spindle post details and dimensions

Notice now that the wool fibres pulled out from the rolag are beginning to twist in with the ready-spun yarn. At each spindle revolution, the thread will flick off and give an additional twist to the fibres. This experiment will be clearer if you use two different wool colours, say red for the ready-spun yarn on the spindle, and a white wool rolag. Thus we have the beginnings of a newly spun yarn. If you extend this process by drawing out more fibres from the rolag, and continue the spinning process, the new yarn will grow in length, and the left hand will move away from the spindle end.

Having spun a length of yarn, it now has to be collected up. To do this simply change the angle of the wool to the spindle axis to 90 degrees (*Fig. 4.9*). Continued rotation of the spindle will then draw the thread in and wind the newly spun yarn onto the spindle. At the same time, your left hand holding the rolag will move back in towards the spindle end.

The twisting and drawing out process is then repeated by moving the yarn angle back to 45 degrees, and when another length of wool is spun the angle is changed to 90 degrees to collect it up again. This alternate procedure is the principle of

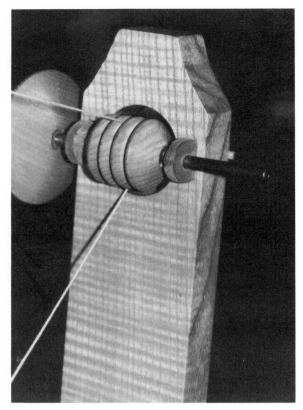

Fig. 4.8 Leather bearings

spinning on the great wheel, and with a little practice you should be able to master the skill quite quickly. Indeed you will notice that compared to the spinning spindle the new spinning process is much faster, and the invention was thus, as intended, a significant step forward in spinning mechanisation.

Finally, a useful tip is to tape a small roll of paper (or thin tube) onto the spindle before spinning. The spun thread, as it is formed, is then wound onto this instead of the spindle. When a quantity of yarn has been produced, the cop can then be easily released for later use.

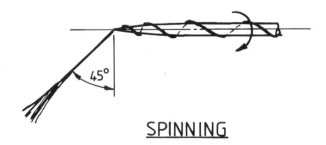

SPINNING

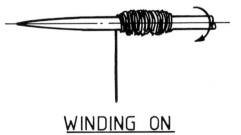

WINDING ON

Fig. 4.9 Spinning and collection on the great wheel

5
HEBRIDEAN SPINNING

INTRODUCTION

It is generally considered that the greatest single advance in the history of spinning was the invention of the flyer spinning wheel. This was a means of producing a continuous thread without stopping, which had never before been possible. As a first design which embodies these principles I have selected a Hebridean spinning wheel as shown in Fig. 5.1. Before discussing the constructional details, however, let us trace the development from the great wheel, and take a look at what flyers are and how they work.

HISTORY

You will recall that up to now spinning had been an intermittent operation, even on the great wheel. An improvement to be able to spin and draw on thread simultaneously would dramatically speed up the spinning process. The flyer spinning wheel which solved this problem, and enabled continuous thread to be spun, was developed around AD 1500–1600. It is variously attributed to Leonardo da Vinci and Jürgen, though some authorities consider that neither of these was responsible. The possible evolution from the great wheel is described below.

From the principles of the spinning spindle and the great wheel, the inventor knew that to spin a thread, wool fibres had to be held either in line, or at an angle to the spindle axis, and that to collect this up the angle had to be changed to 90 degrees. The development which combined both concepts was the introduction of a U-shaped piece or *flyer* fixed to the free end of the spindle (*Fig. 5.2*). One of the spindle bearings was also moved forward to give support to the flyer end.

The wool, instead of twisting off the end of the spindle, now passed through an orifice, the latter

Fig. 5.1 Hebridean spinning wheel

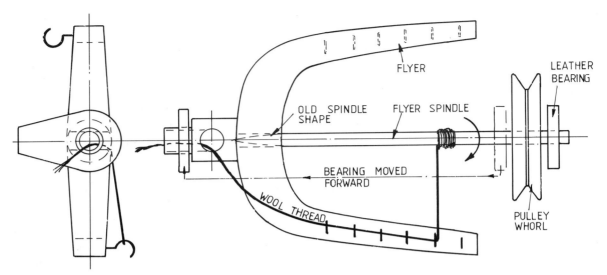

Fig. 5.2 Flyer development (1)

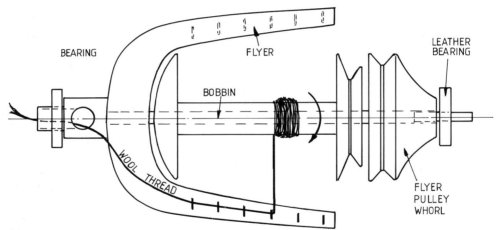

Fig. 5.3 Flyer development (2)

being a means of getting the thread through the front bearing. It then passed out along one of the flyer arms, over a hook, and then radially in at 90 degrees onto the flyer shaft. At first sight this would appear to satisfy the inventor's aims – rotation of the flyer putting in the wool twist, and the shaft being for the collection of the spun yarn. This was not enough, however, for since the flyer twist and the spindle rotation were the same, all that could be achieved was a thread with ever increasing twist but no collection.

The problem was solved by the addition of a bobbin mounted loosely on the shaft behind the flyer (*Fig. 5.3*). One end of the bobbin was arranged as a pulley, so that it could be driven faster or slower than the flyer. Rotating it faster, known as bobbin lead, thus causes the thread to be drawn on while being spun. Conversely rotating the bobbin slower than the flyer, known as flyer lead, also achieves the same result. In the latter case the flyer effectively wraps the spun yarn round the bobbin – another way of collecting it. There are two ways of arranging this: one method is a double band drive, and the second is known as the scotch tension system. These are discussed more fully after the construction of the Hebridean spinning wheel.

One further difficulty remained to be overcome before spinning a continuous thread could be claimed to be a complete success. This was a need to concentrate effort in handling the wool entering the flyer orifice – one hand to guide the wool into the orifice, and the second to draft out new fibres from the rolag. This left no spare hand to rotate the wheel, and the problem was overcome by fitting a crank to the wheel, driven by a treadle through a pitman rod. Powered by foot, this transferred the reciprocating motion of the treadle to continuous rotation of the wheel, and for the first time man now had control in producing a continuously spun thread without having to stop intermittently. The first flyer spinning wheel incorporating the above features is outlined below.

DESIGN

The upright Hebridean spinning wheel is so called because the antique original came from that area. It is quite an attractive little wheel (*Fig. 5.1*) and, being compact, is easily portable. The general arrangement drawings are given in fig. 5.4, and the associated parts list in Table 4. It has a slightly smaller wheel than normal at 360mm (14¼in) diameter, but that is no great sacrifice, the treadling speed being a little greater to compensate. The wheel is of segmented design, and the original is fitted with a scotch tension arrangement for slowing the bobbin down, i.e. flyer lead. However, the design has been adapted also for a double band drive (i.e. bobbin lead), as an alternative choice for the spinner. The flyer orifice is small, indicating it was used for finer threads, but this has been enlarged slightly to make it more suitable for general use. A lazy kate is also fitted. It is probably the easiest flyer type spinning wheel in this book to make, and therefore most suitable for a beginner.

CONSTRUCTION

Since this is the first of the true flyer spinning wheels to be described, its assembly will be discussed in some depth, together with some of the problems to be overcome.

Base Begin construction with the frame, and make a start by cutting out the base (1), machining the legs (2), uprights (10) and (11), and the mother-of-all (15). Dimensions for these items are given in Figs. 5.5, 5.6 and 5.8. The baseblock is of rectangular shape with the rear corners cut obliquely back. Do not cut these off until you have marked out all the holes, as this is

easier to do with the wood square. With regard to drilling holes, this is no problem for those that are square to the block, but getting the leg angles right may prove more difficult. This can be achieved using a leg angle jig, as shown in Fig. 5.9. This is simply a piece of hardboard cut to the required angle, set up on a datum line marked on the baseblock, under the drill press. Note that the holes are blind and do not penetrate right through the block. A flat auger will probably suffice, though a more robust drill, such as a saw tooth bit, will make a cleaner job and not wander. They are more expensive, but worth it.

Progress the assembly by letting the legs into the base. I usually leave the leg centres on until the last moment; this allows some minor adjustments to make the leg ends a nice tight fit in the base holes. The base assembly now needs levelling. To do this, set it up on a flat board, and, using a scribing block, mark circumferentially round the bottom of each leg (*Fig. 5.10*). Cut off the waste material, and sand the ends smooth.The assembly should now stand neat and level, subject perhaps to a few minor adjustments.

Wheel supports The next operation is to fit the previously machined uprights, and the mother-of-all. These items require some transversely drilled holes, so need setting up accurately. Those for the wheel axle are drilled off-centre, which helps to maintain strength in the uprights. A suitable jig for doing this is shown in Fig. 5.11, used in place of the lathe tool rest. Locate the holes accurately along the uprights, so that the wheel, when in position, is square and does not tilt. Keep the power drill on a slow speed when cutting these holes, as otherwise it tends to rip and make an untidy job. Then place the uprights in the baseblock complete with the mother-of-all, and check the steel axle slides freely in the wheel holes. These holes may then be opened up into slots.

Treadle Whilst the frame assembly is still in progress this is a convenient point to add on the treadle (4). The treadle stretcher is pivoted through the bottom of the front legs, and again calls for some tricky drilling. A method of doing this accurately is described in Chapter 7, using the woodturning lathe.

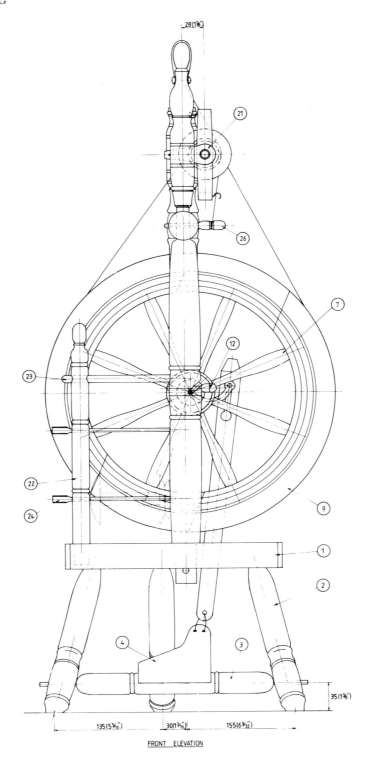

FRONT ELEVATION

Fig. 5.4 General arrangement of Hebridean spinning wheel

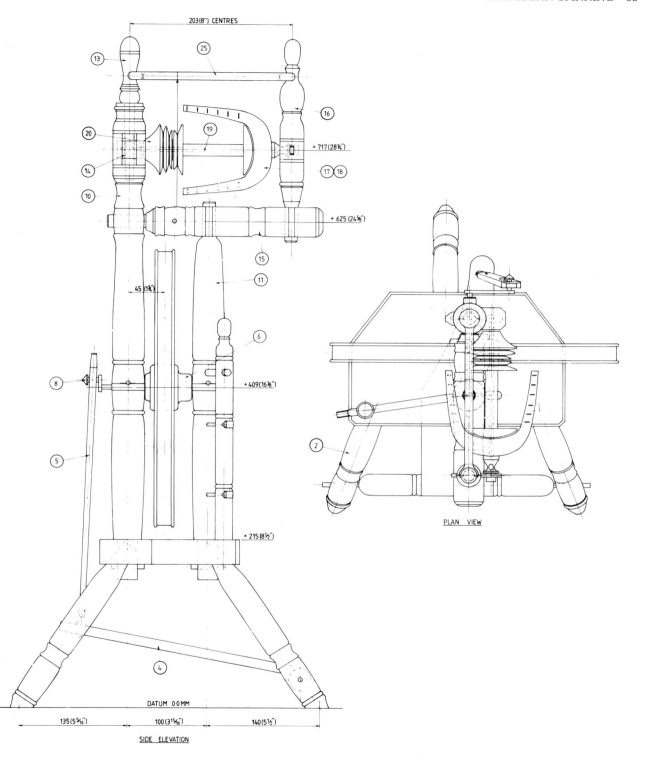

203 (8") CENTRES

+ 717 (28¼")

+ 625 (24⅝")

45 (1¾")

+ 409 (16⅛")

+ 215 (8½")

DATUM 0·0 MM

135 (5⁵⁄₁₆")   100 (3¹⁵⁄₁₆")   140 (5½")

SIDE ELEVATION

PLAN VIEW

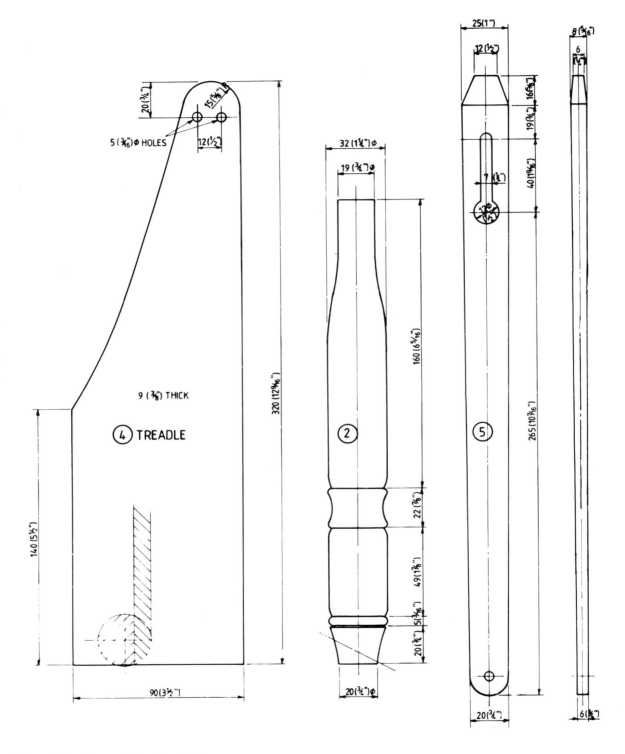

Fig. 5.5 Base, legs and treadle details

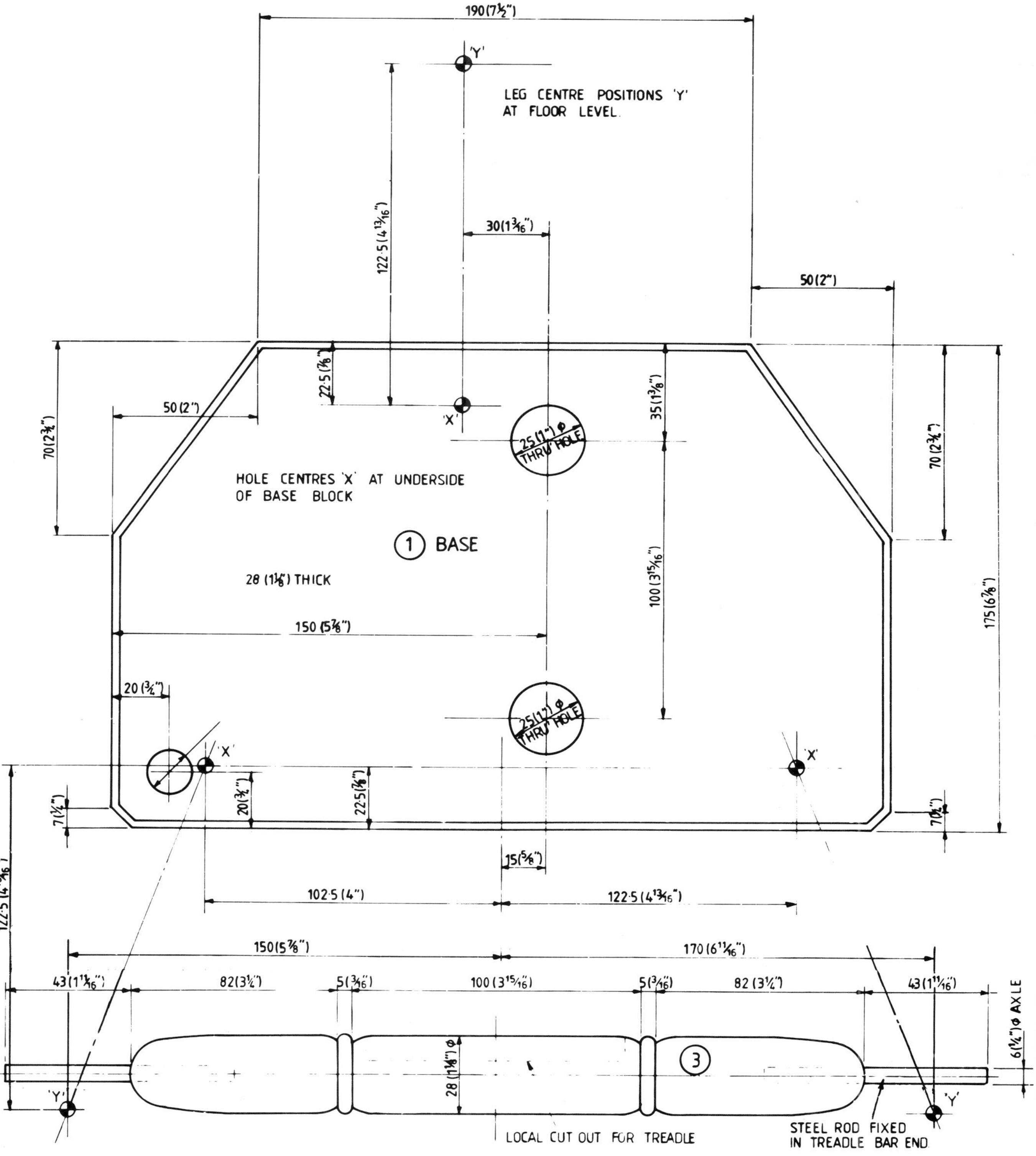
190 (7½")
'Y'
LEG CENTRE POSITIONS 'Y'
AT FLOOR LEVEL.
122·5 (4 13/16")
30 (1 3/16")
50 (2")
70 (2¾")
50 (2")
22·5 (7/8")
'X'
35 (1 3/8")
25 (1") φ THRU' HOLE
70 (2¾")
HOLE CENTRES 'X' AT UNDERSIDE
OF BASE BLOCK
1 BASE
28 (1 1/8") THICK
100 (3 15/16")
175 (6 7/8")
150 (5 7/8")
20 (¾")
25 (1") φ THRU' HOLE
'X'
'X'
7 (¼")
20 (¾")
22·5 (7/8")
7 (¼")
15 (5/8")
102·5 (4")
122·5 (4 13/16")
122·5 (4 13/16")
150 (5 7/8")
170 (6 11/16")
43 (1 11/16")
82 (3¼")
5 (3/16")
100 (3 15/16")
5 (3/16")
82 (3¼")
43 (1 11/16")
6 (¼") φ AXLE
28 (1 1/8") φ
3
'Y'
'Y'
LOCAL CUT OUT FOR TREADLE
STEEL ROD FIXED
IN TREADLE BAR END

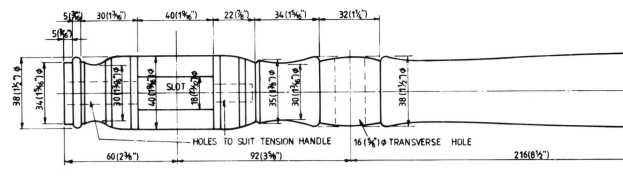

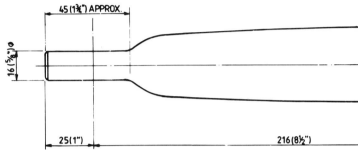

Fig. 5.6 Wheel post dimensions

Table 4: Hebridean Spinning Wheel Parts List

Item	Description	No. off	Material	Dimensions
1	Baseblock	1	Hardwood	175 × 28 × 290 long ($6\frac{7}{8}$ × $1\frac{1}{8}$ × $11\frac{1}{2}$in long)
2	Leg	3	Hardwood	35 sq. × 270 long ($1\frac{3}{8}$in sq. × $10\frac{3}{4}$in long)
3	Treadle stretcher	1	Hardwood	32 sq × 280 long ($1\frac{1}{4}$in sq. × 11in long)
4	Treadle	1	Hardwood	90 × 10 × 320 long ($3\frac{1}{2}$ × $\frac{3}{8}$ × $12\frac{3}{4}$in long)
5	Pitman rod	1	Hardwood	25 × 8 × 340 long (1 × $\frac{5}{16}$ × 13in long)
6	Wheel hub	1	Hardwood	60 sq. × 70 long ($2\frac{3}{8}$sq. × $2\frac{3}{4}$in long)
7	Spoke	8	Hardwood	20 sq. × 150 long ($\frac{3}{4}$in sq. × 6in long)
8	Axle	1	Steel	8 dia. × 200 long ($\frac{1}{4}$in dia. × 8in long)
9	Wheel rim	1	Hardwood	115 × 28 × 1000 long ($4\frac{1}{2}$ × $1\frac{1}{4}$ × $39\frac{1}{2}$in long)
10	Wheel support (long)	1	Hardwood	42 sq. × 630 long ($1\frac{5}{8}$in sq. × 25in long)
11	Wheel support (short)	1	Hardwood	42 sq. × 510 long ($1\frac{5}{8}$in sq. × 20in long)
12	Peg (1)	2	Hardwood	16 sq. × 80 long ($\frac{5}{8}$in sq. × $3\frac{1}{4}$in long)
13	Tension screw	1	Hardwood	28 sq. × 205 long ($1\frac{1}{8}$in sq. × 8in long)
14	Tension screw block	1	Hardwood	30 × 22 × 75 long ($1\frac{3}{16}$ × $\frac{7}{8}$ × 3in long)
15	Mother-of-all	1	Hardwood	42 sq. × 290 long ($1\frac{5}{8}$in sq. × $11\frac{1}{2}$in long)
16	Maiden	1	Hardwood	32 sq. × 280 long ($1\frac{1}{4}$in sq. × 11in long)
17	Flyer	1	Hardwood	115 × 20 × 110 long ($4\frac{1}{2}$ × $\frac{3}{4}$ × 4in long)
18	Flyer axle	1	Steel	6 dia. & 20 dia. bar ($\frac{1}{4}$in dia. & $\frac{3}{4}$in dia. bar)
19	Bobbin	3	Hardwood	70 sq. & 20 sq. material ($2\frac{3}{4}$in sq. & $\frac{3}{4}$ in sq. mat'l)
20	Pulley whorl	1	Hardwood	70 sq. × 40 long ($2\frac{3}{4}$in sq. × $1\frac{9}{16}$in long)
21	Bearing	1	Leather	75 × 38 × 5 thick (3 × $1\frac{1}{2}$ × $\frac{3}{16}$in thick)
22	Bobbin rack upright	1	Hardwood	25 sq. × 330 long (1in sq. × 13in long)
23	Crossbar	1	Hardwood	12 sq. × 160 long ($\frac{1}{2}$in sq. × $6\frac{1}{4}$in long)
24	Bobbin peg	2	Hardwood	10 sq. × 160 long ($\frac{3}{8}$in sq. × 6in long)
25	Bobbin drag crossbar	1	Hardwood	25 × 12 × 225 long (1 × $\frac{1}{2}$ × 9in long)
26	Peg (2)	1	Hardwood	16 sq. × 90 long ($\frac{5}{8}$in sq. × $3\frac{1}{2}$in long)

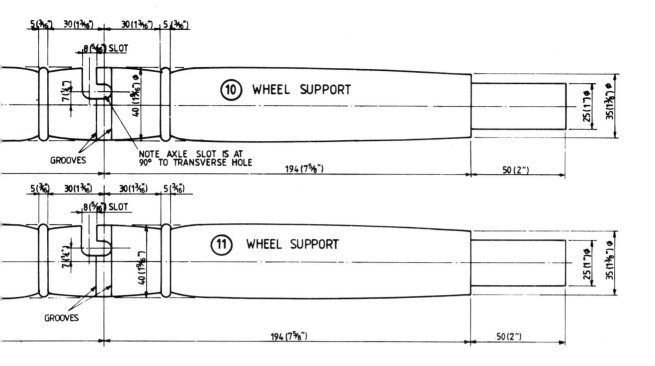

Fig. 5.7 Wheel machining procedure

Wheel rim In building any spinning wheel, it is always the wheel itself which is the most difficult part to construct. The Hebridean wheel has a segmented rim and split hub construction. However, this is not the only method and the reader is referred to another later in this book (p. 72).

Whether you choose radial or parallel segmentation is a matter for personal choice. It is important though that the jointing is accurate, as any mismatch shows up rather glaringly. From this aspect, unless you have machining facilities to cut angles of say 45 or 60 degrees accurately, it is probably easier to use parallel segmentation. This can be accomplished with hand planing and disc sanding. The rim pieces are joined together with loose tenons, and when the fit is to your satisfaction, the assembly is glued and cramped up to set. The next operation is to machine the rim on all four faces, and a set procedure is required to do this, as outlined below (see *Fig. 5.7*).

Step 1 Mount the rim on the bowl turning head, using external waste wood to hold this to the faceplate. Machine the inside diameter, and one side face, using a suitably slow speed, then remove the work from the lathe.

Step 2 Mount a disc blank on the lathe and machine this so that the wheel rim is a tight fit onto it. Reverse the rim and slide this over this centre disc, refixing it onto the faceplate again using screws through the external waste wood. The rim should be a tight fit on the centre disc. If it is not, slip in pieces of paper equally all round to pack out. Now machine the second side face.

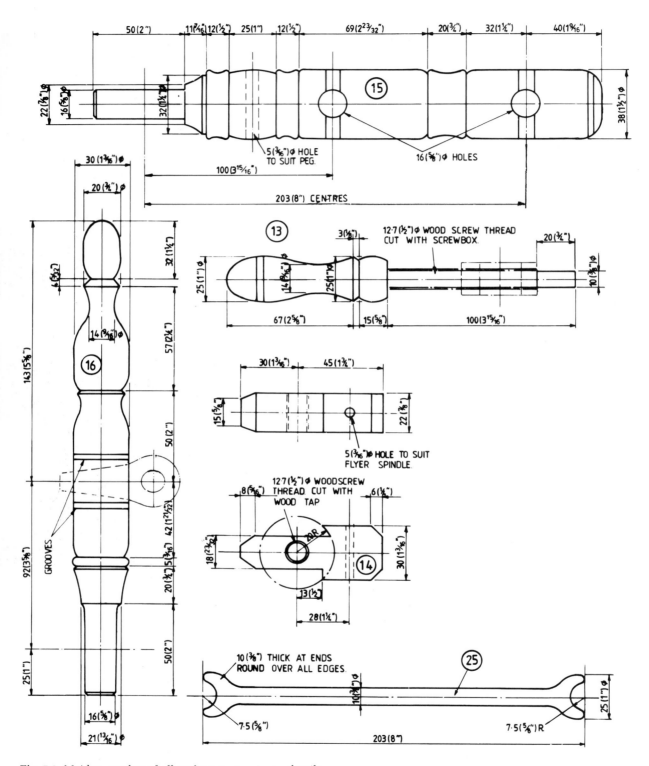

Fig. 5.8 Maiden, mother-of-all and screw tensioner details

Fig. 5.9 Leg angle jig

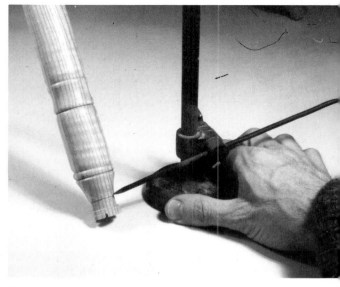

Fig. 5.10 Spinning wheel base levelling

Step 3 Unscrew the wheel rim and reclamp, this time using plywood pieces screw fixed to the centre disc and holding the rim's side face. Finally, machine up the outer circumference of the wheel removing surplus wood.

The rim is now complete apart from machining the radial spoke holes. You may have slight difficulty here drilling these due to the limited wheel inside diameter, but this restriction is a small handicap compared with trying to machine a number of loose segmented rim pieces. Larger wheels are, of course, much easier in this respect. Also, with regard to the above machining procedure, three tips which you may find useful are as follows.

The first is to include a disc of waste wood between the lathe faceplate and the wheel rim, thus preventing damage to the faceplate whilst machining. The second point relates to the screw fixing of the rim to the bowl turning head for the first time. Before doing this, it is preferable to plane flat the surface of the wheel rim adjacent to the faceplate. If this is not done and the surface is irregular, then the screw fixing may subsequently distort or twist the rim slightly. Thus, whilst you can, of course, still

Fig. 5.11 Lathe jig for drilling off-centre holes

turn up a true outer face, when you later release the rim it may unflex a little making the wheel warp slightly. If planing one side of the rim truly flat presents difficulties, then packing pieces between the rim and the faceplate to fill any obvious gaps could be used as an alternative. The third recommendation is slightly to crown the outside diameter of the wheel where the cord drive runs. This makes the drive cord track more efficiently.

Spokes, hub and crank It is important when machining the spokes to make sure that they are all exactly the same length. Fit them into the rim radial spigot holes, and measure the gap left at the centre where the split hub is to fit. The hub is machined to match this, and is turned from two pieces clamped together on a mandrel. The latter should suit the axle size, i.e. 8mm ($\frac{5}{16}$in). The radial spoke holes in the hub are drilled using the same jig as was used for machining the axle holes in the uprights (*Fig. 5.11*). If the lathe has an indexing head, e.g. Myford ML8, then the pitching can be accurately spaced at 45 degree intervals.

The final item to make before proceeding with the wheel assembly is the steel axle and crank. This requires some metal machining for the spigot end. I usually thread the ends of the axle and spigot into the crank arm, and get the local blacksmith to add a spot of weld to fix these. Dimensions of the hub and crank etc. are given in Fig 5.12.

WHEEL ASSEMBLY

Proceeding with the wheel assembly, slide the two halves of the hub onto the axle, and close these onto the inner spoke ends. A trial assembly is recommended first without glue applied to the spoke ends and the hub. The wheel should be perfectly concentric, but some correction for axial wobble may be necessary. When you are satisified, you can set it right, take the wheel gently apart, apply glue sparingly and reassemble again, correcting for any minor errors. A method of checking the axial wobble is to mount the wheel in engineer's vee-blocks, and place a pointer adjacent to the outer rim. Rotate the wheel and measure the varying gap between the pointer and the rim. If the wheel setting is correct, this should be constant. This is similar to the method used for checking the great wheel (*Fig. 4.5*) except the roles are reversed, i.e. the pointer is stationary and the wheel rotates.

After the glue has set, the hub is finally pinned to the axle using a 2mm ($\frac{1}{16}$in) diameter steel pin. The completed wheel can then be dropped into the bearing slots in the uprights, and connected up to the treadle by the pitman rod. It should run easily and smoothly, and work can then proceed to the top section of the spinning wheel.

Maiden and flyer Before the flyer can be mounted, some other items have to be completed. These include the maiden (16), tension screw block (14), and tension screw (13). Details of these components are given in Fig. 5.8. The maiden should be a tight fit in the mother-of-all, but free to twist. Make the end of the maiden marginally tapered to assist this. The tension screw and block are screw threaded 12.7mm ($\frac{1}{2}$in) diameter. A screwbox and tap will be required to complete these items. If you feel the expense of a screwbox too high to justify, an alternative is to consider a steel screw and matching nut set into the tension block (14).

The dimensional information for the flyer arrangement is given in Fig. 5.13. The flyer consists of a machined metal orifice and 6mm ($\frac{1}{4}$in) diameter steel shaft, to which is fitted a U-shaped wooden flyer arm. An alternative to brazing the orifice and shaft together is to screw thread these. The flyer itself requires accurate marking out, and if you intend making other wheels, a perspex template may be worth making. Join the flyer and orifice/axle using epoxy resin glue. This item is then mounted between the bearing (21) and tension screw block (14).

Pulley whorl The pulley whorl (20) screws onto the flyer shaft end, and is machined on a 6mm ($\frac{1}{4}$in) diameter steel mandrel. It has a metal insert threaded M6 Isometric ($\frac{1}{4}$in Whitworth) fitted into it using epoxy glue. However, a threaded nut will suffice if necessary. Older wheels originally had a left-hand thread, but this is not really critical as a spinner uses the wheel in both directions, say clockwise for spinning the yarn, and anti-clockwise for plying. Screwed up tight, the arrangement should be perfectly adequate.

Bobbins Bobbins are made in three pieces and glued together, as shown in Fig. 5.14. The bobbin shaft is first machined on a 6mm ($\frac{1}{4}$in) diameter mandrel, and then 75mm (3in) diameter blanks are drilled with a 16mm ($\frac{5}{8}$in) hole and glue fixed either end of this (epoxy resin). Final machining is then completed and, after withdrawal, from the mandrel, the centre hole is eased to be a clearance fit on the flyer shaft, so that it runs smoothly. An important point to check is that, if the wheel is set up for double band drive, then there must be a differential speed ratio between the flyer and bobbin, the latter usually running faster. Typically 10–20mm ($\frac{3}{8}$–$\frac{3}{4}$in) difference in pulley diameter is required. This is explained further under the wheel operation (see below).

Fig. 5.12 Wheel component details

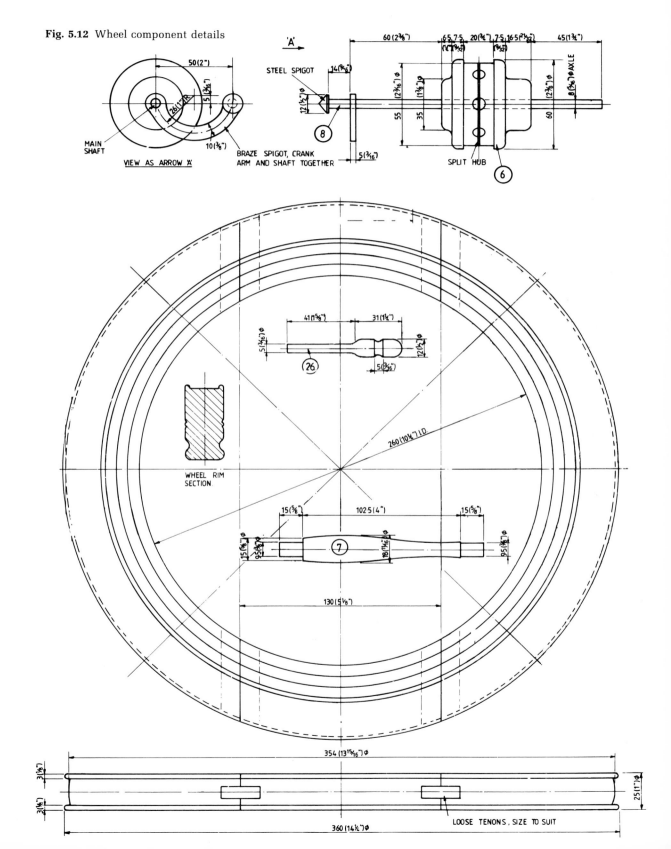

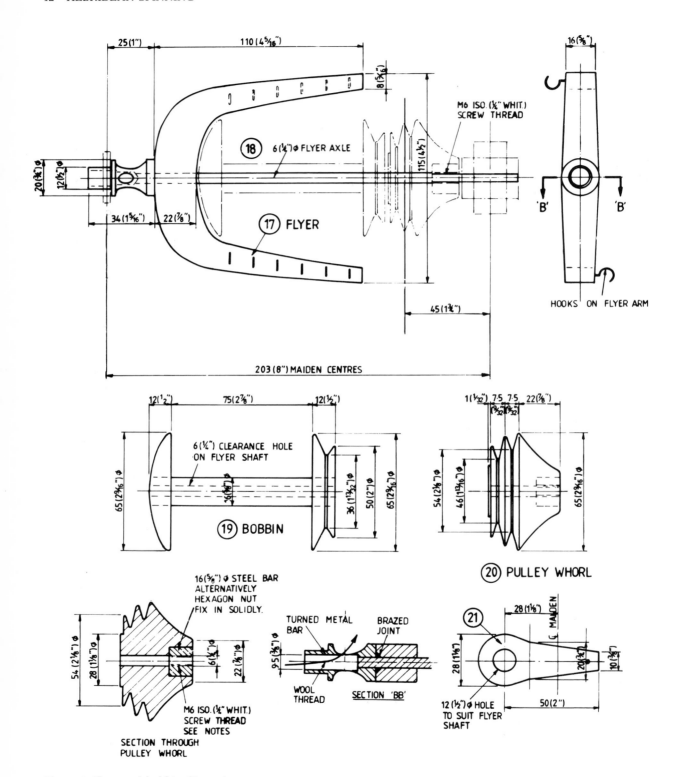

Fig. 5.13 Flyer and bobbin dimensions

Fig. 5.14 Bobbin construction

Finishing touches The last remaining items to add are the pegs (12) and (26), the crossbar (25), and also the lazy kate arrangement items (22), (23) and (24). Details of the latter are given in Fig. 5.15. The lazy kate permits thread to be drawn from two bobbins to ply yarns together. The wheel is now complete and the drive band is finally added to make it fully operational.

USING THE WHEEL

The spinner sits beside the wheel, with the flyer to the front, and pitman rod at the back. Treadle operation rotates the wheel, which, via the drive cords, spins the flyer/bobbin arrangement. A length

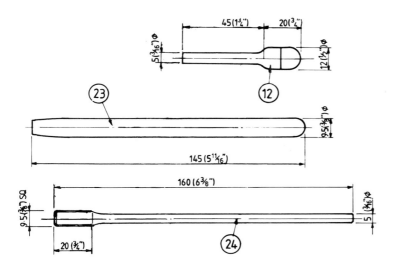

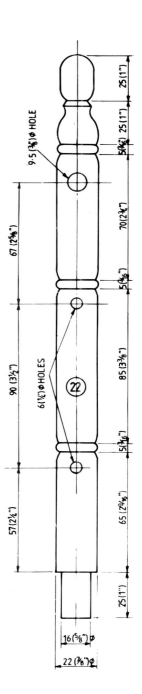

Fig. 5.15 Lazy kate dimensions

of ready-spun yarn is attached to the bobbin, hooked onto one of the flyer arms, finally passing through the flyer orifice, as in Fig. 5.3.

Wool to be spun is prepared by teasing and carding into rolags. As for the great wheel, wool fibres are pulled out from the rolag, and laid over 50–75mm (2–3in) of the ready-spun yarn. Now, with gentle treadling of the wheel in a clockwise direction, the flyer will begin to twist the wool fibres over the spun yarn, and start to produce new thread. As the yarn is made it is drawn onto the bobbin. The process is continuous, and after some practice the spinner should become quite skilful.

As mentioned earlier, the spinning wheel is fitted with two options for regulating the *draw-on* – scotch tension or double band drive. For the beginner the double band drive is probably the easiest, but as the spinner gains experience, it is more a question of individual preference.

Scotch tension arrangement In the scotch tension spinning mode, the wheel, via a single driven cord loop, spins only the flyer and pulley whorl (17 and 20), the bobbin (19) remaining loose on the shaft between these items. A friction cord is stretched across the bobbin whorl, between the crossbar (25) and the adjusting peg (26) fixed in the mother-of-all (*Fig. 5.4*). Wool is connected as described above.

If the drag cord is slack, spinning the flyer through treadle operation, and with the thread held steady, causes the bobbin to rotate at the same speed. Thus wool is twisted to form a thread, but there is no *draw on*. If the drag cord is now tightened, by applying light friction to the bobbin whorl, the speed of the latter is caused to retard slightly relative to the flyer (i.e. flyer lead). The wool will now be drawn on by the flyer wrapping it round the bobbin at the same time as it is being spun. If, in the limit, the bobbin is totally stopped, then the thread is simply wrapped round the bobbin with little or no twist, providing the spinner allows this.

The experienced spinner adjusts the drag cord to allow just the right amount of bobbin drag to produce the desired thread. In this arrangement, because only the flyer is driven, the relative size between the bobbin whorl and flyer whorl is not important. However, if the wheel is also to be used in the double band drive mode, this ratio is critical, as outlined below.

Double band drive In the double band drive arrangement, both the bobbin and the flyer are caused to rotate by the wheel, using a single continuous drive cord formed into a double loop. To make the system work it is essential that there is a differential ratio between the bobbin and flyer speed. As described earlier, the flyer spins the thread and the bobbin collects it up. To do this, the bobbin is usually set to rotate faster than the flyer (i.e. bobbin lead), so the thread is drawn on as it is being spun. In this design a two step flyer whorl is provided to cover the spinner's needs from fine to coarse spun yarn. It is always best to err on the side of a larger difference between these two diameters. If the draw on is too fast (i.e. coarse yarn), the spinner can retard the thread to give it more twist by holding it back. Thus the bobbin will slip slightly against the drive cord, but a perfectly spun thread to the spinner's requirements will result.

PLYING

A last point to mention is the use of the spinning wheel to ply threads together. Plying is necessary for knitted garments, as, if made in single ply, the item will not lie flat and instead becomes twisted up – the result of the thread being spun all one way. A balancing force is needed, and this is achieved by spinning two threads together, with the wheel rotating in the opposite direction to when making a singly ply yarn. Spinning with clockwise rotation produces a 'Z' twisted thread, and plying with rotation in the opposite direction folds the yarns together with an 'S' twist. A bobbin rack, otherwise known as a lazy kate, is fitted to the wheel for this purpose.

6
SLOPING SPINNING WHEEL

INTRODUCTION

Having discussed the detailed construction of a flyer spinning wheel in the last chapter, the designs which follow in this and succeeding chapters concentrate on some variations in style from the past and present, to give the woodworker a selection to choose from to build. There are four basic types of wheel – the upright, sloping bed, Scandinavian, and the frame type. There are designs for all of these except the last, which is not so well known, and which also takes up more floor space. Looking now at the second type of wheel, the sloping bed design, this has a completely different arrangement. In this the flyer, instead of being mounted above the wheel, is now moved to one side, and the base is accordingly sloped up under the mother-of-all to give it support.

DESIGN

There are myriad sloping bed wheel designs, but the one shown in Fig. 6.3 has some particularly attractive turnings which the craftsman woodturner who likes a challenge will enjoy. The 486mm (19¼in) diameter wheel is of hoop rimmed construction; thus a lathe equipped for spindle turning only will suffice. The dimensions are taken from an original wheel known to date from at least 1878, but the hoop rim style suggests it could possibly be earlier. An interesting point is that the beadings and features are not dissimilar to Samuel Crompton's wheel, which dates from about the mid eighteenth century. The wheel/flyer drive uses the double band connection.

The wheel is fitted with a distaff; the flyer orifice is small and the flyer hooks are closely spaced. These features all indicate that it was a wheel for spinning flax. The orifice and hook spacing have been modified slightly in the design to make it more suited to general purpose usage with wool as well as flax. Spinning flax is briefly discussed at the end of the chapter. A further point of interest is the screw tension arrangement for tightening the drive cord. Sloping bed wheels often have this fixed into the end of the base (see the Arkwright wheel in Chapter 8). This one is rather different in being mounted off the base on support blocks.

CONSTRUCTION

A full description of the construction is not offered here, since much of what was discussed on the Hebridean wheel applies, and would only be repetitive. The account is therefore shorter, and concentrates on the special features and construction issues with which readers may have difficulty. The general arrangement is given in Fig. 6.3, and the associated parts lists in Table 5.

Base In the same way as for the Hebridean wheel, construction should begin with the baseblock (1), and this is assembled together with the legs (2), and wheel supports (10). Detailed dimensions of these items are given in Fig. 6.4. The principal difficulty with these is in machining the holes in the baseblock to fit the tapered ends of items (2) and (10). The most troublesome are the leg holes, which are blind ended. I have been asked on numerous occasions how to do this, and there is really no simple answer, but the following tips are offered.

Cutting tapered holes

Step 1 The first step in cutting any tapered hole is to mark the positions accurately on the baseblock top and bottom, and the true elliptic shape of the item which fits into it (*Fig. 6.1*). In the case of the wheel

Table 5: Sloping Spinning Wheel Parts List

Item	Description	No. off	Material	Dimensions
1	Baseblock	1	Hardwood	$170 \times 57 \times 428$ long ($6\frac{3}{4} \times 2\frac{1}{4} \times 17$in long)
2	Leg	3	Hardwood	42 sq. $\times 460$ long ($1\frac{5}{8}$in sq. $\times 18\frac{1}{4}$in long)
3	Treadle stretcher	1	Hardwood	32 sq. $\times 470$ long ($1\frac{1}{4}$in sq. $\times 18\frac{1}{2}$in long)
4	Treadle	1	Hardwood	$100 \times 10 \times 405$ long ($4 \times \frac{3}{8} \times 16$in long)
5	Pitman rod	1	Hardwood	$22 \times 7 \times 485$ long ($\frac{7}{8} \times \frac{1}{4} \times 19\frac{1}{4}$in long)
6	Wheel hub	1	Hardwood	80 sq. $\times 80$ long ($3\frac{1}{8}$in sq. $\times 3\frac{1}{8}$in long)
7	Wheel axle	1	Steel	7 dia. $\times 200$ long ($\frac{1}{4}$in dia. $\times 8$in long)
8	Spoke	12	Hardwood	32sq. $\times 240$ long ($1\frac{1}{4}$in sq. $\times 9\frac{1}{2}$in long)
9	Hoop rim	1	Hardwood	$50 \times 6 \times 1800$ long ($2 \times \frac{1}{4} \times 72$in long)
10	Wheel support	2	Hardwood	48 sq. $\times 450$ long ($1\frac{7}{8}$in sq. $\times 17\frac{3}{4}$in long)
11	Peg	2	Hardwood	22 sq. $\times 120$ long ($\frac{7}{8}$in sq. $\times 4\frac{3}{4}$in long)
12	Tension screw support	2	Hardwood	$57 \times 22 \times 155$ long ($2\frac{1}{4} \times \frac{7}{8} \times 6\frac{1}{4}$in long)
13	Tension screw	1	Hardwood	38 sq. $\times 320$ long ($1\frac{1}{2}$in sq. $\times 12\frac{1}{2}$in long)
14	Tension screw handle	1	Hardwood	38 sq. $\times 130$ long ($1\frac{1}{2}$in sq. $\times 5\frac{1}{8}$in long)
15	Mother-of-all	1	Hardwood	50 sq. $\times 300$ long (2in sq. $\times 12$in long)
16	Maiden	2	Hardwood	48 sq. $\times 270$ long ($1\frac{7}{8}$in sq. $\times 10\frac{1}{2}$in long)
17	Flyer	1	Hardwood	$115 \times 20 \times 120$ long ($4\frac{1}{2} \times \frac{3}{4} \times 4\frac{3}{4}$in long)
18	Flyer axle	1	Steel	6 dia. & 20 dia. bar ($\frac{1}{4}$in dia. & $\frac{3}{4}$in dia. bar)
19	Bobbin	1	Hardwood	75 sq. & 20 sq. material (3in sq. & $\frac{3}{4}$in sq. mat'l)
20	Pulley whorl	1	Hardwood	80 sq. $\times 50$ long ($3\frac{1}{4}$in sq. $\times 2$in long)
21	Bearing	2	Leather	75 sq. $\times 5$ thick total (3in sq. $\times \frac{3}{16}$in thick)
22	Distaff (1)	1	Hardwood	42 sq. $\times 280$ long ($1\frac{5}{8}$in sq. $\times 12$in long)
23	Distaff (2)	1	Hardwood	28 sq. $\times 220$ long ($1\frac{1}{8}$in sq. $\times 8\frac{3}{4}$in long)
24	Distaff arm	1	Hardwood	38 sq. $\times 290$ long ($1\frac{1}{2}$in sq. $\times 11\frac{1}{2}$in long)
25	Lower distaff	1	Hardwood	48 sq. $\times 460$ long ($1\frac{7}{8}$in sq. $\times 18\frac{1}{4}$in long)

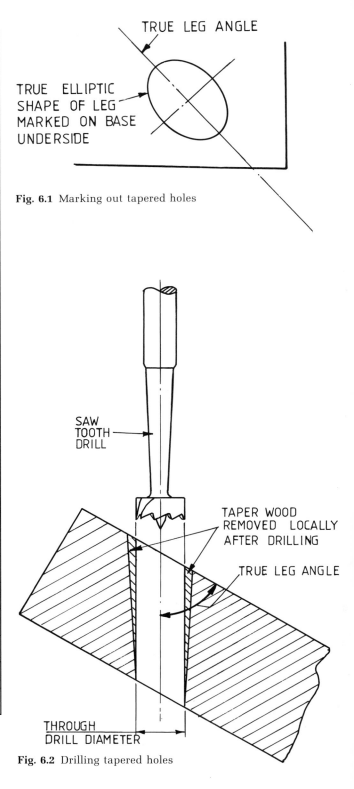

Fig. 6.1 Marking out tapered holes

Fig. 6.2 Drilling tapered holes

support holes the elliptic shape can be marked on both sides of the base, and for the leg holes only on one side.

Step 2 Mount the baseblock under a drill press at the correct angle. Calculate this angle from the dimensions given, and use a leg angle jig, as shown in Fig. 5.9. Select the largest drill which will pass through the narrow end of the taper hole, and drill through. In the case of the blind holes, drill to the depth of the hole only, making sure you do not break through. Fig. 6.2 shows this operation.

Step 3 Complete the taper by carefully paring out with a gouge, until the final shape is achieved. Lastly, wrap glasspaper round the leg end or taper fitting, and twist this into the hole to clean up the latter. If the hole is uneven a way of revealing the high spots in the hole is to put a little beeswax on the leg taper before twisting in. The high spots will be disclosed by the beeswax rubbing onto these areas, and they can then be locally removed. It also helps to retain the turning centres on the leg/wheel support for as long as possible. These items can then be remounted on the lathe to carry out any last minute local sanding/trimming.

Another method of machining a tapered hole is to obtain a tapered drill/reamer, but these are few and far between, and may need to be specially made. Most that are available are for machining in metalwork, and tend to have rather narrow tapers. A novel solution along these lines is to machine a wooden taper section to match the leg end, then cut a longitudinal groove in it, and fix a fine-tooth metal saw-blade edge into this. Use this combination as a tapered scraper to clean out the hole.

Finally, there is the easy way out, which is simply to drill parallel holes in the baseblock using a saw tooth bit, and to modify the ends of the items also being let into this section by lathe machining.

Wheel As the wheel is hoop rimmed, the same method of construction as outlined in Chapter 4 can be followed. The spoke and hub details are given in Fig. 6.8. The shaping and grooving on the outer face of the hoop rim should be completed whilst the wood strip is straight, and before steam bending. You could consider routing this, though due to the thin section it may be more practical to use scrapers

of various patterns. The assembly is carried out following the method in Fig 4.5, with checks for concentricity and axial wobble, and then glued. When complete, it should drop neatly into the axle slots in the end of the wheel supports (10), and be held in place by pegs (11).

Treadle The treadle details are given in Fig. 6.4, and construction of items (3), (4) and (5) is straightforward. The stretcher (3) is pivoted through the bottom of the front legs. A method of doing this accurately is described in Chapter 7. The pitman rod design is from the original, plain and simple; it can be improved upon, and some notes on this are given in Chapter 10.

Mother-of-all/tension screw support The mother-of-all (15) is mounted on a tension screw (13), which in turn is set off the baseblock on two supports (12). These items are detailed in Fig. 6.10 and 6.9. Note that two small pegs are fitted in the underside of the mother-of-all. These act as levelling blocks, to hold the mother-of-all against twisting. In making the tension screw and mother-of-all, these items have to be screw threaded. This is a specialized technique, so it is worth digressing for a moment to discuss this.

Cutting wood screw threads Because of the fibrous nature of wood, you cannot simply cut a screw thread on a dowel using a steel die as you would to cut a metal thread. If you do try it, the result is a rather crumbly mess, aggravated by the fact that the thread pitch is far too fine for wood. The die quite simply cracks off any thread which is formed. Wood threads are consequently much coarser than the metal equivalent, and are cut instead with a wooden screwbox, as shown in Fig. 6.5. In use, the wood dowel is entered on one side, and twisted against an internal vee shaped cutter, which forms the thread. Behind the cutter is a preformed female thread of the size being cut, which the new dowel thread screws into. It uses the latter as a means of drawing the dowel through the screwbox, as new thread is cut.

A special feature of the vee cutter is its backward rake towards the root (*Fig. 6.6*); hence it does not cut the thread abruptly, but instead with a slicing action. The crown is cut in advance of the root, and the risk of thread fracture is much reduced. The

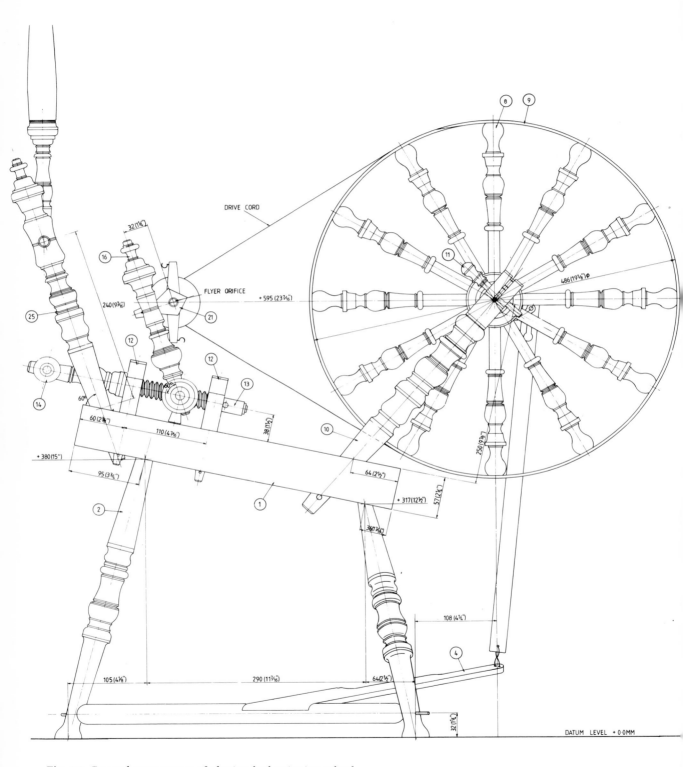

DRIVE CORD

FLYER ORIFICE

Fig. 6.3 General arrangment of sloping bed spinning wheel

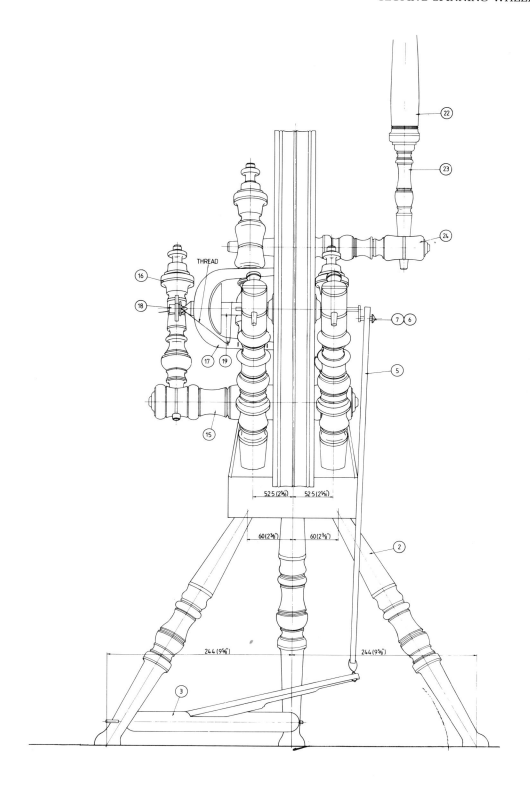

THREAD

52·5 (2¹⁄₁₆") 52·5 (2¹⁄₁₆")

60 (2³⁄₈") 60 (2³⁄₈")

244 (9⁵⁄₈") 244 (9⁵⁄₈")

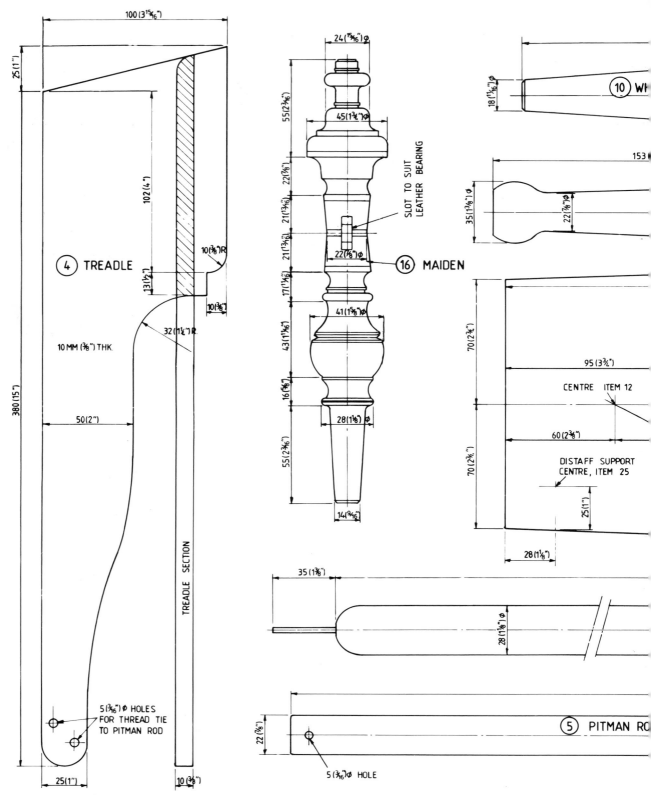

Fig. 6.4 Base, leg, treadle and maiden details

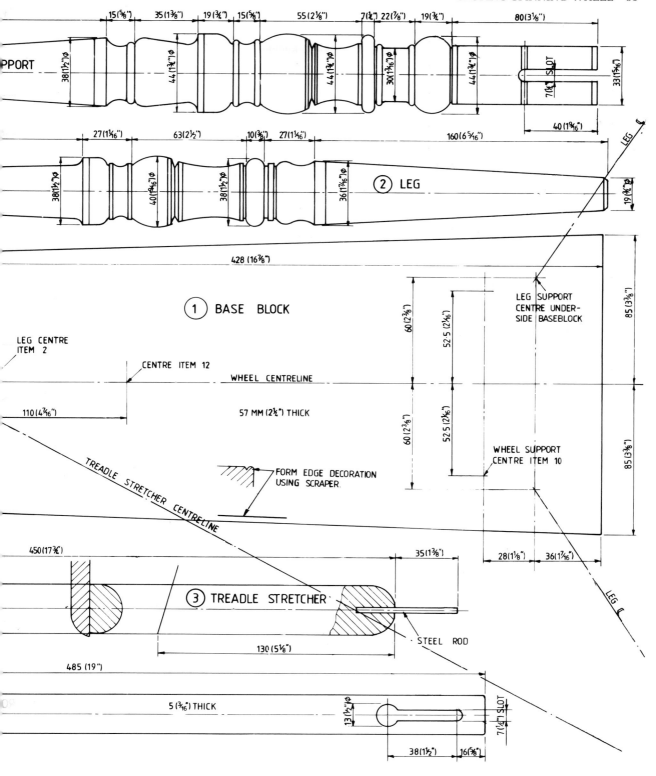

PPORT

38(1½")Φ   15(⅝")   35(1⅜")   19(¾")   15(⅝")   55(2⅛")   7(¼")   22(⅞")   19(¾")   80(3⅛")

44(1¾")Φ   44(1¾")Φ   30(1³/₁₆")Φ   44(1¾")Φ   33(1⁵/₁₆")   SLOT   7(¼")   40(1⁹/₁₆")

27(1¹/₁₆")   63(2½")   10(⅜")   27(1¹/₁₆")   160(6⁵/₁₆")

38(1½")Φ   40(1⁹/₁₆")Φ   38(1½")Φ   36(1⁷/₁₆")Φ   ② LEG   19(¾")Φ   LEG ℄

428 (16⅞")

① BASE BLOCK

LEG SUPPORT CENTRE UNDER-SIDE BASEBLOCK

85 (3⅜")

LEG CENTRE ITEM 2

CENTRE ITEM 12

WHEEL CENTRELINE

60 (2⅜")   52.5 (2¹/₁₆")

110 (4³/₁₆")

57 MM (2¼") THICK

60 (2⅜")   52.5 (2¹/₁₆")

WHEEL SUPPORT CENTRE ITEM 10

85 (3⅜")

TREADLE STRETCHER CENTRELINE

FORM EDGE DECORATION USING SCRAPER.

450 (17¾")   35 (1⅜")   28 (1⅛")   36 (1⁷/₁₆")

③ TREADLE STRETCHER

STEEL ROD

130 (5⅛")

LEG ℄

485 (19")

5 (³/₁₆") THICK   13 (½")Φ   7 (¼") SLOT

38 (1½")   16 (⅝")

Fig. 6.5 Screwbox and tap

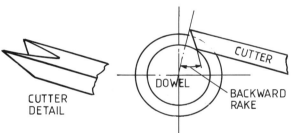

Fig. 6.6 Screwbox vee cutter showing backward rake

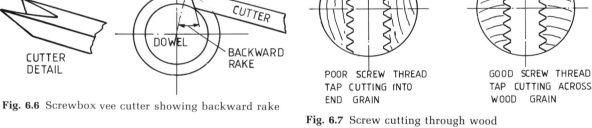

Fig. 6.7 Screw cutting through wood

preformed screwbox thread also assists in stopping the new dowel screw from breaking out. The key to using the screwbox successfully is to maintain the vee cutter in razor sharp condition and accurately set.

With regard to the use of the screw tap, this is conventional, except for one or two reservations. The first is to grip the wood on each side of the area being tapped, so that it does not break out under the pressure of this. The second point is to note that tapping across the grain gives a much cleaner result than cutting into end grain (*Fig. 6.7*), so study the wood item before deciding in which direction to drill the tapping hole.

Flyer and bobbins Details of the flyer components (17) and (18), and the leather bearings (21), are given

in Fig. 6.9. The pulley whorl is provided with a three step groove to give a choice of speed ratios between this and the bobbin. The bobbin dimensions are given in Fig. 6.10. Construction of these items has been discussed earlier.

Distaff The last items to add are the distaff components, the dimensions of which are given in Fig. 6.11. The lower distaff is in two pieces to make turning easier (items 22 and 23). Taper connections are used and the previous tips, i.e. marking/out drilling etc., should be followed. When not in use, the distaff is swung to the back of the wheel away from the spinner.

SPINNING FLAX

In the last chapter, basic wool spinning was

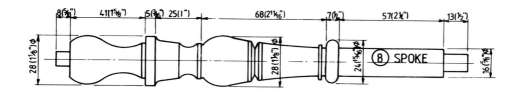

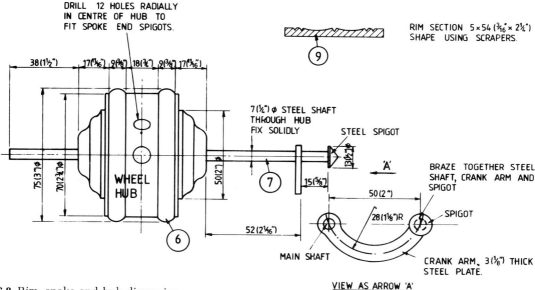

Fig. 6.8 Rim, spoke and hub dimensions

discussed, and, as the sloping bed wheel is fitted with a distaff for flax spinning, this is a good point to relate briefly the differing approach to working with this fibre. The first question a newcomer will ask is 'What do we need a distaff for; why can't we just card the flax as we do wool?' The answer lies in its staple length, which is typically 900mm (36in), compared to 50–150mm (2–6in) for wool. Thus you cannot card in the normal sense because you would need a pair of rather long carders, and also some long arms to go with it! Instead, the fibres are drawn through a hackle (*Fig. 6.12*) to straighten them, and then *dressed* onto a distaff, the latter being a means of holding the flax in an ordered manner ready for spinning.

Dressing a distaff with flax is not difficult, but the technique does demand a certain amount of skill. In principle, what you do is first build up a paper cone stuffed with tissue on the distaff. You then *dress* a small quantity of flax into a flat fan-shape on your lap, usually on a cloth. In this the fibres must never run straight, i.e. radial, but be allowed to criss-cross naturally over one another. Build up several thin fan-shaped layers, then wrap the flax fan gently round the distaff paper cone with the apex at the top. Usually this is done by rolling the cone into the flax. Secure the flax with a 2m (7ft) length of ribbon tied at the top of the distaff; then criss-cross it back and forth round the outside of the cone of flax to hold it all in position. Now mount the dressed distaff on the end of the distaff arm (24) ready for spinning. To spin, the flax fibres are drawn from the bottom of the distaff for spinning in the normal way. Flax is usually purchased as a *strick*, i.e. already

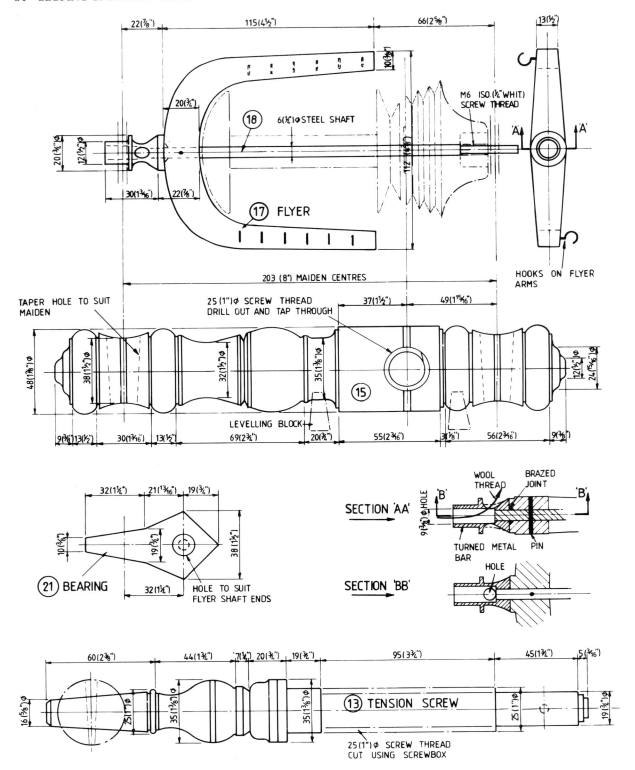

Fig. 6.9 Flyer, mother-of-all and tension screw details

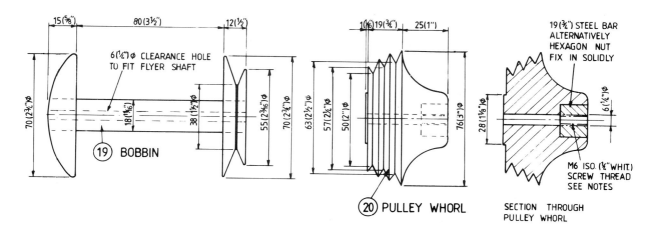

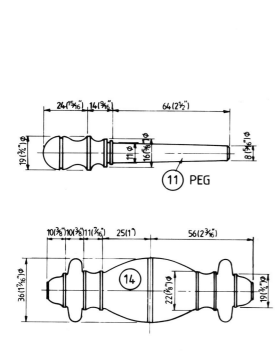

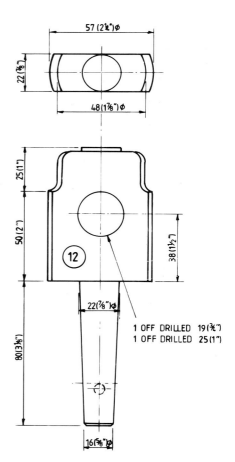

Fig. 6.10 Bobbin and miscellaneous details

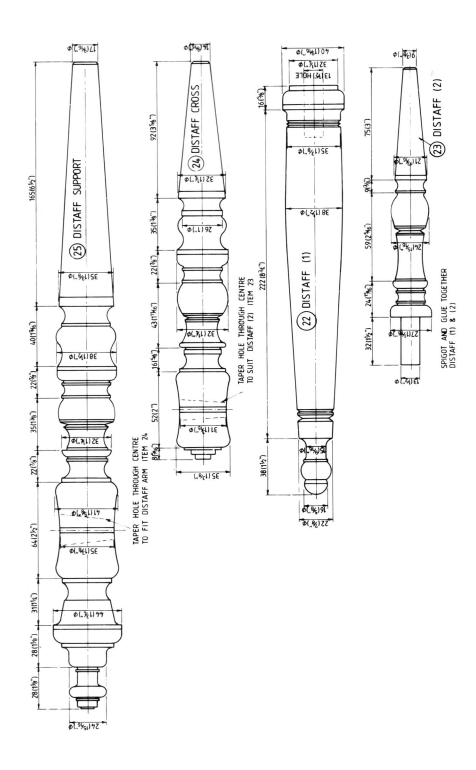

Fig. 6.11 Distaff details

Fig. 6.12 Hackle

Fig. 6.13 Lazy kate

combed, and as such does not need to be drawn through a hackle.

This description is a simplistic one aimed at explaining the principle, and encouraging the inexperienced to experiment. Some references are given in the bibliography for readers wishing to pursue this in greater depth.

LAZY KATE

The sloping bed wheel, unlike the Hebridean upright, is not fitted with a lazy kate, so it is handy to have an independent one such as that shown in Fig. 6.13. The dimensional information is given in Fig. 6.14. It is a very simple project, comprising a box frame to hold up to four bobbins.

It consists of two tapered end boards from $165 \times 22 \times 215$mm ($6\frac{1}{2} \times \frac{7}{8} \times 8\frac{1}{2}$in) long softwood fixed to $75 \times 18 \times 340$mm ($3 \times \frac{3}{4} \times 13\frac{3}{8}$in) long side pieces. A

25mm (1in) diameter ramin dowel is fitted into recesses in each end board to make a handle. Four 6mm ($\frac{1}{4}$in) holes are drilled in the sides to take the steel rods on which the bobbins are mounted, and should spin freely. Matching 6mm ($\frac{1}{4}$in) holes are drilled in the handle to line up with the bobbin axles. A plywood base is also fitted. This is optional but can actually be quite useful, so that the lazy kate doubles as a box for carrying the many spinning bits and bobs around. A useful tip with regard to the bobbin rods is to kink these slightly at one end, where they fit in the side strips. They will thus be held firmly, and not fall out of the box. To do this it may be necessary to reduce the rod size to 5mm ($\frac{3}{16}$in) diameter.

In use, the yarn is lead from the bobbins through the handle holes, as in Fig. 6.14, and then plied on the spinning wheel.

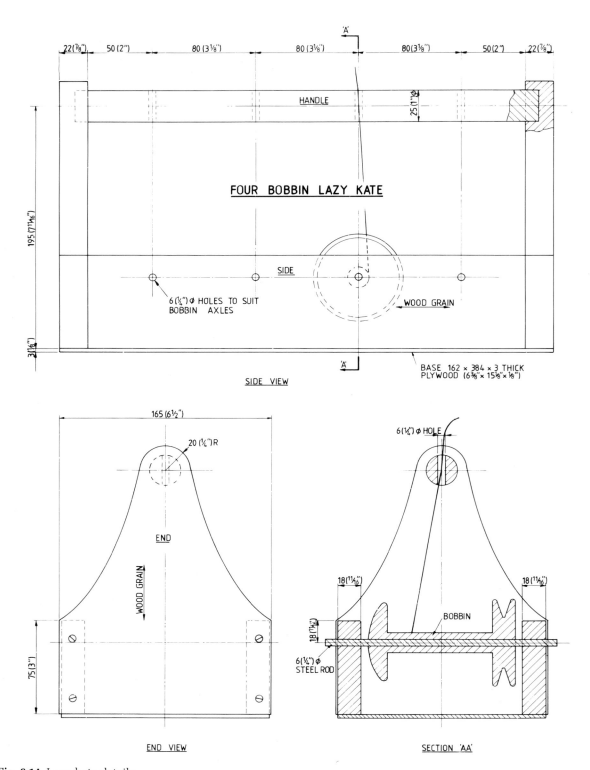

Fig. 6.14 Lazy kate details

7
UPRIGHT SPINNING WHEEL

INTRODUCTION

The wheels examined so far have been based on antique originals, so it is appropriate at this point to introduce something a little more modern. The subject is an upright wheel in the traditional style, with simple gracious lines. Looking at the design, and referring to the general arrangement in Fig. 7.3, there are similarities in the base (1) to the Hebridean wheel, but otherwise the form is completely different. The wheel is 460mm (18in) diameter and of segmented pattern. This is a fairly common size for spinning wheels, be they of upright or sloping bed type. This aspect and the general issue of wheel momentum/inertia will be discussed later.

DESIGN

The flyer arrangement, instead of being mounted directly above the wheel, is displaced slightly to one side on maidens (15) which fit horizontally into the mother-of-all (14). The latter fits in a slot in the rear wheel support (10), and slides in this and on the front wheel support (11), through a hole in the mother-of-all. A tension screw (13) adjusts the belt drive, and when this is correct a clamp knob (23) stiffens up the flyer arrangement. The wheel is fitted for double band drive, and a lazy kate for plying is included. The parts list is given in Table 6.

CONSTRUCTION

Start construction by making the baseblock (1), legs (2) and the treadle details (3) and (4). Dimensions of these items are given in Fig. 7.4. Assemble these in accordance with the general arrangement. A difficulty which has been previously raised, but not yet discussed, is that of drilling the 6mm ($\frac{1}{4}$in) diameter treadle stretcher pivot holes through the bottom ends of the front legs. Drilling, even with the

assistance of a straight edge as a guide, will never produce a satisfactory job. The solution is to make use of the centring capabilities of the woodturning lathe as follows.

The axle hole positions are first marked on the outside of the legs and centre popped. The base assembled with the front pair of legs is then mounted on the lathe, using a revolving centre in the tailstock, and a jacobs chuck/drill in the headstock, set on these hole positions. The centreline of the lathe is now the centreline of the treadle stretcher, and drilling will hence give a perfectly aligned hole. The lathe should be run at a slow speed during this operation to minimise the risk of damage, and it is also recommended that a small pilot hole is drilled first. To drill the hole in the opposite leg, the base arrangement is reversed.

Wheel supports The wheel supports (10) and (11) are rather slender, so may need the use of a steady when woodturning. Leave the turning centres on these items until the last possible moment, to allow for final trimming. This applies particularly to wheel support (11), where at the top end the 19mm ($\frac{3}{4}$in) diameter parallel section may need to be dressed, to make it fit smoothly in the matching hole in the mother-of-all (14). For the wheel support dimensions see Fig. 7.7.

Wheel The wheel is of segmented rim and split hub construction, and this method has been discussed earlier. Dimensional information is given in Fig. 7.5. Fig. 7.2 illustrates wheel machining in progress. Using the standard checks for wheel alignment, it should be possible to achieve a wheel wobble of less than $\frac{1}{2}$mm ($\frac{1}{32}$in), which is hardly noticeable and generally acceptable. However, if you wish to make

Table 6: *Upright Spinning Wheel Parts List*

Item	Description	No. off	Material	Dimensions
1	Baselock	1	Hardwood	230 × 32 × 380 long ($9\frac{1}{16}$ × $1\frac{1}{4}$ × 15in long)
2	Leg	3	Hardwood	35 sq. × 280 long ($1\frac{3}{8}$in sq. × 11in long)
3	Treadle stretcher	1	Hardwood	32 sq. × 395 long ($1\frac{1}{4}$in sq. × $15\frac{1}{2}$in long)
4	Treadle	1	Hardwood	120 × 10 × 350 long ($4\frac{3}{4}$ × $\frac{3}{8}$ × $13\frac{3}{4}$in long)
5	Pitman rod	1	Hardwood	25 × 10 × 436 long (1 × $\frac{3}{8}$ × $17\frac{1}{4}$in long)
6	Wheel hub	1	Hardwood	70 sq. × 100 long ($2\frac{3}{4}$in sq. × 4in long)
7	Spoke	8	Hardwood	28 sq. × 200 long ($1\frac{1}{8}$in sq. × 8in long)
8	Axle	1	Steel	8 dia. × 300 long ($\frac{5}{16}$ in dia. × 12in long)
9	Wheel rim	1	Hardwood	150 × 32 × 1250 long (6 × $1\frac{1}{4}$ × $49\frac{1}{4}$in long)
10	Wheel support (1)	1	Hardwood	65 sq. × 690 long ($2\frac{1}{2}$in sq. × $27\frac{1}{4}$in long)
11	Wheel support (2)	1	Hardwood	48 sq. × 700 long (1in sq. × $27\frac{1}{2}$in long)
12	Peg (1)	2	Hardwood	16 sq. × 85 long ($\frac{5}{8}$in sq. × 3in long)
13	Tension screw	1	Hardwood	42 sq. × 225 long ($1\frac{5}{8}$in sq. × 8in long)
14	Mother-of-all	1	Hardwood	48 sq. × 300 long ($1\frac{7}{8}$in sq. × 12in long)
15	Maiden	2	Hardwood	32 sq. × 250 long ($1\frac{1}{4}$in sq. × 10in long)
16	Flyer	1	Hardwood	115 × 20 × 115 long ($4\frac{1}{2}$ × $\frac{3}{4}$ × $4\frac{1}{2}$ in long)
17	Flyer axle	1	Steel	6 dia × 200 long ($\frac{1}{4}$in dia. × 8in long)
18	Bobbin	3	Hardwood	75 sq. & 20 sq. material (3in sq. & $\frac{3}{4}$in sq. mat'l)
19	Pully whorl	1	Hardwood	75 sq. × 40 long (3in sq. × $1\frac{9}{16}$in long)
20	Bearing	2	Hardwood	75 × 35 × 5 thick (3 × $1\frac{1}{2}$ × $\frac{3}{16}$in thick)
21	Bobbin rack upright	2	Hardwood	22 sq. × 170 long ($\frac{7}{8}$in sq. × $6\frac{3}{4}$in long)
22	Peg (2)	2	Hardwood	10 sq. × 170 long ($\frac{3}{8}$in sq. × $6\frac{3}{4}$in long)
23	Clamp knob	1	Hardwood	50 sq. × 60 long (2in sq. × 2in long)

Fig. 7.1 Wheel machining in progress

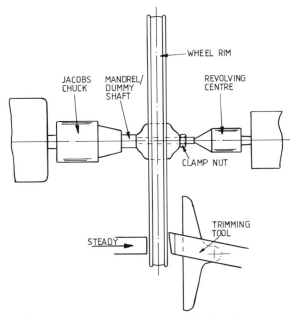

Fig. 7.2 Jig for accurate machining of wheel rim

an absolutely true wheel, then the only way is to carry out a final trim after the assembly has been glued together, i.e. rim, spokes and axle. This involves mounting the wheel between centres, as shown in Fig. 7.6, using a dummy axle. The large diameter usually necessitates a special slow speed drive being constructed. A suggested arrangement is to mount the axle at one end in a revolving centre, and drive at the opposite end through a jacobs chuck. A means of temporarily clamping the wheel to the dummy axle (e.g. screw nuts/washers) is also required. When carrying out the final trim a steady may need to be used behind the wheel rim to stop undue vibration during this operation. This should be reversible to enable the second side face to be machined. The details are left to the reader, but whatever is decided upon, do make sure the arrangement is safe and rigid.

Wheel momentum Wheels are built of varying sizes, indeed this book features designs with diameters ranging from 360mm (14in) to 610mm (24in). A general purpose segmented wheel design is typically 460–510mm (18–20in) diameter, with a radial width of 50mm (2in) and about 25mm (1in) thick. This gives a good momentum and is nice and steady to treadle. Wheels of smaller diameter will spin just as well, but need treadling faster, so can be a little wearing after a time. Larger ones, by contrast, can be treadled slowly and regularly.

Table 7: Comparison of Wheel Inertia Ratios

Outside diameter	Inside diameter	Inertia ratio relative to 460mm (18in) diameter wheel.	Inertia ratio relative to 360mm (14in) diameter wheel.
360 (14in)	250 (10in)	0.46	1.0
405 (16in)	305 (12in)	0.65	1.41
460 (18in)	360 (14in)	1.0	2.17
510 (20in)	410 (16in)	1.41	3.05
560 (22in)	460 (18in)	1.92	4.16
610 (24in)	510 (20in)	2.53	5.49

Table 7 compares the inertia ratios of wheels of different diameters and similar thicknesses, but ignores the effect of the hub and spokes, which is generally small. Thus a wheel of 460mm (18in) diameter has over twice the inertia of one of 360mm (14in) diameter. Similarly, one of 610mm (24in) diameter has about five and a half times the inertia of the smallest wheel. Larger wheels can therefore be reduced in radial width and still maintain sufficient momentum. It is not uncommon, for example, to find wheels of 610mm (24in) diameter and over to have smaller radial widths.

Flyer, maidens, mother-of-all Details of the flyer, maidens and mother-of-all are given in Fig. 7.6. In

making the mother-of-all, check that the end flats where it fits in the wheel support (10) are in line with the 19mm (¾in) diameter hole which slides on the wheel support (11), so as to ensure a smooth movement. The latter also has a 16mm (⅝in) wood screw tapped transversely through the end, into which the tension screw (13) fits (*Fig. 7.9*). A clamp knob (23) screws onto the end of the mother-of-all. Note that this knob has an M8 Isometric (5/16in Whitworth) captive nut embedded in it. This is achieved by machining it in two pieces, inserting the nut, and gluing the parts back together.

Miscellaneous items The last items to add are the bobbins, the lazy kate arrangement, and the wheel pegs. Dimensions of these parts are given in Fig. 7.9. The lazy kate is designed for two bobbins, but by doubling the height of the bobbin upright (21), this could be increased to four if required. A tip worth remembering when turning small items such as the wheel pegs (12) is to grip the wood in a jacobs chuck rather than using a two or four pronged drive centre. This holds the work much firmer, with less risk of the wood splitting. It also reduces vibration, so that a good finish can be achieved.

IMPROVED FEATURES

The flyer and bobbin details given so far in this book will work quite successfully. This is not to say, however, that they cannot be improved upon, and some suggestions for better design are made as follows.

Flyer orificies The flyer orifice in Fig. 7.6 is traditional in that it has a locally reduced section where the wool comes through the transverse hole behind the leather bearing to pass out along the flyer arms. This can be difficult to make, requiring local filing etc. Fig. 7.8 shows a much simpler and more modern design which is easier to machine. Two sizes are given, a standard one with a 10mm (⅜in) orifice, and a larger one with a 12mm (15/32in) orifice for use with chunkier wools. If you want to spin flax you might consider a slightly smaller version than the standard, with say an 8mm (5/16in) orifice.

Disposition of flyer eye It is usual to arrange the wool guide hooks on the trailing arms of the flyer as shown in Fig. 7.10, when viewed in normal

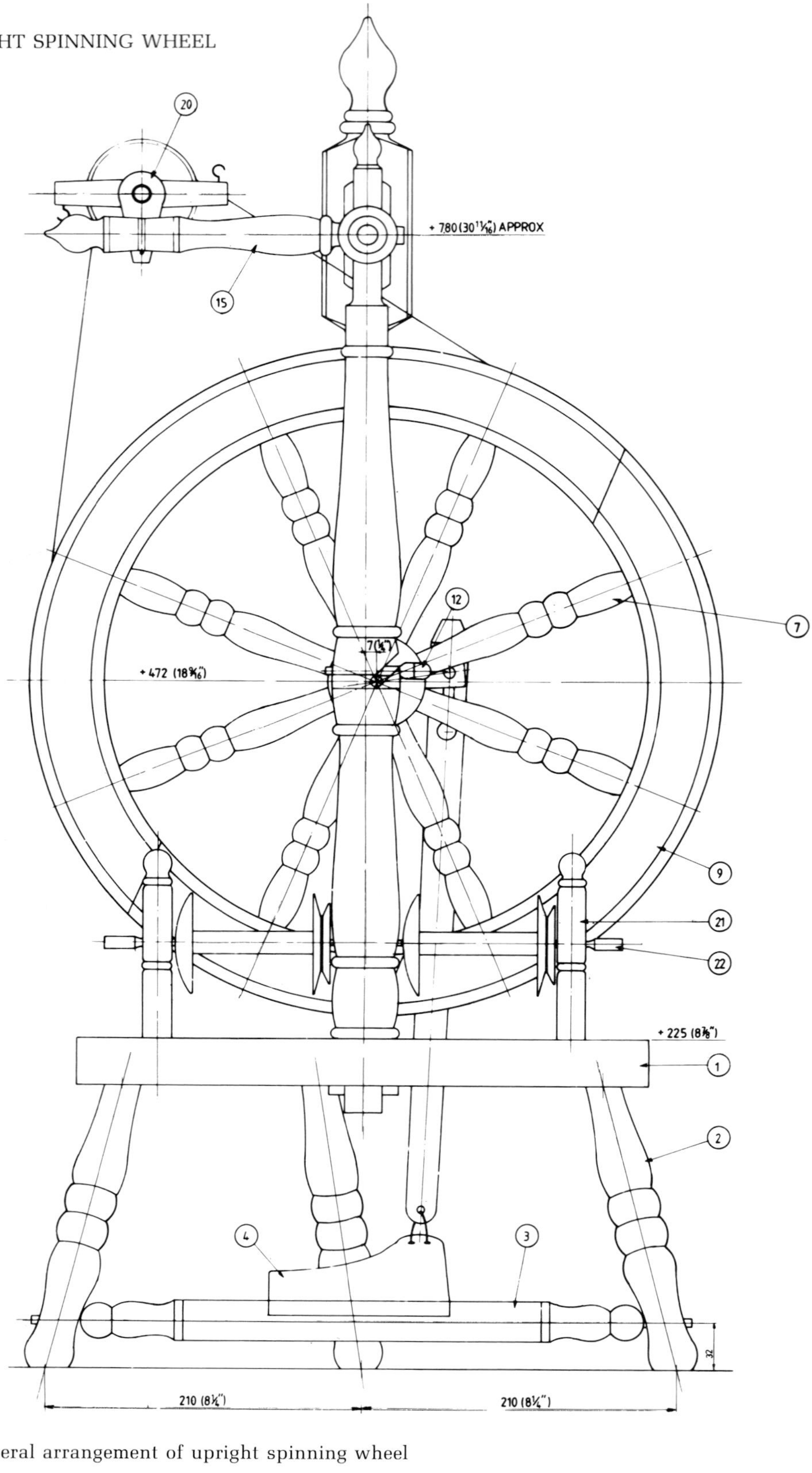

+ 780 (30¹¹⁄₁₆") APPROX

7

12

7 (¼")

+ 472 (18⁹⁄₁₆")

9

21

22

+ 225 (8⅞")

1

2

4

3

210 (8¼")   210 (8¼")

Fig. 7.3 General arrangement of upright spinning wheel

DATUM LEVEL + 0·0MM

115 (4½")   140 (5½")   115 (4½")

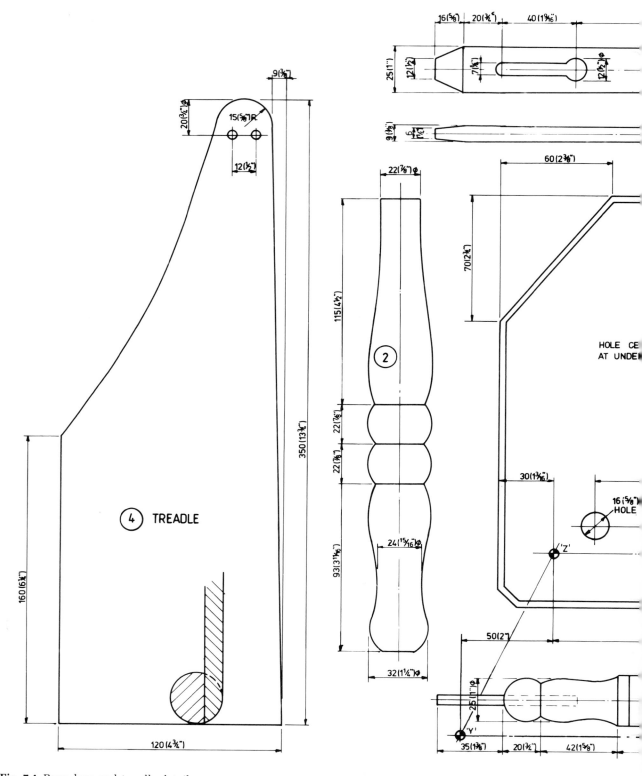

Fig. 7.4 Base, legs and treadle details

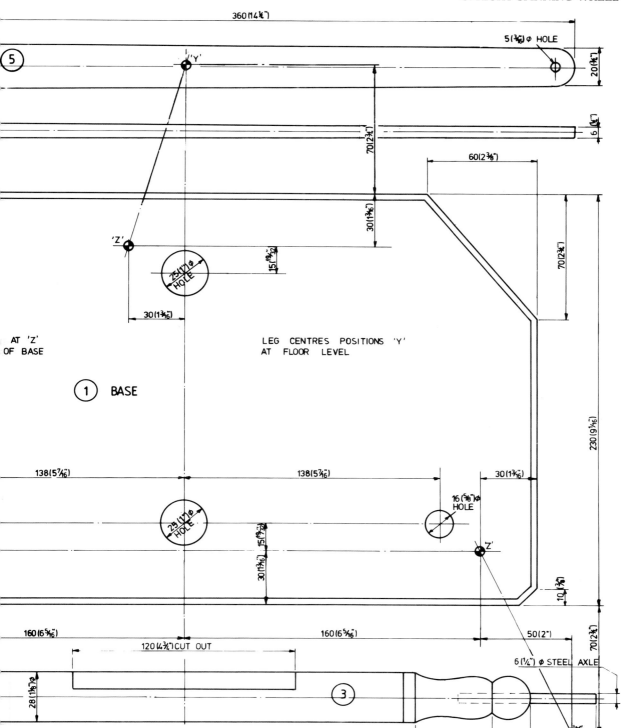

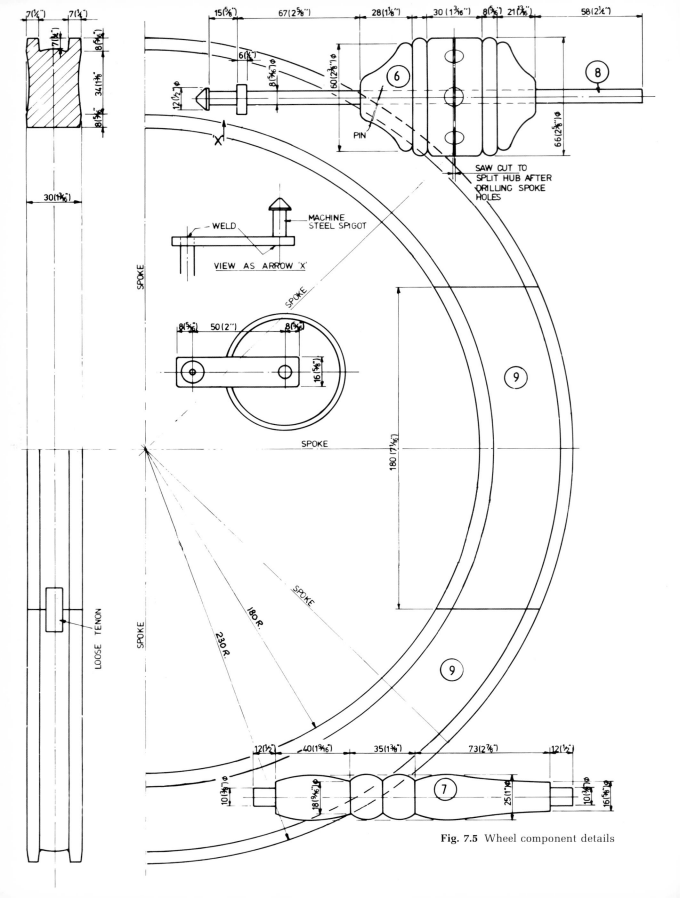

Fig. 7.5 Wheel component details

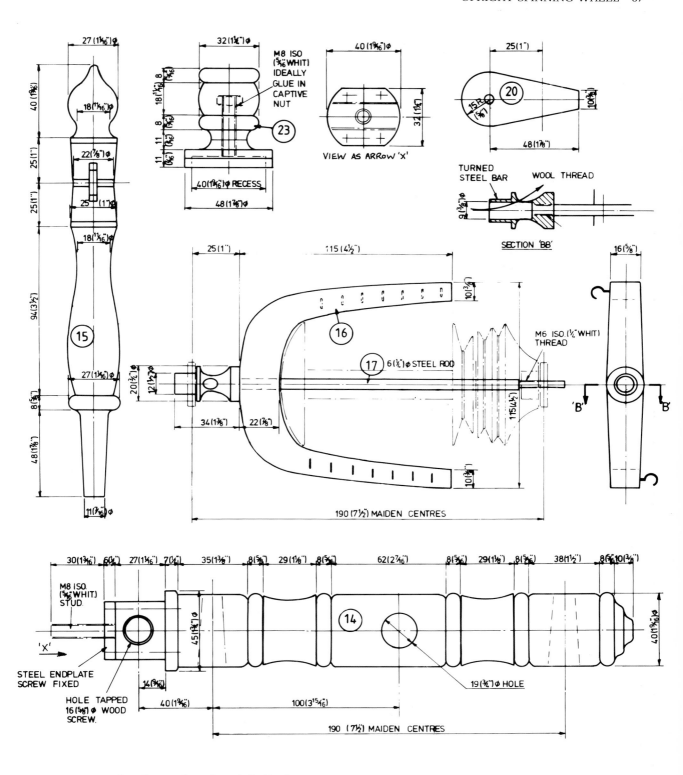

Fig. 7.6 Maiden, flyer and mother-of-all details

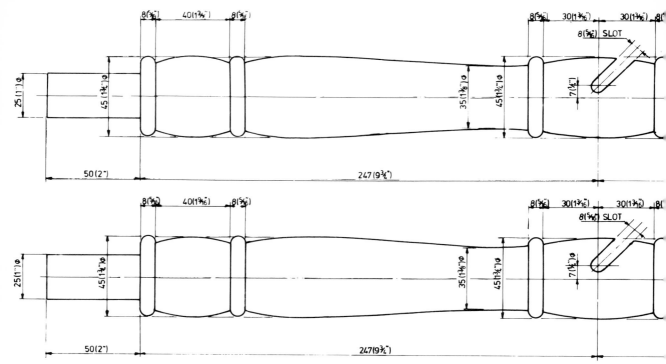

Fig. 7.7 Wheel support dimensions

clockwise rotation. The hooks on one arm are sometimes staggered relative to the set on the other. Thus by switching the wool from one side to the other as thread is spun, the yarn can be evenly distributed over the bobbin. The disadvantage with the arrangement in Fig.7.10 is that the wool has to be rethreaded through the orifice at every switch. An improvement is to put both sets of hooks on the same side of the flyer, and centre up the orifice transverse hole as in Fig. 7.11. With this arrangement you can then lift the threads off the hooks 'A' and transfer them to 'B' and vice versa, without having to rethread the wool through the orifice.

Orifice threader A very useful little device is an orifice threader. This consists of either a wire hook or a loop embedded in a short handle. Fig. 7.12 gives details of a suitable threader you can make. The spring wire loop is best made of piano wire.

Bobbin improvements One of the irritating things about bobbins is that, unless the centre hole is a snug but loose fit on the flyer axle, it tends to rattle a little when in use, even though the belt tension is adequate. An improvement is to use a brass tube for the bobbin centre, which is a close tolerance fit on the flyer axle. The bobbin ends can be glued on with epoxy resin before machining on a mandrel.

Alternatively, if you wish to preserve the wooden centre section of the bobbin, the brass tube could be inserted down the centre of this. Fig. 7.13 gives details of these two options.

Pulley whorl fixture In designs we have looked at so far the pulley whorls have been secured by screwing them onto the end of the flyer axle, e.g. Fig. 7.9. The pulley whorl has a screwed metal insert or nut to facilitate this. On old wheels this was a left-hand thread, so it tended to tighten whilst spinning clockwise, but, as explained in Chapter 5, this is not really necessary. As an alternative, antique wheels sometimes used pulley whorls with a square section hole, which fitted over a matching square section of the flyer axle. A simple adaptation of this which uses a flat on the shaft as a key is shown in Fig. 7.14.

In this design the pulley whorl is drilled right through to the flyer axle diameter, and finish machined on a mandrel this size. A thin piece of 6mm ($\frac{1}{4}$in) wide steel strip is then inserted in the hole and bent over as shown. This metal strip matches a local flat at the end of the flyer axle. The pulley whorl will then slide on but cannot rotate. It should be a spring fit, and not sloppy. To incorporate this design the flyer axle needs to be larger, of the order of 8–10mm ($\frac{5}{16}$–$\frac{3}{8}$in) diameter. Below this size it is just not practical.

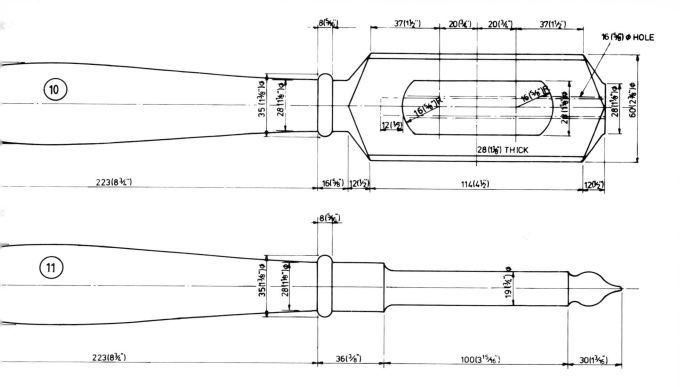

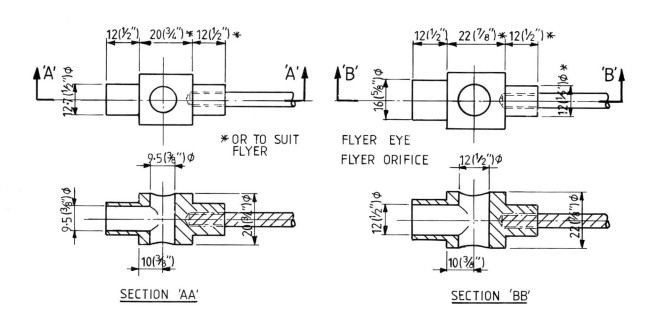

SECTION 'AA'

SECTION 'BB'

Fig. 7.8 Modern flyer orifice design

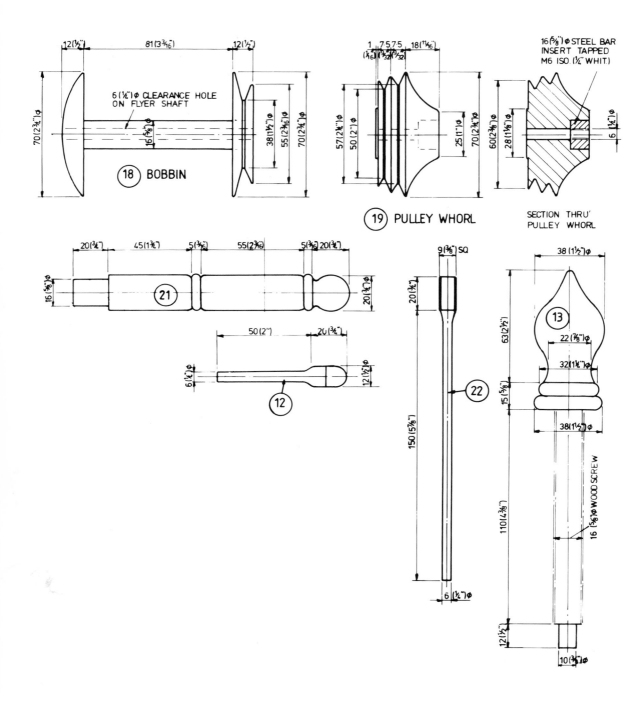

Fig. 7.9 Bobbin, tension screw and lazy kate details

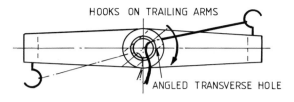

Fig. 7.10 Flyer orifice/hook arrangement (1)

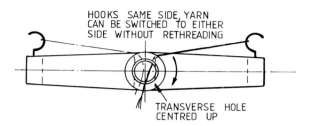

Fig. 7.11 Flyer orifice/hook arrangement (2);
right hook = A, left hook = B.

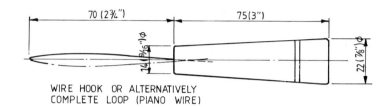

Fig. 7.12 Orifice threader

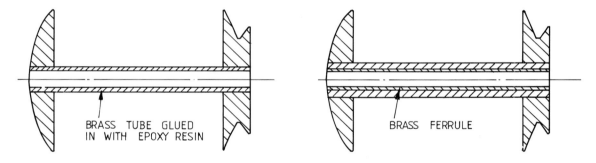

Fig. 7.13 Improved bobbin bearings

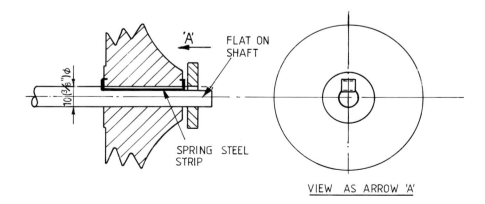

Fig. 7.14 Alternative pulley whorl fixing

8
ARKWRIGHT SPINNING WHEEL

Fig. 8.1 Arkwright spinning wheel

INTRODUCTION

We come now to a spinning wheel design with its name indelibly marked in history, the *Arkwright wheel*, as shown in Fig. 8.1. Strangely, not a lot is known about the wheel, except that it has been in the Science Museum, London, for over 100 years, and was donated by 'B. Fothergill' along with other items including Arkwright's improved spinning machine and also a carding machine. Arkwright was born in Preston in 1732 and lived until 1792, so the wheel probably dates from the mid to late eighteenth century.

DESIGN

The design is of sloping bed style, and features an unusually steep base, supporting a 488mm (19$\frac{1}{4}$in) diameter segmented wheel with 16 spokes. The latter is of stepped rim construction, a method not yet discussed but which will be detailed later. It is a flax wheel and is fitted with a lantern distaff for dressing this fibre. The turnings on the legs and distaff etc. are neither plain nor elaborate, consisting of beaded sections contrasting with short lengths of undulating contour. The flyer is quite unconventionally set on a rather tall support post, indeed the height at 890mm (35in) above the floor is such that it exceeds many upright style wheels. This arrangement also tends to give the wheel an unbalanced appearance, as though tipped to the right, and some alternative proposals to correct this are given later in the chapter. The flyer itself is almost horseshoe-shaped, with long slender arms and numerous closely spaced hooks. Within this is a rather diminutive bobbin. The original is made of oak and stained a dark brown.

CONSTRUCTION

The general arrangement drawings are given in Fig. 8.2, and the associated parts list in Table 8. The measured drawings here are, with one or two exceptions, the originals. Where there are differences, the changes have been to make the wheel more practical and aesthetically acceptable. These are principally in the flyer details, and the base slope. But so that the purist can make an original if he so wishes, the differences have been highlighted in the text.

Table 8: Arkwright Spinning Wheel Parts List

Item	Description	No. off	Material	Dimensions
1	Baseblock (1)	1	Hardwood	170 × 60 × 440 long ($6\frac{3}{4} \times 2\frac{3}{8} \times 17$in long)
2	Leg	3	Hardwood	50 sq. × 525 long (2in sq. × $20\frac{3}{4}$in long)
3	Treadle stretcher	1	Hardwood	35 sq. × 490 long ($1\frac{3}{8}$in sq. × 19in long)
4	Treadle backbar	1	Hardwood	45 × 10 × 405 long ($1\frac{3}{4} \times \frac{3}{8} \times 16$in long)
5	Treadle	1	Hardwood	60 × 7 × 235 long ($2\frac{3}{4} \times \frac{1}{4} \times 9\frac{1}{4}$in long)
6	Wheel hub	1	Hardwood	75 sq. × 75 long (3in sq. × 3in long)
7	Wheel axle	1	Steel	8 dia. × 200 long ($\frac{5}{16}$in dia. × 8in long)
8	Spoke	16	Hardwood	16 sq. × 165 long ($\frac{5}{8}$in sq. × $6\frac{1}{2}$in long)
9	Wheel rim	1	Hardwood	140 × 28 × 1400 long ($5\frac{1}{2} \times 1\frac{1}{8} \times 55$in long)
10	Connector	1	Leather	60 × 25 × 5 thick ($2\frac{3}{8} \times 1 \times \frac{3}{16}$in thick)
11	Wheel support	2	Hardwood	60 sq. × 400 long ($2\frac{3}{8}$in sq. × $15\frac{3}{4}$in long)
12	Peg	2	Hardwood	20 sq. × 90 long ($\frac{3}{4}$in sq. × $3\frac{1}{2}$ long)
13	Tension screw (1)	1	Hardwood	45 sq. × 230 long ($1\frac{3}{4}$in sq. × $9\frac{1}{16}$in long)
14	Mother-of-all support	1	Hardwood	60 sq. × 410 long ($2\frac{3}{8}$in sq. × $16\frac{1}{4}$in long)
15	Collar	1	Hardwood	100 × 20 × 100 long ($4 \times \frac{3}{4} \times 4$in long)
16	Mother-of-all	1	Hardwood	50 sq × 260 long (2in sq. × $10\frac{1}{4}$in long)
17	Maiden (1)	2	Hardwood	38 sq. × 190 long ($1\frac{1}{2}$in sq. × $7\frac{1}{2}$in long)
18	Flyer	1	Hardwood	115 × 20 × 115 long ($4\frac{1}{2} \times \frac{3}{4} \times 4\frac{1}{2}$in long)
19	Flyer axle	1	Steel	6 dia. & 20 dia. bar ($\frac{1}{4}$in dia. & $\frac{3}{4}$in dia. bar)
20	Bobbin	1	Hardwood	75 sq. & 20 sq. material (3in sq. & $\frac{3}{4}$in sq. material)
21	Pulley whorl	1	Hardwood	80 sq. × 50 long ($3\frac{1}{4}$in sq. × 2in long)
22	Bearing	2	Leather	80 × 60 × 5 thick ($3\frac{1}{4} \times 2 \times \frac{3}{16}$in thick)
23	Lower distaff	1	Hardwood	45 sq. × 430 long ($1\frac{3}{4}$in sq. × 17in long)
24	Distaff arm	1	Hardwood	40 sq. × 310 long (1in sq. × $12\frac{1}{4}$ in long)
25	Lantern base	1	Hardwood	110 sq. × 7 thick (4in sq. × $\frac{1}{4}$in thick)
26	Lantern upright	3	Hardwood	7 dia. × 380 long ($\frac{1}{4}$in dia. × 15in long)
27	Lantern spigot	1	Hardwood	32 sq. × 80 long ($1\frac{1}{4}$in sq. × $3\frac{1}{4}$in long)
28	Crown piece	1	Hardwood	38sq. × 90 long ($1\frac{1}{2}$in sq. × $3\frac{1}{2}$in long)
29	Baseblock (2)	1	Hardwood	170 × 60 × 460 long ($6\frac{3}{4} \times 2 \times 18\frac{1}{4}$in long)
30	Maiden (2)	2	Hardwood	38 sq. × 240 long ($1\frac{1}{2}$in sq. × $9\frac{1}{2}$in long)
31	Mother-of-all support	1	Hardwood	75 sq. × 170 long (3 in sq. × $6\frac{3}{4}$in long)
32	Tension screw	1	Hardwood	45 sq. × 250 long ($1\frac{3}{4}$in sq. × 10in long)
33	Finial	1	Hardwood	30 sq. × 30 long (1in sq. × 1in long)

Base, legs and wheel supports The dimensions of the baseblock (1), legs (2), and wheel supports (11) are given in Fig. 8.3. As just mentioned, the base has an unusually high tilt, and in the general arrangement (*Fig. 8.2*) this slope has been reduced to make it less severe. This also has the advantage of making the legs all about the same length. If you prefer to maintain the original base angle, the height dimension of the left leg at +444mm ($17\frac{1}{2}$in), should be increased to about +480mm (19in).

Treadle The treadle details are given in Fig. 8.4. This is a three-part construction used quite commonly on spinning wheels. What is different, however, is the method of pivoting the treadle stretcher (3). Instead of passing through holes in the bottom of the legs, the axles are mounted in steel hoops set into the side of them. It is suggested that these are made in stainless steel rather than mild steel so that they do not discolour.

Wheel The wheel is of segmented stepped rim

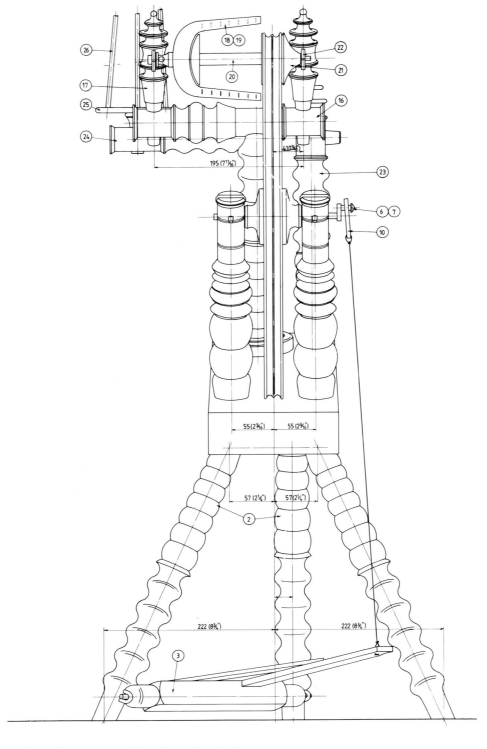

Fig. 8.2 General arrangement of Arkwright wheel

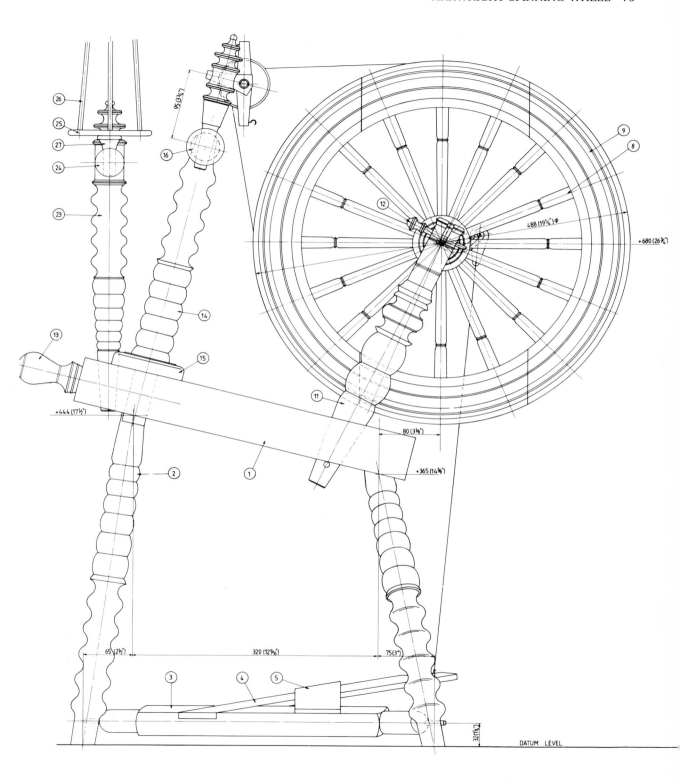

construction, and the dimensions of this, the spokes (8) and the hub (6) are given in Fig. 8.5. In this arrangement the rim is machined in the normal way, but with a step on the inside diameter (see rim section). The spokes are made with matching ends to fit this step. The hub can be turned as a whole (i.e. not split), and the spokes are then spigoted into this. The assembly is then let sideways into the previously machined rim. The spokes are positioned circumferentially at the rim by small wooden pegs, and glued. The usual alignment and concentricity checks should, of course, be carried out. The completed wheel is then slotted into the wheel supports (11) and pegged. The crank is connected to the treadle via a cord link instead of the usual pitman rod. The leather connector (10) at the crank end is detailed in Fig. 8.7.

Flyer, mother-of-all and bobbins The flyer/mother-of-all is mounted off a support bar (14). The details of this, the collar (15) and the tension screw (13) for drive band adjustment are given in Fig. 8.7. In the original, the support bar/collar is made from one piece of hardwood, but it is less wasteful of material if this is made in two parts. The tension screw (13) fits in a longitudinal hole in the end of the baseblock (1), and screws through the end of the support bar (14). A 25mm (1in) screwbox and tap will be required to cut the threads.

The bobbins are tiny, being only 35–40mm ($1\frac{1}{2}$in) diameter each end, and hence can hold very little spun yarn. The flyer is also rather fragile, and the maiden centre pitching is narrow at 175mm ($6\frac{7}{8}$in). This is not a very practical arrangement for modern-day usage, and some changes have therefore been made. Firstly, the maiden centre distance has been increased by 20mm ($\frac{3}{4}$in) to 195mm ($7\frac{11}{16}$in). Secondly, the opportunity has been taken to fit a more robust flyer, and also larger bobbins. The flyer diameter of 115mm ($4\frac{1}{2}$in) has been maintained as in the original. The modified flyer and bobbin details are given in Fig. 8.6. No changes have, however, been made to the maidens.

Distaff The distaff arrangement follows the usual pattern on a sloping bed wheel comprising of three parts: the lower distaff (23), a radial arm (24), and finally the distaff itself. For details of these items see Fig. 8.7. On the Arkwright wheel a lantern distaff is

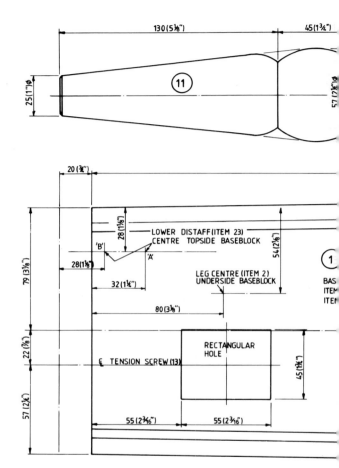

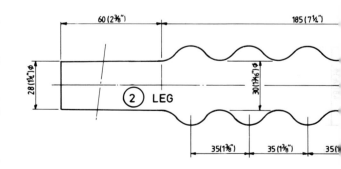

Fig. 8.3 Base, leg and wheel post details

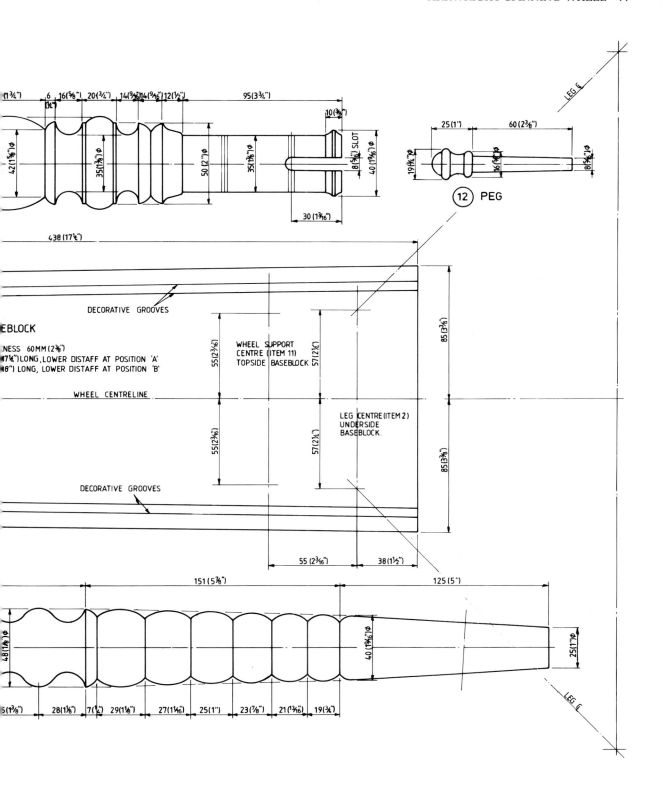

(1¾")   6   16(⅝")   20(¾")   14(9⁄16")14(9⁄16")12(½")   95(3¾")

10(⅜")

42(1⅝")⌀

35(1⅜")⌀

50(2")⌀

35(1⅜")⌀

8(⁵⁄₁₆") SLOT

40(1⁹⁄₁₆")⌀

30(1³⁄₁₆")

438(17¼")

25(1")   60(2⅜")

19(¾")⌀

16(⅝")⌀

8(⁵⁄₁₆")⌀

(12) PEG

DECORATIVE GROOVES

EBLOCK

NESS 60MM (2⅜")

17¼") LONG, LOWER DISTAFF AT POSITION 'A'

8") LONG, LOWER DISTAFF AT POSITION 'B'

WHEEL CENTRELINE

55(2³⁄₁₆")

WHEEL SUPPORT
CENTRE (ITEM 11)
TOPSIDE BASEBLOCK

57(2¼")

85(3⅜")

55(2³⁄₁₆")

57(2¼")

LEG CENTRE (ITEM 2)
UNDERSIDE
BASEBLOCK.

85(3⅜")

DECORATIVE GROOVES

55 (2³⁄₁₆")   38(1½")

151(5⅞")   125 (5")

48(1⅞")⌀

40(1⁹⁄₁₆")⌀

25(1")⌀

LEG ₵

6(1⅜")   28(1⅛") 7(¼") 29(1⅛")   27(1¹⁄₁₆") 25(1")   23(⅞") 21(¹³⁄₁₆") 19(¾")

fitted, so called because of the similarity to old-fashioned lamps. It has an advantage over the plain spindle type in that it is generally easier to dress with flax, and its conical shape stops this from sliding down.

Alternative flyer/mother-of-all

As mentioned earlier, the original Arkwright wheel tends to have a rather unbalanced look about it, due to the tall, ungainly flyer/mother-of-all. Also the flyer orifice is somewhat high for normal usage. Generally this height above floor level is between 600mm (24in) for sloping bed wheels, and up to 800mm ($31\frac{1}{2}$in) for upright style wheels. With a very simple adaptation, however, you can both improve the wheel appearance and, at the same time, reduce the flyer orifice height to an acceptable level. This involves a modification to the flyer arrangement, as shown in Fig. 8.8, rather similar to the sloping bed wheel in Chapter 6.

The principal change is to eliminate the tall mother-of-all support (14), and then to slope the maidens back away from the wheel. The maidens have also been extended slightly to bring the orifice height in line with the wheel centre at +680mm ($26\frac{3}{4}$in) above the floor. It is also necessary to slope the lower distaff (23) back in line with the maidens, so that it does not clash with the latter. In addition, the baseblock (1), and tension screw (13) need to be made slightly longer (now items 29 and 32) to accommodate this change. The dimensions of the modified maidens (30) and mother-of-all support (31) are given in Fig. 8.9.

The resulting wheel is therefore *Arkwright style* rather than *Arkwright original*, but it is, I feel, an acceptable compromise, in which the least change has been made to make the wheel appearance more pleasing and also more practical for modern-day usage.

WOODS

It has been mentioned in passing that oak and ash are common choices for the construction of spinning wheels – indeed the Arkwright wheel is made of oak – and to be authentic one would consider nothing else. But other woods can be used for wheels, the most common of which are the temporate hardwoods such as beech and cherry, and also yew which, strictly speaking, is not a hardwood.

Fig. 8.4 Treadle dimensions

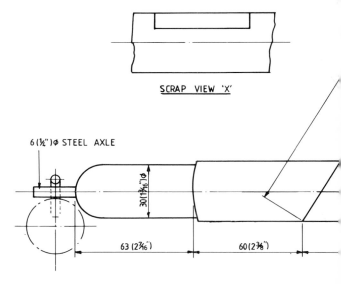

SCRAP VIEW 'X'

6 ($\frac{1}{4}$")⌀ STEEL AXLE

30 (1$\frac{3}{16}$")⌀

63 (2$\frac{7}{16}$")

60 (2$\frac{3}{8}$")

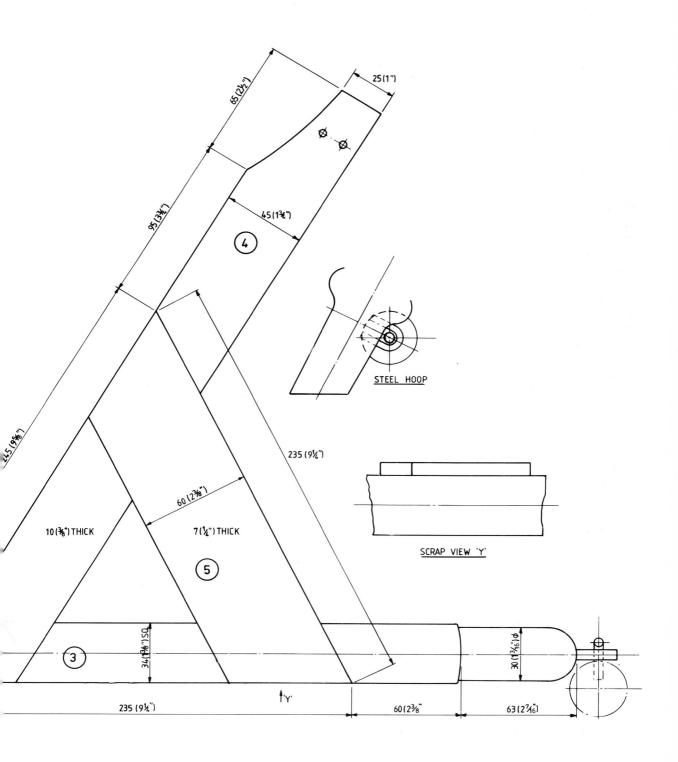

65 (2½")

25 (1")

95 (3¾")

45 (1¾")

④

245 (9⅝")

235 (9¼")

60 (2⅜")

10 (⅜") THICK

7 (¼") THICK

⑤

STEEL HOOP

SCRAP VIEW 'Y'

③

34 (1⅜") SQ.

30 (1³⁄₁₆") ∅

235 (9¼")

'Y'

60 (2⅜")

63 (2⁷⁄₁₆")

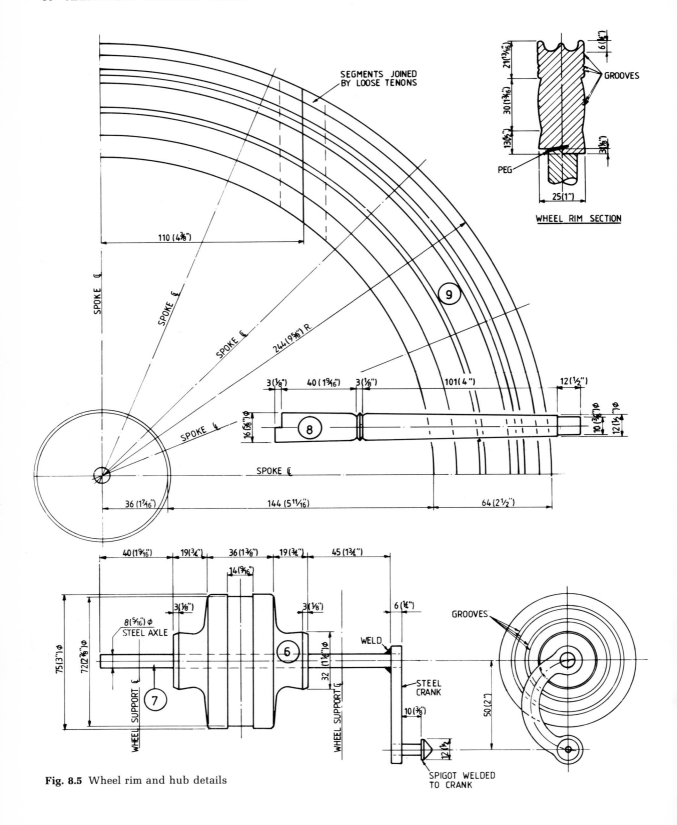

Fig. 8.5 Wheel rim and hub details

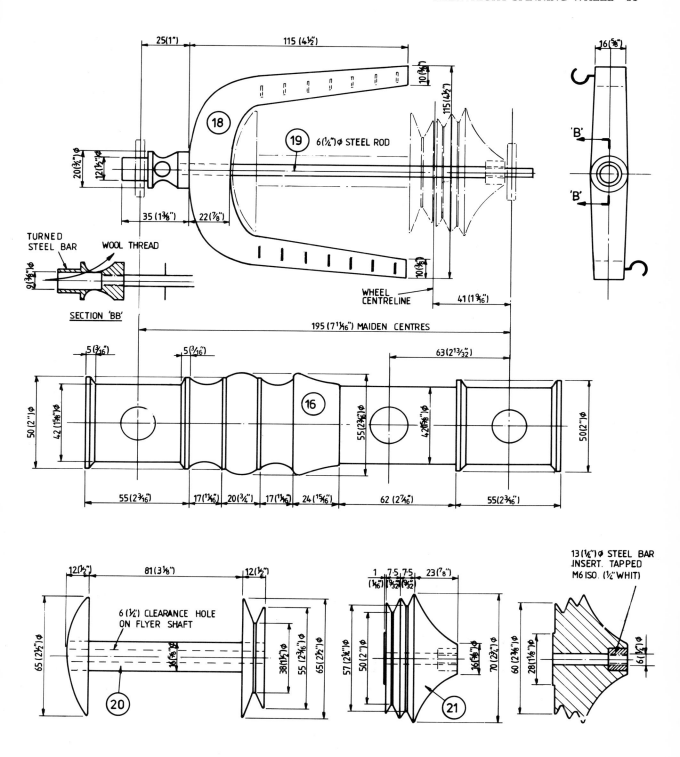

Fig. 8.6 Flyer; mother-of-all and bobbin details

Fig. 8.7 Maiden, tension screws and distaff details

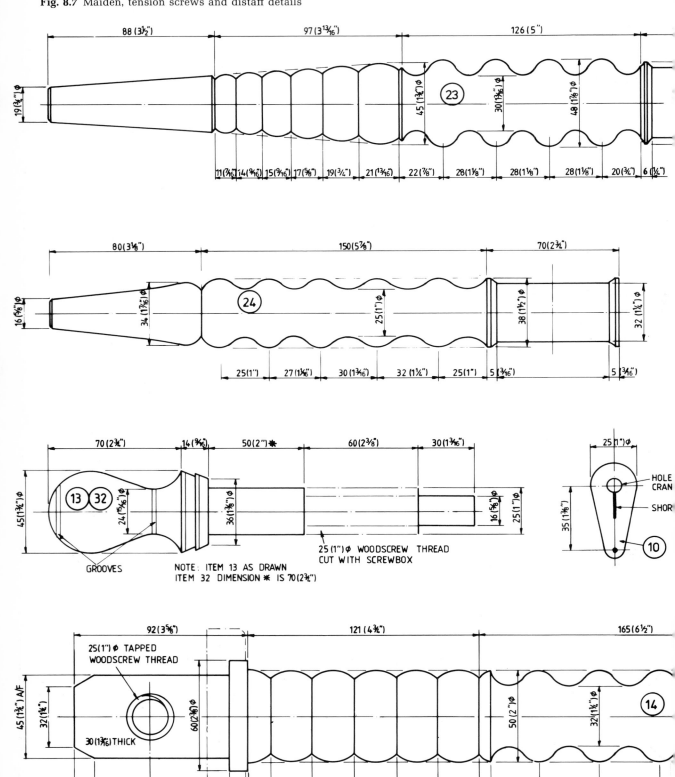

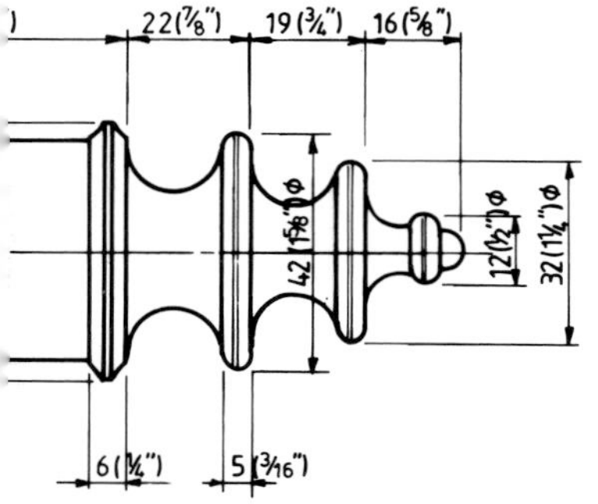
22(7/8")
19(3/4")
16(5/8")
42(1 5/8")ϕ
12(1/2")ϕ
32(1 1/4")ϕ
6(1/4")
5(3/16")

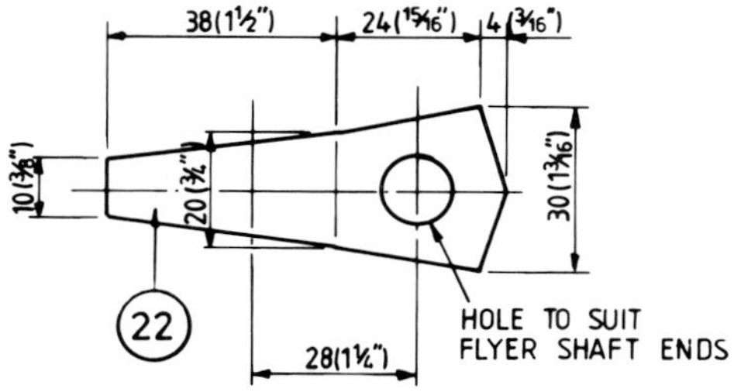
38(1 1/2")
24(15/16")
4(3/16")
10(3/8")
20(3/4")
30(1 3/16")
22
HOLE TO SUIT
FLYER SHAFT ENDS
28(1 1/4")

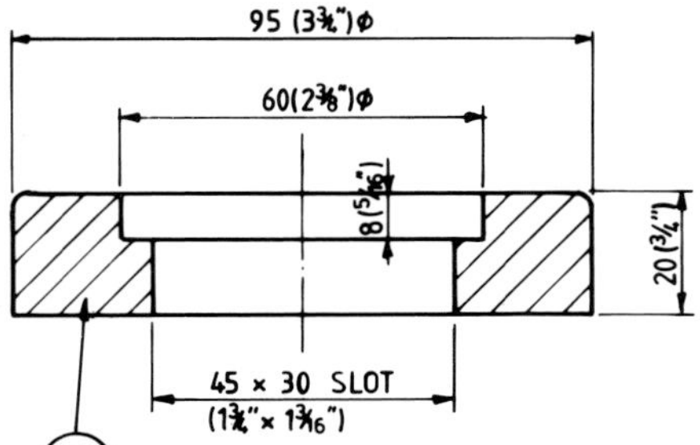
95 (3 3/4")ϕ
60(2 3/8")ϕ
8(5/16")
20(3/4")
45 × 30 SLOT
(1 3/4" × 1 3/16")

15 COLLAR

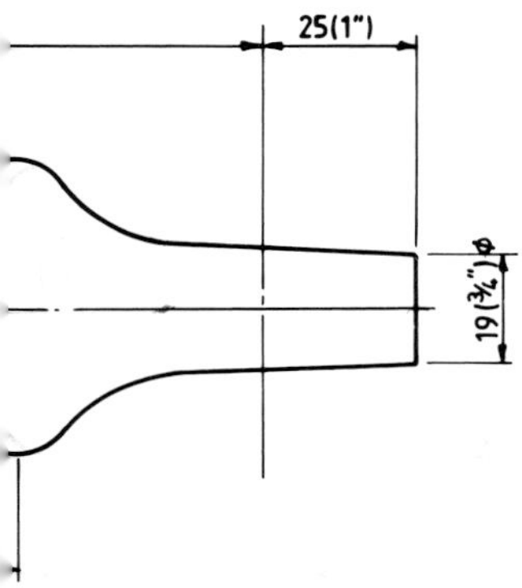
25(1")
19(3/4")ϕ

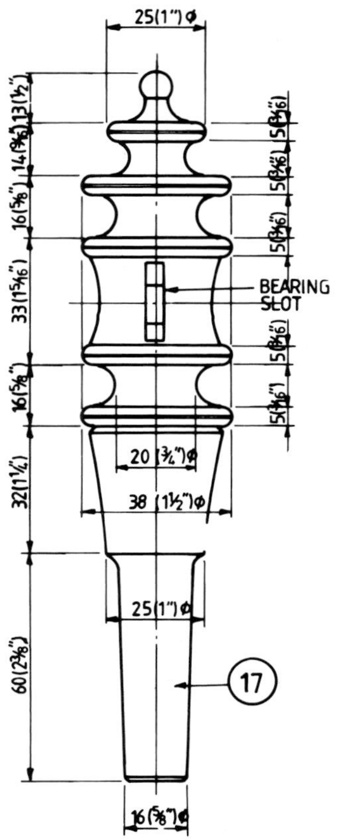
25(1")ϕ
13(1/2")
14(9/16")
16(5/8")
33(1 5/16")
16(5/8")
32(1 1/4")
60(2 3/8")
5(3/16")
5(3/16")
5(3/16")
5(3/16")
5(3/16")
BEARING
SLOT
20 (3/4")ϕ
38 (1 1/2")ϕ
25(1")ϕ
17
16(5/8")ϕ

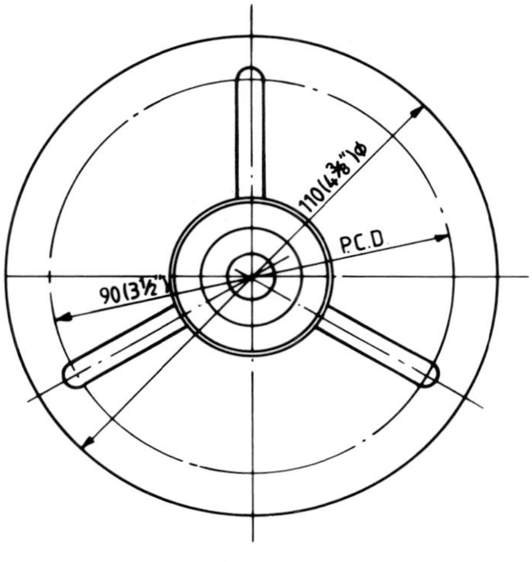
110(4 3/8")ϕ
P.C.D
90(3 1/2")

PLAN VIEW - LANTERN DISTAFF

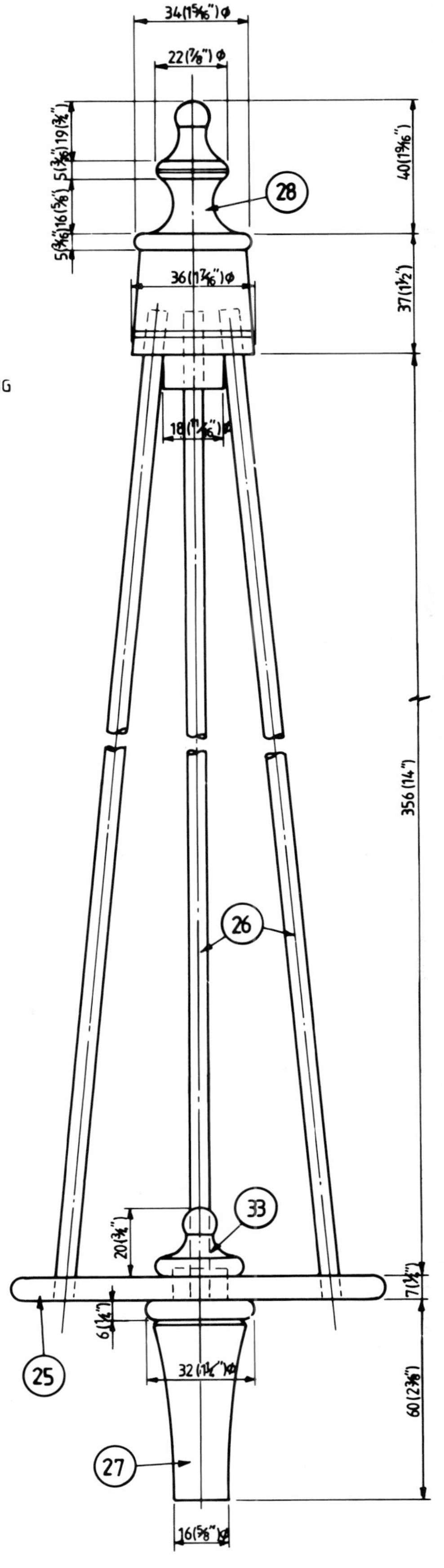
34(1 5/16")ϕ
22(7/8")ϕ
19(3/4")
5(3/16")
16(5/8")
5(3/16")
40(1 9/16")
28
36(1 7/16")ϕ
37(1 1/2")
18(11/16")ϕ
356 (14")
26
33
20(3/4")
7(1/4")
6(1/4")
25
32 (1 1/4")ϕ
60(2 3/8")
27
16(5/8")ϕ

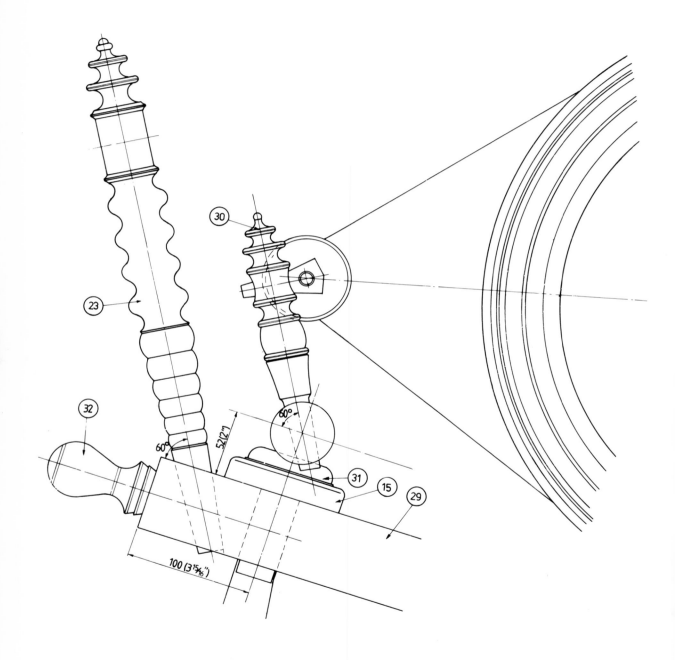

Fig. 8.8 Modified Arkwright flyer and distaff arrangement

Oak

English oak is light brown in colour, and features a very attractive ray fleck when quarter sawn. It also has a distinctive smell. American oak is similar, but has a slight pinkish tinge.

Ash

A light coloured wood with brown streaks. Quite a pretty wood, easy to steam bend, and probably suited to the more gracious looking wheels. Usually cheaper than oak.

Beech

A utilitarian hardwood, light brown or pinkish according to whether it has been air or kiln dried. Does not have much of a figure, and therefore not a particularly attractive wood to use for effect. Many commercial wheels are made in this because it is cheaper.

Cherry

A warm brown wood, which can be quite attractive, and has a nice straight grain.

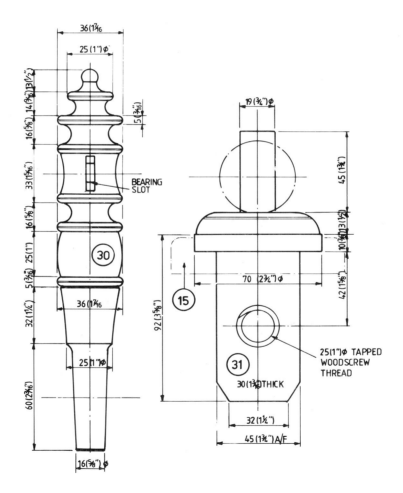

Fig. 8.9 Alternative Arkwright *style* maiden and mother-of-all support

Yew

Almost an orange coloured wood at times. It is hard and the figure is extremely variable, which sometimes makes it difficult to get straight pieces sufficiently long to make a wheel. Having said that, it can make a very beautiful wheel.

Elm

Although it has a nice rich brown colour, it is not so strong as some woods, and in turning up long lengths less easy to get a good finish. Not very often selected for making spinning wheels.

Tropical hardwoods

Common tropical hardwoods are mahogany, sapele, iroko and teak. Whilst spinning wheels can be made from these, they are not usually the first choice. But if you were making a really special wheel you might consider using a more exotic (and expensive) hardwood such as rosewood.

9
SPINNING STOOL

INTRODUCTION

Having considered in previous chapters a number of different spinning wheel types, I cannot pass without including a design for a traditional spinning stool to complement these. As a subject I have chosen a carved four legged stool, as shown in Fig. 9.1. It is a pretty example of what is termed *chip carving*, and offers a challenge to a patient woodworker perhaps not experienced in this craft, and which a practised carver will no doubt accomplish with ease. The original is made of beech and stained a warm brown.

DESIGN

With regard to design it should be noted that stools of this type generally have a height of about 350mm (14in) or perhaps a little more. They are thus principally suited to spinning with sloping bed wheels, or those where the flyer orifice is about + 600mm (24in). When, however, the orifice height is about 700mm (27½in), as for example in upright wheels, a generally taller stool or chair is needed, and this design is not really suitable.

With regard to the number of legs, most have four rather than three, because of the greater stability offered. Four also make it easier to fit the backrest, because the rear legs are positioned to each side of this in the seat. In the case of a three legged stool, the single rear leg can foul the backrest unless care is exercised in the design to avoid this.

CONSTRUCTION

The general arrangement is shown in Fig. 9.1, and the associated parts list is given in Table 9. It is suggested that you begin construction by first assembling the stool and checking the parts fit together correctly, and tackle the carving aspect as a

Table 9: Spinning Stool Parts List

Item	Description	No. off	Material	Dimensions
1	Seat	1	Hardwood	300 × 35 × 390 long (11⅞ × 1⅜ × 15⅜in long)
2	Leg	4	Hardwood	42 sq. × 380 long (1⅝in sq. × 15in long)
3	Backrest	1	Hardwood	130 × 22 × 600 long (5⅛ × ⅞ × 24in long)
4	Peg	2	Hardwood	10 × 12 × 75 long (⅜ × ½ × 3in long)

separate, second stage of the project. Make a start, therefore, by forming the seat (1), and the backrest (3) to the dimensions in Fig. 9.1, 9.2 and 9.4, and complete these with the bevel edges. These items require selected pieces of kiln dried hardwood, and should have even straight grain to permit later carving. Beech, of which the original was made, is a close grained timber and so probably a good choice.

The leg (2) dimensions are given in Fig. 9.3 and, apart from the decoration, these require only simple woodturning and letting into the seat underside. They should not penetrate right through as this spoils the carved pattern. The seat holes are machined under a drill press using a leg angle jig as a guide (*Fig. 5.9*). The slot for the backrest can be cut in a similar way. A trial assembly is then made, but the legs are not glued in place until after the carving is completed. Proceeding on to this aspect, details of the seat, backrest and leg carvings will now be given. These are followed by some useful notes on carving practice.

Seat carving As mentioned earlier, the stool is an example of chip carving, in which the cuts are principally triangular, although some of the edges may be curved. Thus there are no flat bottoms to the carving, and the pattern takes the form of *ridges and* *valleys*. The carving consists of a central floral motif, surrounded by a broad perimeter decoration.

The 45mm ($1\frac{7}{8}$in) wide border pattern consists of two outer rows of lined dog's tooth carvings, between which is a chip carved zigzag design, which alternates back and forth between a second row of nicked dog's teeth. The centre pattern, by contrast, is a six lobed petal-like shape inset with nicked diamonds. This is surrounded by a circle of lined dog's tooth carvings. The centre pattern is completed with twelve semi-circular star-like arrays, with an appearance not dissimilar to a ship's compass. The space between the central motif and the border pattern is a flat surface with a stippled finish.

Backrest carving The backrest carving is given in Fig. 9.4. The design is complementary to the seat, and the border likewise features a row of lined dog's teeth. Within this are two vertical rows of sloped chip carvings not dissimilar to the zigzag pattern in the seat border. These are inset with pairs of nicked diamonds. The centre section consists of a series of eleven fan-shaped motifs. The flat surface surrounding these has a stipple finish as used on the seat.

Leg carving The leg pattern is relatively simple. Referring to Fig. 9.4, the centre section below the triple beading is carved with a series of alternate long and short longitudinal grooves, finished with a circumferential dog's tooth pattern at either end. The bottom of the leg is completed with a series of longitudinal narrow tapered flutes.

Marking out/carving Rather than give a detailed treatise on carving techniques, I will restrict this discussion to two points with regard to marking out and cutting which may be useful to the reader. Firstly, to make any success of chip carving it is essential to transfer and mark the pattern accurately onto the item being carved. Secondly, on the question of basic tools you need little more than a knife and a gouge, both of which should be kept razor sharp. The procedure for cutting the zigzag in the seat border is to use the knife to line out the deep grooves (i.e. the valleys), and the gouge to slice the wood away. Fig. 9.5 clarifies this, and also shows the cuts for the dog's tooth carving. If you wish to

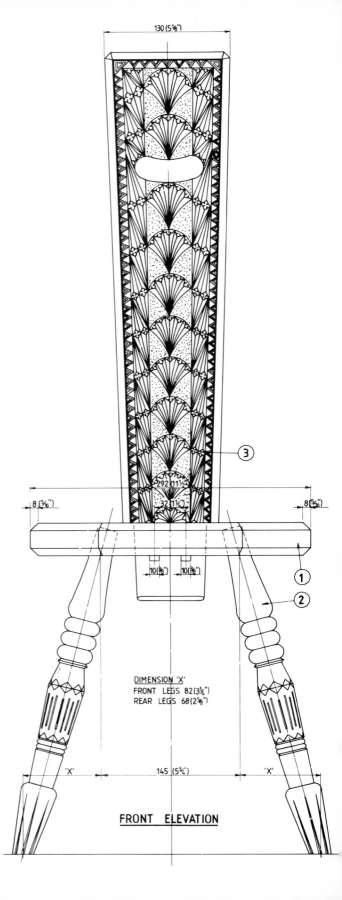

FRONT ELEVATION

study carving techniques in greater detail, some references are given in the bibliography.

Stool completion The carving completed, the stool can now be finally assembled, and the legs glued into the seat. The backrest is slotted into the seat and pegs (4) fitted to hold this in place. It only remains to add a finish to personal choice.

Fig. 9.1 General arrangement of spinning stool

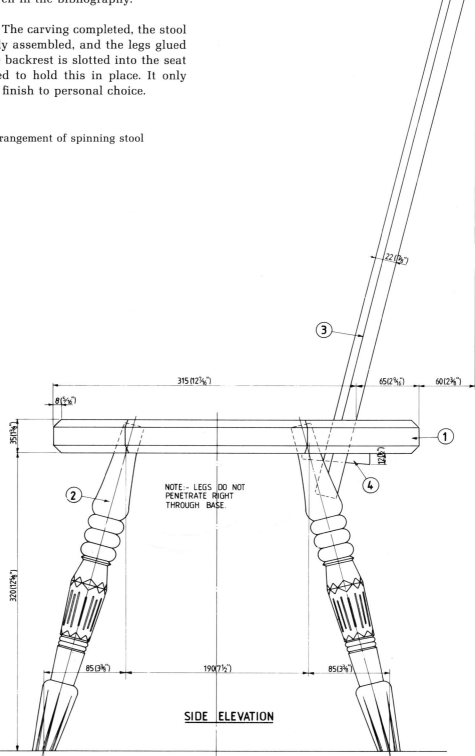

NOTE:- LEGS DO NOT PENETRATE RIGHT THROUGH BASE.

SIDE ELEVATION

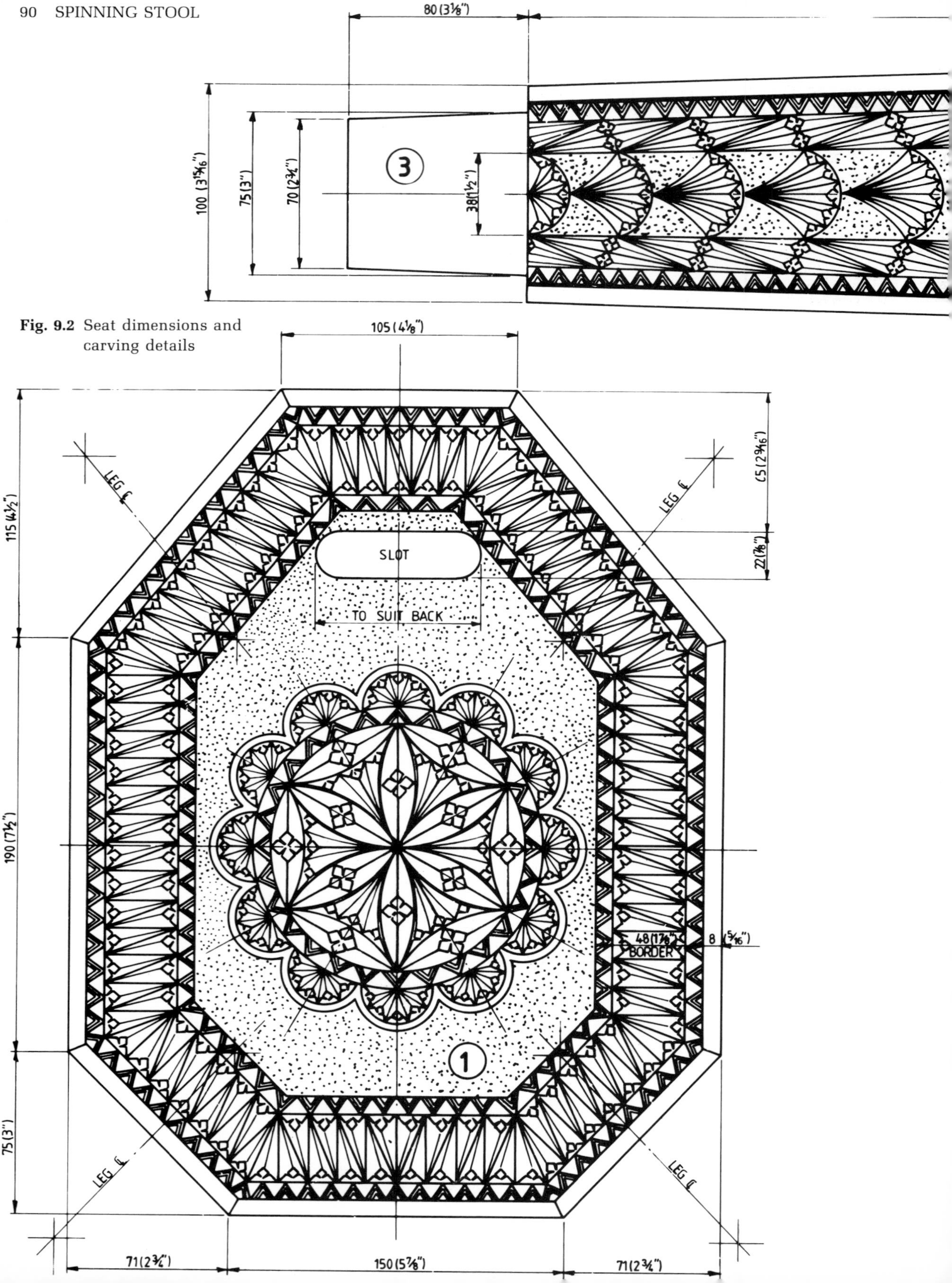

Fig. 9.2 Seat dimensions and carving details

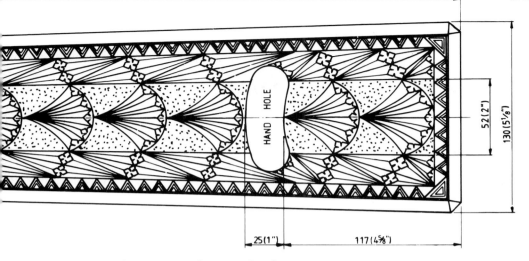

520 (20½")

130 (5⅛")

52 (2")

HAND HOLE

25 (1") 117 (4⅝")

Fig. 9.4 Backrest dimensions and carving details

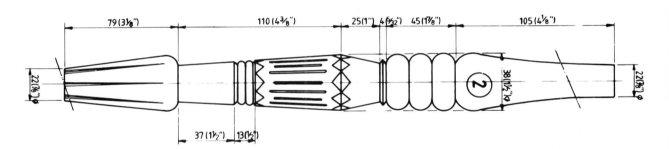

79 (3⅛")   110 (4⅜")   25 (1") 4 (½") 45 (1⅞")   105 (4⅛")

22 (⅞") φ   37 (1½") 13 (½")   38 (1½") φ   22 (⅞") φ

Fig. 9.3 Leg dimensions

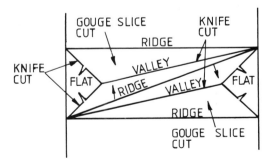

Fig. 9.5 Chip carving procedure

10
NORWEGIAN SPINNING WHEEL

INTRODUCTION

The Norwegian wheel, sometimes referred to as Scandinavian, is a third type of spinning wheel, known as *horizontal bed*.

DESIGN

The design here is for one with a 610mm (24in) diameter wheel, as shown in Fig. 10.3. This is typical of the size, though they are sometimes as much as 690mm (27in) diameter. They are similar to sloping bed in that the flyer position is to the side, but to accommodate such a large wheel requires a rather low bed on short legs. This makes it difficult to support the conventional flyer/mother-of-all arrangement, except perhaps on some sort of tall post (see the great wheel in Chapter 4).

In the Norwegian wheel this problem is neatly overcome by making the bedblock (1) horizontal, and mounting an auxiliary platform (13) on pillars (12) on this, which in turn provides the support for the flyer arrangement (*Fig. 10.3*). Thus the orifice level is maintained at roughly the same level as for sloping style wheels, i.e. at about +600mm (24in) above the floor.

The wheel itself is mounted on vertical rather than sloping supports, and this design lends itself to a unique method of wheel tracking to line up the double band drive with the bobbin/flyer pulley whorls. Details of this tracking arrangement are described below (p. 93). The wheel is of stepped rim pattern and is fitted with a distaff, so both wool and flax may be spun.

CONSTRUCTION

The general arrangement drawings are given in Fig. 10.3 and the associated parts list is in Table 10.

Base, legs and platform The bedblock design is rectangular, with two semi-elliptic fiddle-like cutouts along each side, and edge decoration which is completed with a scraper. Dimensions of this and the legs (2) are given in Fig. 10.4. The legs penetrate right through the bedblock. The taper shape of the legs should be sufficient to hold, but may be pegged with wedges if necessary, though not before the treadle stretcher (3) is fitted, nor before the holes 'U', 'V' and 'W' are drilled in the bedblock. After levelling, the pillars (12) and platform (13) are then fitted. Details of these items are in Fig. 10.6. The platform has a centre cutout, and holes 'R', 'S' and 'T' should be machined before assembling on the pillars. The longitudinal holes 'R' and 'S' should be accurately drilled.

Wheel supports and treadle The next items to add are the wheel supports (9), which should be initially machined to fit snugly in the bedblock holes 'W', but will be opened up slightly on the underside later to allow them to rock slightly. The treadle stretcher (3) is of square section with turned ends. The treadle itself is made from a tapered board, and tied to the pitman rod (28) via a horizontal hole instead of the usual vertical ones. For the dimensions of these items see Fig. 10.5.

Wheel The wheel construction uses the same stepped rim assembly as for the Arkwright wheel. This allows the hub (5) to be machined whole, as described above. The wheel rim (8), spokes (7) and hub (5) dimensions are given in Fig. 10.7. It should be clear now from earlier discussion in this book that to make a segmented type rim a purpose-made slow speed woodturning head is required to machine this; this head should be strong and vibration free to achieve a smooth finish.

Wheel tracking As mentioned earlier the wheel is fitted with a unique method for wheel tracking. Referring to the general arrangement (*Fig. 10.3*), this is achieved by setting the vertical wheel supports (9) so that they pivot slightly in the bedblock holes, and controlling the movement by two horizontal wheel track adjusters (14). The latter are fixed into the platform (13) in holes 'S', but left free to rotate, and screwed through the wheels supports (9). Screwing the front wheel support towards the flyer, and the rear one away from this, thus twists the wheel slightly, i.e. the wheel rim nearest the flyer will move away from you. Conversely, screwing the front wheel support away from the flyer, and the rear one to close up, changes the wheel adjustment towards you. Fig. 10.1 shows this schematically in plan view for clarity.

Dimensions of the wheel track adjusters (14) are given in Fig. 10.5. A 19mm ($\frac{3}{4}$in) diameter screwbox and tap will be required for cutting the threads on this and through the wheel support. An interesting point is the method of retaining the track adjusters in the end of the platform whilst still allowing them to rotate. This is achieved by means of a holding peg (31) fixed into the side of the platform, and located in a 4mm ($\frac{5}{32}$in) wide groove turned in the end of the track adjuster. Thus the latter is held in position but is free to turn. To get a good fit it is suggested that the turning centres on the adjusters are left on until after the peg holes are drilled. The groove in the track adjuster ends can then be matched to suit. The peg arrangement is used again to fix the tension screw (15), and can be used on other wheels for a similar purpose.

At this point the bedblock holes 'W' for the wheel supports (9), which were previously drilled to a close fit, now need opening up slightly on the underside. This should be just sufficient to allow the supports to rock a little back and forth, but not sideways. You will find that very little wood needs removing. The finished movement should not be sloppy.

The wheel can then be fitted into the vertical slots at the end of the wheel supports, and pegged to hold them in place. Instead of using a simple peg, a finial cap (10) is first fitted, and this is then secured by a

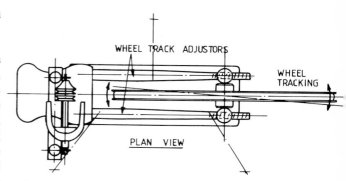

Fig. 10.1 Wheel tracking schematic

peg (11). With this arrangement the drilling of the peg hole in the wheel support is not so critical. The pitman rod can then be connected to make the wheel functional. Pitman rods are always arranged to operate at a slight angle away from the wheel crank so that they do not foul it, though because of this they also sometimes scrape the crank at the top end. This can be overcome by extending the end and

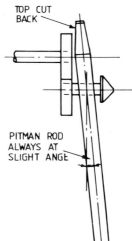

Fig. 10.2 Pitman rod crank connection

Table 10: Norwegian Spinning Wheel Parts List

Item	Description	No. off	Material	Dimensions
1	Bedblock	1	Hardwood	175 × 35 × 460 long (6$\frac{7}{8}$ × 1 × 18$\frac{1}{4}$in long.)
2	Leg	3	Hardwood	42 sq. × 400 long (1$\frac{5}{8}$ in sq. × 15$\frac{3}{4}$in long)
3	Treadle stretcher	1	Hardwood	35 sq. × 450 long (1$\frac{3}{8}$in sq. × 17$\frac{3}{4}$in long)
4	Treadle	1	Hardwood	150 × 20 × 450 long (5$\frac{7}{8}$ × $\frac{3}{4}$ × 17$\frac{3}{4}$in long)

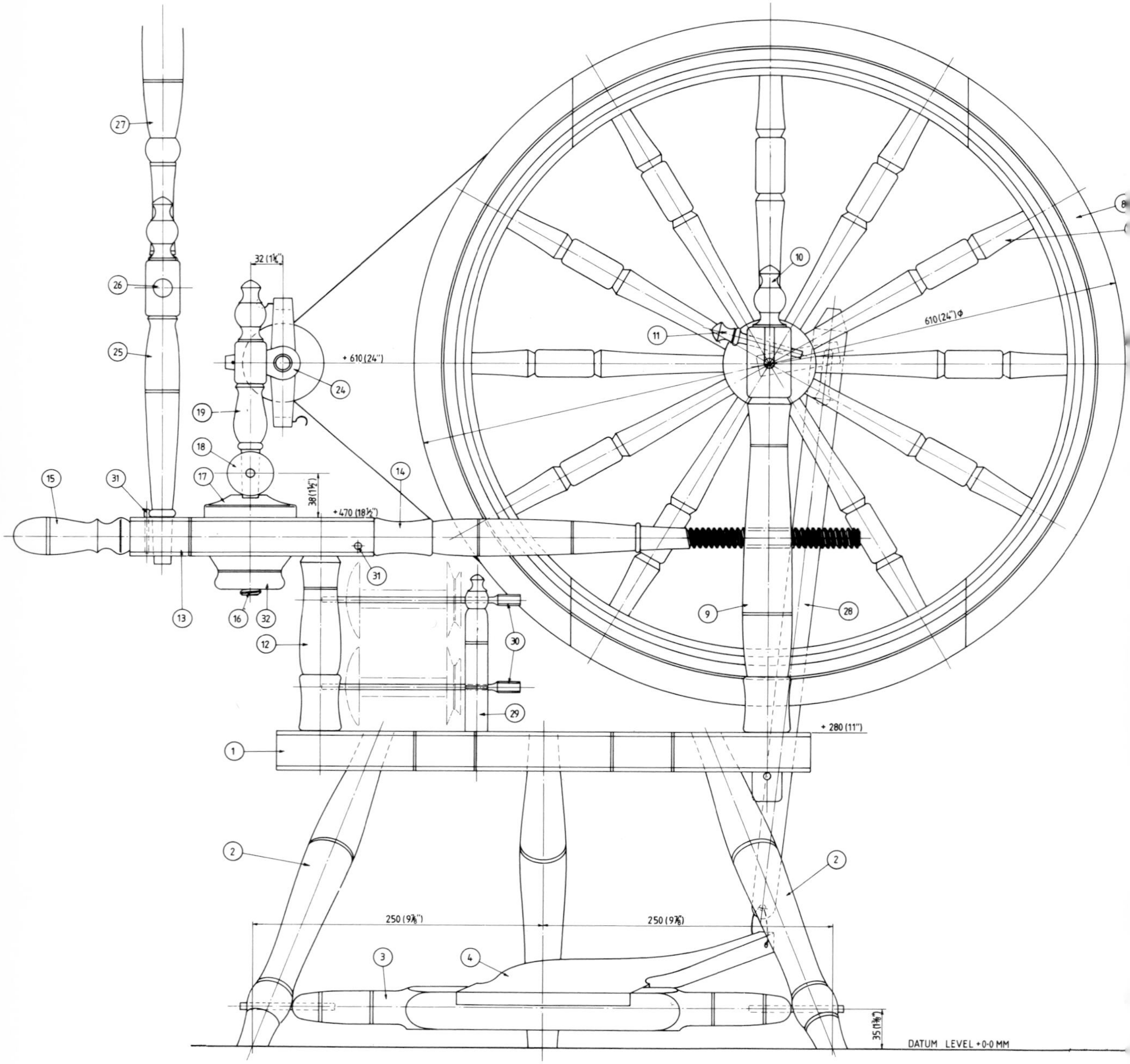

Fig. 10.3 General arrangement of Norwegian spinning wheel

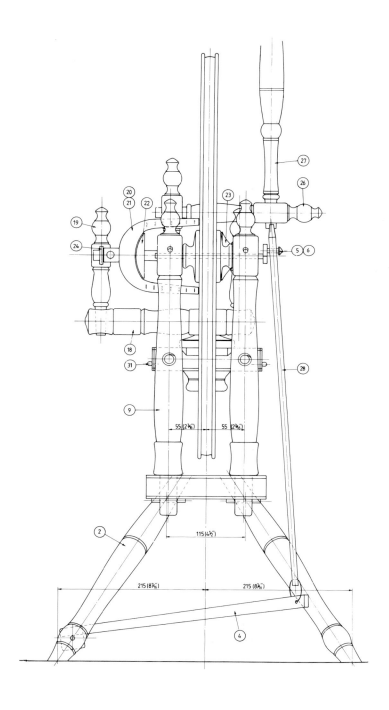

5	Wheel hub	1	Hardwood	85 sq. × 70 thick ($3\frac{3}{8}$in sq. × $2\frac{3}{4}$in thick)
6	Wheel axle	1	Steel	8 dia. × 200 long ($\frac{5}{16}$in dia × 8in long)
7	Spoke	12	Hardwood	28sq. × 250 long ($1\frac{1}{8}$in sq. × 10in long)
8	Rim	1	Hardwood	140 × 30 × 1700 long ($5\frac{1}{2}$ × 1 × 67in long)
9	Wheel support	2	Hardwood	45 sq. × 440 long ($1\frac{3}{4}$in sq. × $17\frac{3}{8}$in long)
10	Wheel support cap	2	Hardwood	30 sq. × 100 long ($1\frac{3}{16}$in sq. × 4in long)
11	Peg	2	Hardwood	20 sq. × 100 long ($\frac{3}{4}$in sq. × 4in long)
12	Pillar	2	Hardwood	38 sq. × 220 long ($1\frac{1}{2}$in sq. × $8\frac{3}{4}$in long)
13	Platform	1	Hardwood	165 × 35 × 210 long ($6\frac{1}{2}$ × 1 × $8\frac{1}{4}$in long)
14	Wheel track adjuster	2	Hardwood	38 sq. × 460 long ($1\frac{1}{2}$in sq. × $18\frac{1}{4}$in long)
15	Tension screw	1	Hardwood	38 sq. × 280 long ($1\frac{1}{2}$in sq. × 11in long)
16	Mother-of-all support	1	Hardwood	55 sq. × 150 long ($2\frac{1}{4}$in sq. × 6in long)
17	Collar	1	Hardwood	85 × 20 × 85 long ($3\frac{3}{8}$ × $\frac{3}{4}$ × $3\frac{3}{8}$in long)
18	Mother-of-all	1	Hardwood	45 sq. × 270 long ($1\frac{3}{4}$in sq. × $10\frac{3}{4}$in long)
19	Maiden	2	Hardwood	32 sq. × 220 long ($1\frac{1}{4}$in sq. × $8\frac{3}{4}$in long)
20	Flyer	1	Hardwood	115 × 22 × 120 long ($4\frac{1}{2}$ × $\frac{7}{8}$ × $4\frac{3}{4}$in long)
21	Flyer axle	1	Steel	6 dia. & 22 dia. bar ($\frac{1}{4}$in dia. & $\frac{7}{8}$in dia. bar)
22	Bobbin	3	Hardwood	80 sq. & 20 sq. mat'l ($3\frac{1}{8}$in sq. & $\frac{3}{4}$in sq. mat'l)
23	Pulley whorl	1	Hardwood	80 sq. × 45 × 80 long ($3\frac{1}{8}$in sq. × $1\frac{3}{4}$ × $3\frac{1}{8}$in long)
24	Bearing	2	Leather	70 sq. × 5 thick ($2\frac{3}{4}$in sq. × $\frac{3}{16}$in thick)
25	Lower distaff	1	Hardwood	35 sq. × 350 long ($1\frac{3}{8}$in sq. × $13\frac{3}{4}$in long)
26	Distaff arm	1	Hardwood	35 sq. × 270 long ($1\frac{3}{8}$in sq. × $10\frac{3}{4}$in long)
27	Upper distaff	1	Hardwood	38 sq. × 370 long ($1\frac{1}{2}$in sq. × $14\frac{1}{2}$in long)
28	Pitman rod	1	Hardwood	28 × 10 × 550 long ($1\frac{1}{8}$ × $\frac{3}{8}$ × $21\frac{1}{4}$in long)
29	Bobbin rack upright	1	Hardwood	25 sq. × 180 long (1in sq. × $7\frac{1}{4}$in long)
30	Bobbin peg	2	Hardwood	10 sq. × 180 long ($\frac{3}{8}$in sq. × $7\frac{1}{4}$in long)
31	Holding peg	3	Hardwood	10 sq. × 60 long ($\frac{3}{8}$in sq. × $2\frac{3}{8}$in long)
32	Clamp screw	1	Hardwood	75 × 35 × 75 long (3 × 1 × 3in long)

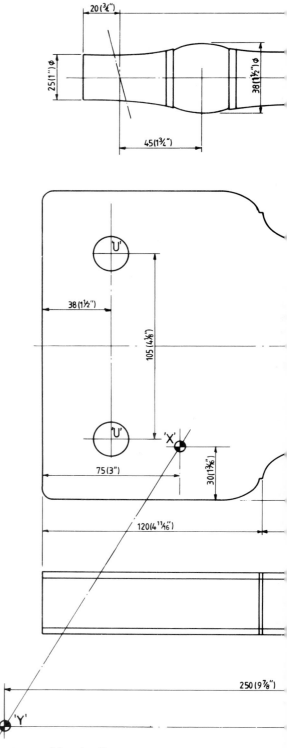

Fig. 10.4 Base and leg details

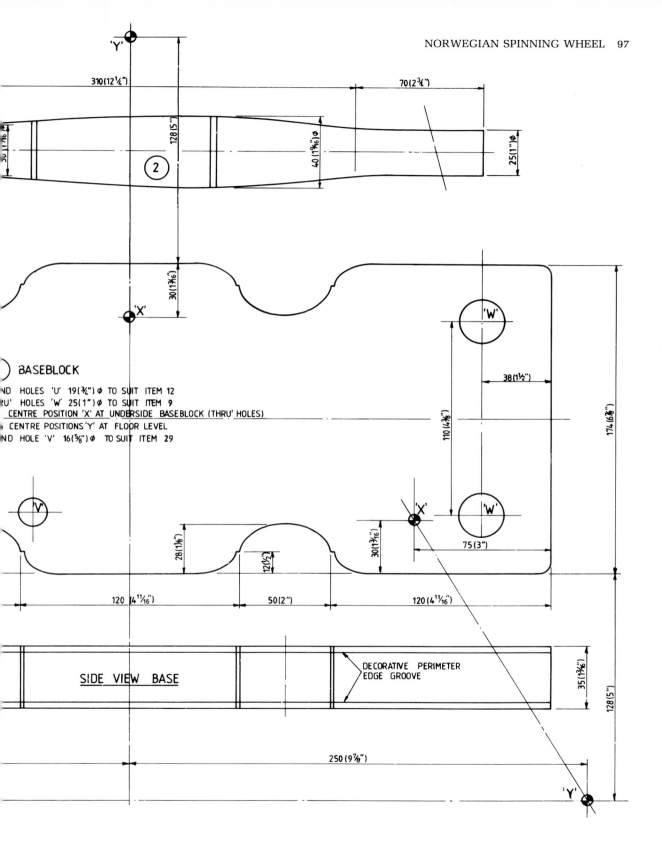

310(12¼")

70(2¾")

128(5")

40(1⁹⁄₁₆")ø

25(1")ø

30(1³⁄₁₆")

②

30(1³⁄₁₆")

'Y'

'X'

'W'

38(1½")

110(4³⁄₈")

174(6⅞")

BASEBLOCK

ND HOLES 'U' 19(¾")ø TO SUIT ITEM 12
RU' HOLES 'W' 25(1")ø TO SUIT ITEM 9
CENTRE POSITION 'X' AT UNDERSIDE BASEBLOCK (THRU' HOLES)
CENTRE POSITIONS 'Y' AT FLOOR LEVEL
ND HOLE 'V' 16(⅝")ø TO SUIT ITEM 29

'V'

'X'

'W'

75(3")

30(1³⁄₁₆")

28(1⅛")

12(½")

120 (4¹¹⁄₁₆")

50(2")

120 (4¹¹⁄₁₆")

SIDE VIEW BASE

DECORATIVE PERIMETER
EDGE GROOVE

35(1³⁄₈")

128(5")

250(9⅞")

'Y'

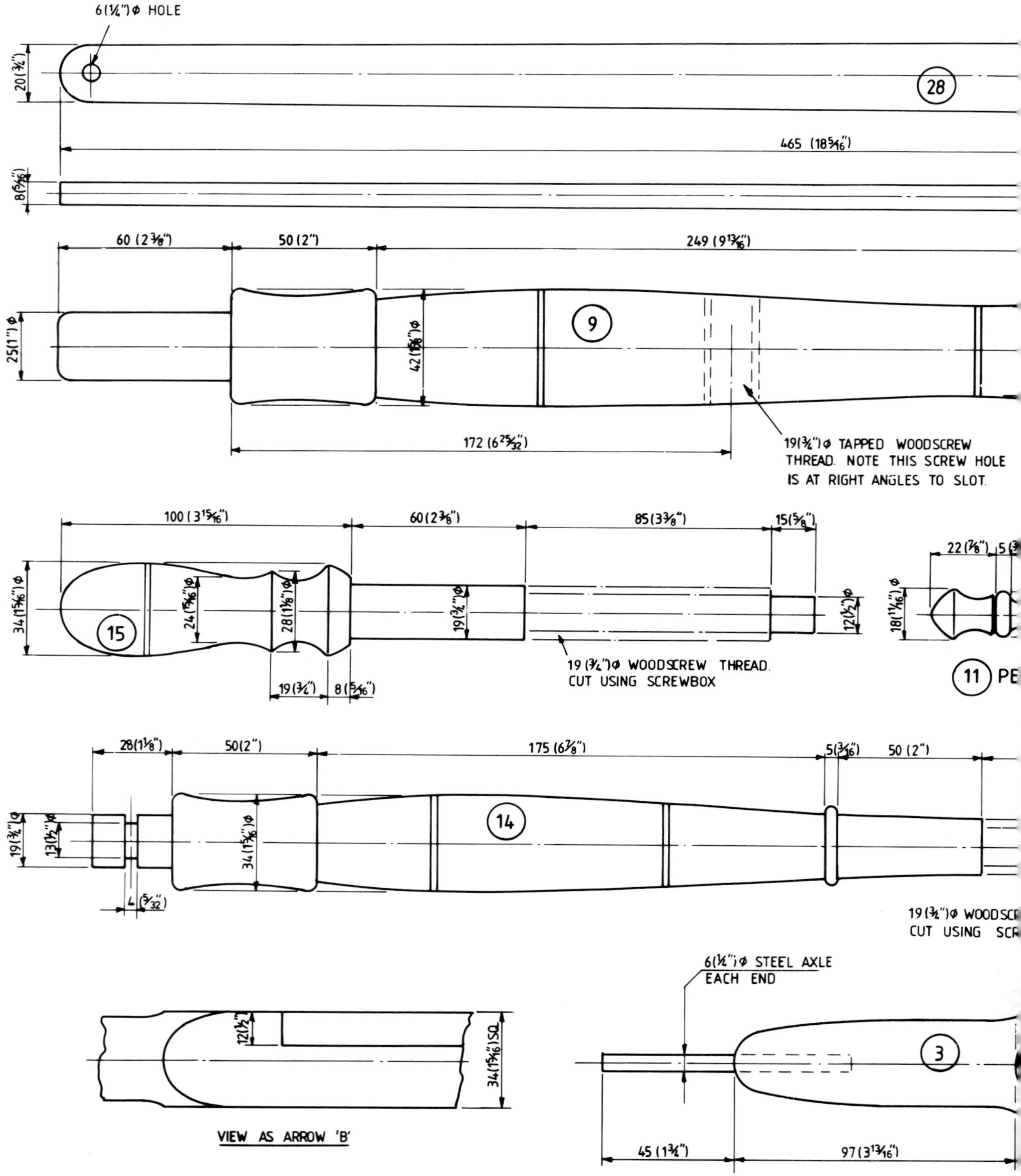

6 (¼") ⌀ HOLE

20 (¾")

465 (18⁵⁄₁₆")

8 (⁵⁄₁₆")

60 (2⅜") 50 (2") 249 (9¹³⁄₁₆")

25 (1") ⌀

4.2 (⅛") ⌀

9

172 (6²⁵⁄₃₂")

19 (¾") ⌀ TAPPED WOODSCREW
THREAD. NOTE THIS SCREW HOLE
IS AT RIGHT ANGLES TO SLOT.

100 (3¹⁵⁄₁₆") 60 (2⅜") 85 (3⅜") 15 (⅝")

34 (1⁵⁄₁₆") ⌀

24 (¹⁵⁄₁₆") ⌀

28 (1⅛") ⌀

19 (¾") ⌀

12 (½") ⌀

15

19 (¾") 8 (⁵⁄₁₆")

19 (¾") ⌀ WOODSCREW THREAD.
CUT USING SCREWBOX

22 (⅞") 5 (³⁄₁₆")

18 (¹¹⁄₁₆") ⌀

11 PE

28 (1⅛") 50 (2") 175 (6⅞") 5 (³⁄₁₆") 50 (2")

19 (¾") ⌀

13 (½") ⌀

34 (1⁵⁄₁₆") ⌀

14

4 (⁵⁄₃₂")

19 (¾") ⌀ WOODSCR
CUT USING SCR

12 (½")

34 (1⁵⁄₁₆") SQ.

VIEW AS ARROW 'B'

6 (¼") ⌀ STEEL AXLE
EACH END

3

45 (1¾") 97 (3¹³⁄₁₆")

Fig. 10.5 Treadle, wheel support and miscellaneous details

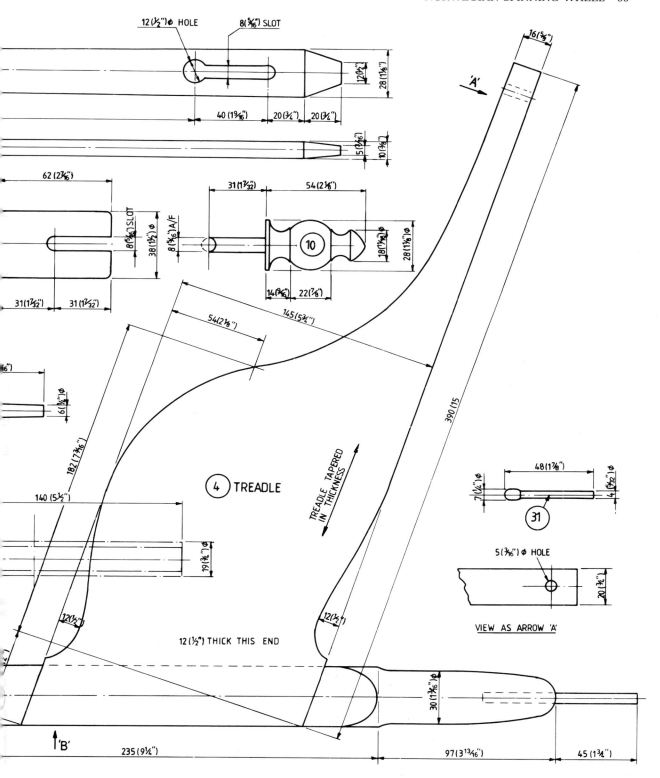

12(½")ϕ HOLE

8(⁵⁄₁₆") SLOT

12(½")

28 (1⅛")

40 (1⁹⁄₁₆")   20 (¾")   20 (¾")

5 (³⁄₁₆")

10 ⅜")

62 (2⁷⁄₁₆")

8(⁵⁄₁₆") SLOT

38 (1½") ϕ

8 (⁵⁄₁₆") A/F

31 (1⁷⁄₃₂")

54 (2⅛")

18 (¹¹⁄₁₆") ϕ

28 (1⅛") ϕ

31(1⁷⁄₃₂")   31(1⁷⁄₃₂")

14 (⁹⁄₁₆")   22 (⁷⁄₈")

10

54 (2⅛")

145 (5¾")

6 (¼") ϕ

182 (7³⁄₁₆")

390 /15

'A'

16 (⁵⁄₈")

140 (5½")

④ TREADLE

TREADLE TAPERED IN THICKNESS

19 (¾") ϕ

48 (1⅞")

7 (¼") ϕ

4 (⁵⁄₃₂") ϕ

31

5 (³⁄₁₆") ϕ HOLE

20 (¾")

VIEW AS ARROW 'A'

12(½")

12 (½")

12 (½") THICK THIS END

30 (1³⁄₁₆") ϕ

'B'

235 (9¼")

97 (3¹³⁄₁₆")

45 (1¾")

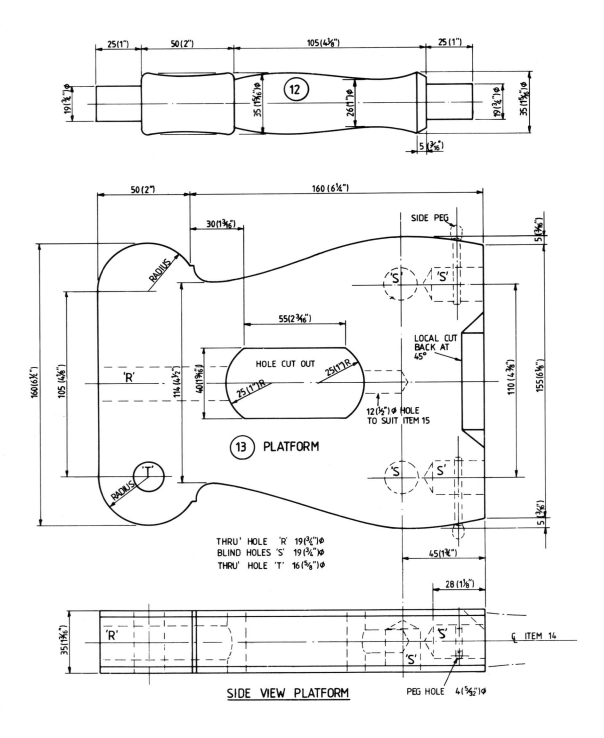

Fig. 10.6 Platform and pillar details

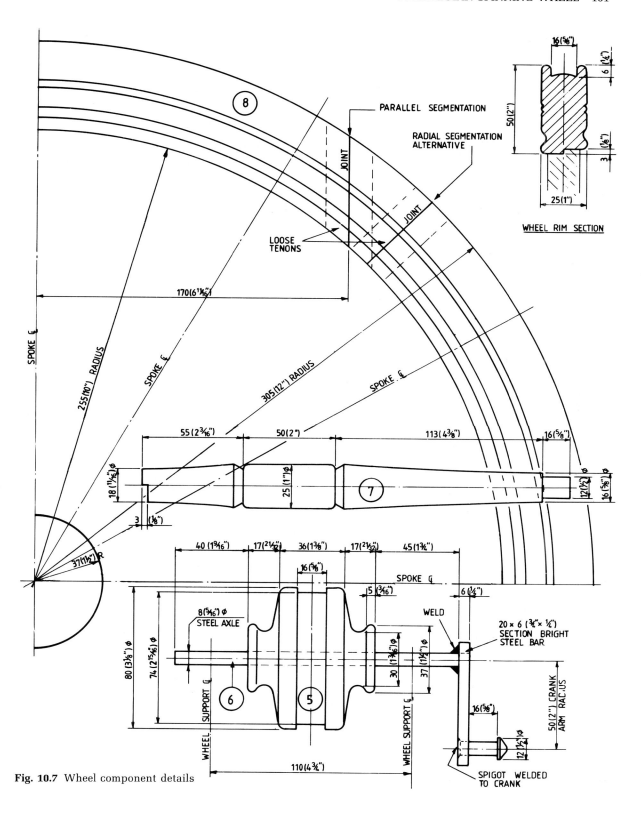

Fig. 10.7 Wheel component details

tapering it down, as in this design. Fig. 10.2 illustrates this point. The pitman rod on the sloping bed wheel (Chapter 6) could be improved to advantage along these lines.

Flyer, maidens and mother-of-all The flyer/maiden support arrangement follows the same principle as the modified Arkwright design, that is with a screw tensioner fitting endwise into the block, in this case the platform (13). The mother-of-all (18) sits on a collar (17), and is glued and pegged to hold it square. Dimensions of these items, including the maidens and flyer, are given in Figs. 10.5, 10.9 and 10.8. The screw movement of the mother-of-all/flyer features a useful clamp screw (32) fitted beneath the platform

on to the end of the mother-of-all support (16). To economise on screwboxes, the wood thread for the tension screw (15) and the clamp screw (32) is 19mm (¾in), the same as used for the wheel track adjusters. The flyer uses the large 12.7mm (½in) diameter orifice design as in Fig. 76, but if you prefer you can fit the standard 10mm (⅜in) size.

Distaff The dimensions of the distaff parts are given in Fig. 10.10, along with the lazy kate details. These feature turnings complementary to the maidens.

BEARING IMPROVEMENTS
Wheel bearings Traditionally wheels are fitted in

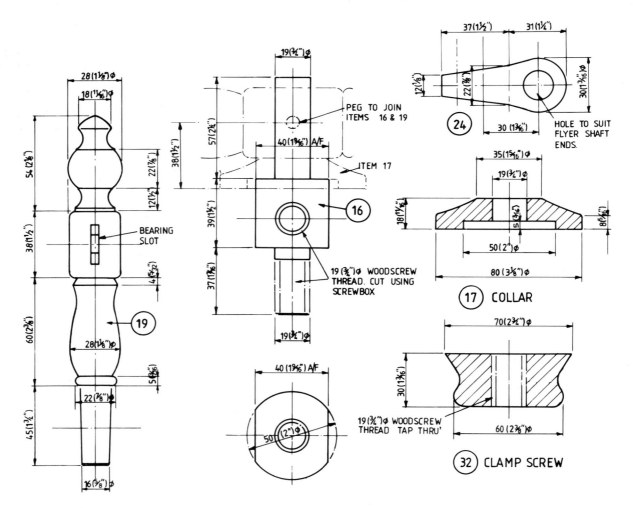

Fig. 10.8 Maiden and mother-of-all support details

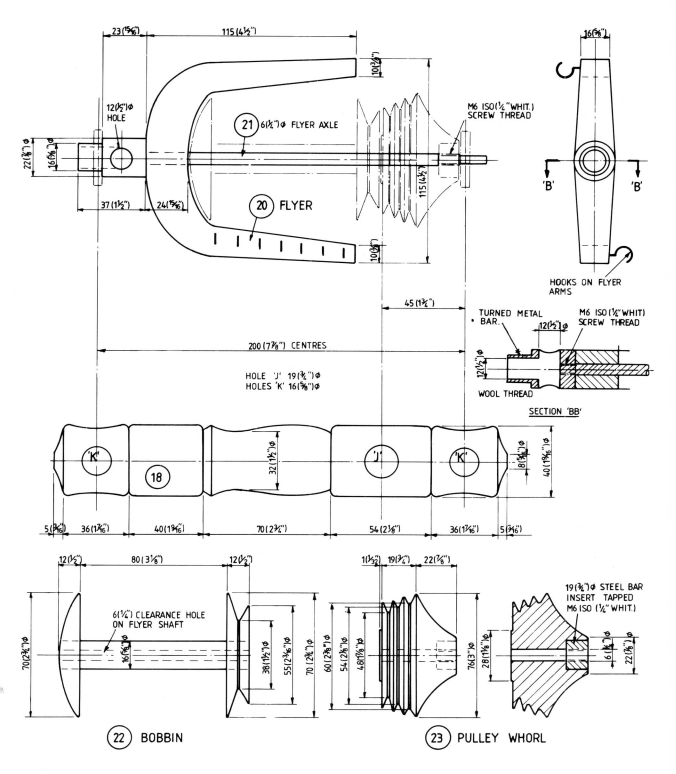

Fig. 10.9 Flyer, mother-of-all and bobbin details

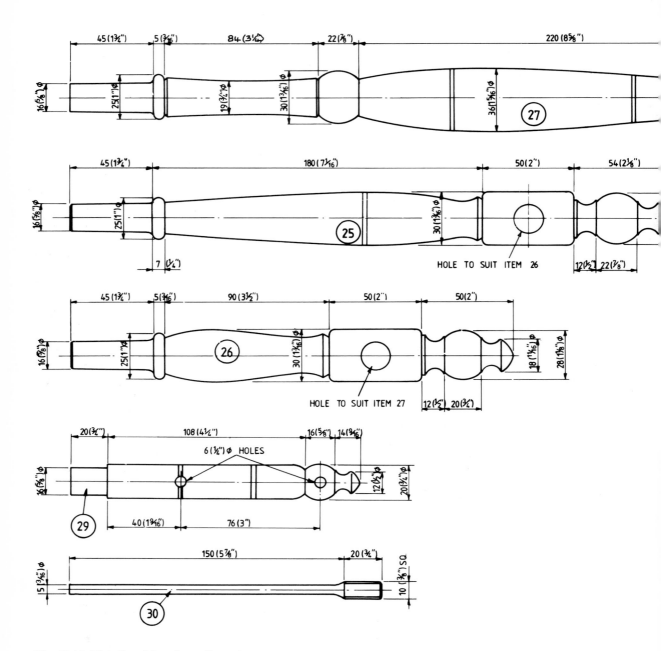

Fig. 10.10 Distaff and lazy kate dimensions

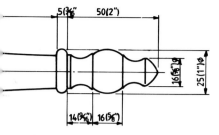

accept these each wheel support will require a slot shape to fit the bearing as well as the axle. Fig. 10.11 shows the ferrule and bearing alternatives. Which you use is a matter of personal preference. You may feel that the ball bearing is introducing engineering, and breaks with tradition. On the other hand the arrangement is discreet, and it does make the wheel spin beautifully.

Flyer bearings There is little to beat the traditional leather bearing, and although they wear down they are replaceable. They are also flexible, so that flyers can be removed. Some designs are amenable to the use of ferrules, and the great wheel in Chapter 4 is a case in point. Mostly it depends on the application, and those in this book generally suit leather bearings.

slots of one form or another in the wheel support, and the axles held in position by small pegs. This arrangement will work quite satisfactorily, but oil lubrication on the steel shaft tends to leach out and stain the wood after a time. Wood also wears down, and it is not uncommon in old wheels to find the support grooves worn away to some degree.

The simplest way of improving this is to slip close fitting brass, nylon or plastic ferrules over each axle end, and the wheel support slots need only be marginally larger to accommodate these. A more sophisticated arrangement is to press a small ball bearing onto the axle on each side of the hub. To

Alternative base support Whilst the design here features a base supported on three legs, horizontal bed wheels are sometimes made with four legs to give greater stability. If you wish you could amend the base design to fit four legs, but if you do, take care to make sure that the back leg beneath the wheel does not foul the treadle/pitman rod.

SPINNING SUMMARY

At the conclusion of this, the last spinning wheel design, I would like to summarise on a couple of points and definitions which are occasionally mis-understood. Firstly it should be quite clear that the

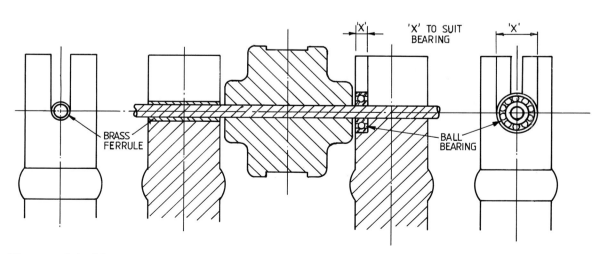

Fig. 10.11 Wheel bearing improvements

ability of a flyer wheel to spin and at the same time collect the yarn does not depend on the wheel size, nor on the speed ratio (twist ratio) with the flyer. This is purely a function of the mechanics between the flyer and the bobbin, the flyer causing the actual thread twist, and the differential speed between this and the bobbin causing the draw on or thread collection. Two terms often referred to are *twist ratio* and *twist per unit length* and are clarified as follows.

Twist ratio Wheels are often spoken of as having a certain twist ratio, say 9:1, this being the difference in speed between the flyer and wheel. If you examine the spinning wheel designs in this book, you will see that the twist ratios range from six and a half to twelve, yet they will all spin satisfactorily. In practice a small wheel will be treadled fast to maintain its momentum, and a larger one, being not so demanding, will be treadled more slowly (see Chapter 7, wheel inertia). In either way the flyer tends to run at a reasonably constant speed, and my own experiments suggest that this is usually between nine and twelve revolutions per second, although on occasions I have found one lower than this. Thus within certain bounds the spinner is presented with a fairly constant speed at which the fibres are twisted into thread. If the spinner then controls the rate of draw on, the twist per unit length can be governed to produce a soft, medium or hard thread as required. It is the flyer/bobbin differential speed which accomplishes this, although as we shall see later the spinner can also exercise some direct control.

Twist per unit length Spun yarn has a varying twist per unit length according to the fibre and its use. Common values for wool are as in Table 11. These are not by any means definite figures and may vary between, say, 2 and 20. Flax and silk, for example, are very thin fibres, and consequently have a proportionately higher twist per unit length compared to wool. In a scotch tension arrangement the degree of twist control is infinite, since the bobbin can be slowed as necessary in relation to the flyer, by adjusting the friction band tension. Looking at the double band drive system, Table 12 shows typical flyer/bobbin pulley whorl ratios, and the theoretical twist per 25mm (1in) length obtainable based on a 16mm ($\frac{5}{8}$in) diameter bobbin shaft. The twist per unit length will, of course, decrease as yarn is collected on the bobbin, and the diameter of this increases.

Table 11: Wool twist per unit length

No. twists per 25mm (1in)	Yarn
4	Soft spun
7	Medium spun
12	Hard spun

Table 12: Double Band Drive Flyer/Bobbin Ratios

Flyer pulley diameters mm (in)	42 (1$\frac{5}{8}$in)	45 (1$\frac{3}{4}$in)	50 (2in)	57 (2$\frac{1}{4}$in)
Bobbin pulley diameter mm(in)	38 (1$\frac{1}{2}$in)	38 (1$\frac{1}{2}$in)	38 (1$\frac{1}{2}$in)	38 (1$\frac{1}{2}$in)
Speed ratio	1.105	1.184	1.315	1.50
Collection rate per bobbin revolution mm (in)	5.2 ($\frac{3}{16}$in)	9.2 ($\frac{3}{8}$in)	15.8 ($\frac{5}{8}$in)	25.1 (1in)
Theoretical twists per 25mm (1in)	4.8	2.8	1.6	1.0

You will note that the values quoted in Table 12 are rather lower than the typical twist/unit length required for wool (Table 11), and may wonder why we do not reduce the flyer pulley whorl diameters further to increase these. In practice, however, the spinner exercises a degree of control by holding back the thread collection (i.e. making the bobbin slip on the drive cord), in order to build up the required number of twists per unit length. Slight adjustment of the drive band tension can also aid this. You should find the flyer/bobbin pulley whorl ratios suggested generally acceptable. If you try to reduce these too much, you run the risk of insufficient draw on. The lowest speed ratio of 1.105 has not been used in the designs in this book, as I have found this a little too fine. It might, however, be advantageous in certain applications, e.g. flax or silk spinning, where a higher twist per unit length is required.

11
DRUM CARDER

INTRODUCTION

Sooner or later anyone who takes up handspinning seriously considers getting a small drum carder. Whilst hand carding can produce fine rolags, it is laborious if much wool has to be carded, and thus a drum carder becomes an attractive proposition. This is an expensive piece of equipment, however, and it is worth considering making one, such as that shown in Fig. 11.4.

Fig. 11.1 Carding cloth detail

In Chapter 2 you will recall that carding cloth consists of a bed of closely spaced hooked wires fixed into a tough fabric base. The carding action is such that with a pair of boards the hooked wires oppose each other, as in Fig. 11.1.

In a drum carder the carding cloth, instead of being attached to flat boards, is fixed to a pair of revolving drums, one small and one large. These are engaged in contra motion where the wires mesh, as shown in Fig. 11.2.

DESIGN

Drum carders consist of a wood or metal frame, within which is mounted a pair of carding drums, the larger usually 175–200mm (7–8in) diameter, and the smaller one 50–80 (2–3¼in) diameter. The larger drum is rotated by a handle, and, through a suitable drive connection, this turns the smaller one, such that the carding wires mesh in contra motion, as described above. The drive mechanism also has to allow for movement between the two cylinders. This is to permit the meshing between these to be adjusted for the correct carding action, and also separation to enable the carded wool to be removed from the larger drum.

Instead of laying the wool on the carding cloth as in hand carding, a wool feeder board is arranged on the underside of the smaller drum as in Fig.11.2. You will, however, note that this presents a problem in that although the contra motion between the cylinders is correct, the feeder drum is rejecting, rather than drawing in, the wool. The solution is to reverse the rotation of the feeder drum, and to arrange for the larger one still to rotate in the same way but at a faster speed, as in Fig.11.3. Thus the smaller drum rotating slowly draws the wool in, and the larger

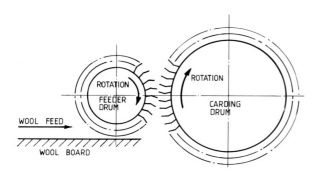

Fig. 11.2 Drum carder scheme (1)

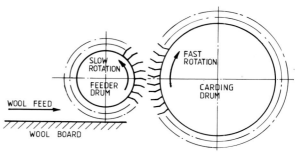

Fig. 11.3 Drum carder scheme (2)

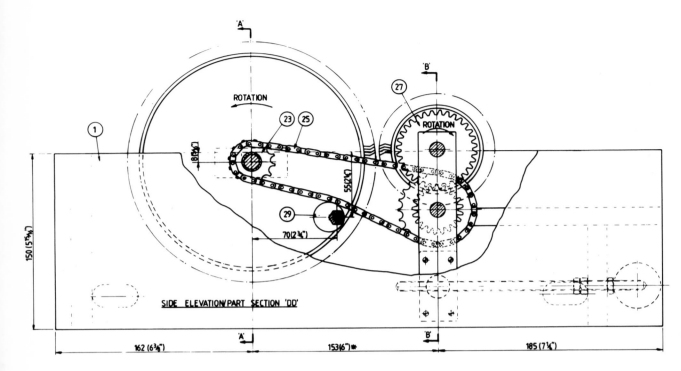

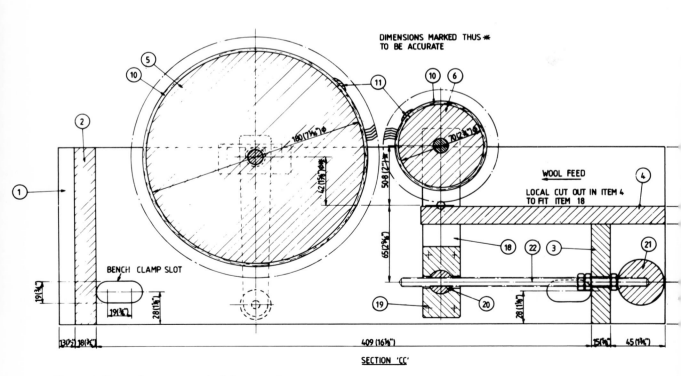

Fig. 11.4 General arrangement of drum carder

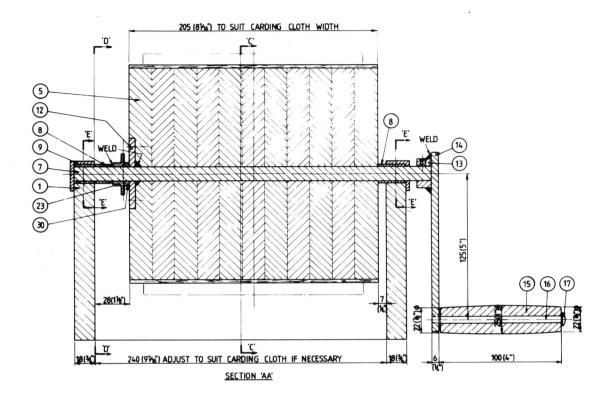

205 (8¹⁄₁₆") TO SUIT CARDING CLOTH WIDTH

WELD

WELD

125(5")

22(⅞")⌀ 25(1")⌀ 22(⅞")⌀

28(1⅛")

7 (¼")

18(¾") 240 (9¹⁄₂") ADJUST TO SUIT CARDING CLOTH IF NECESSARY 18(¾")

6 (¼") 100(4")

SECTION 'AA'

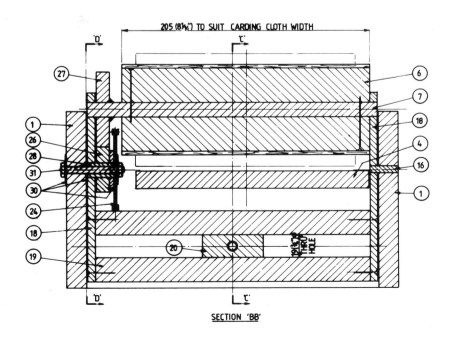

205 (8¹⁄₁₆") TO SUIT CARDING CLOTH WIDTH

18⌀×75 THRO' HOLE

SECTION 'BB'

cylinder rotating faster overtakes the feeder drum, thus providing the correct motion between these. The speed ratio between the drums is usually 3 or 4:1.

DRIVE MOTION

There are two ways of providing the above drive motion. One is a belt and pulley arrangement, and the second is a gear/sprocket and chain interconnection. The design presented here is of the latter arrangement, being selected for its more positive drive compared to the pulley/belt system.

The details of the gear/sprocket drive are given in Fig. 11.4, sections CC and DD. The larger drum is fixed within the frame, and is rotated by a handle. Adjacent is the feeder drum which swings on a fulcrum arm about a centre pivot. By arranging for the drive connection between the drums to be transmitted through this pivot point, the smaller cylinder can still be moved to mesh or separate from the larger one as required.

The primary drive between the larger drum and the fulcrum point is an 8mm ($\frac{5}{16}$in) pitch sprocket and chain connection with a 2:1 reduction ratio. The secondary drive between the fulcrum pivot and the feeder drum is through a pair of spur gears with a ratio 1.67:1. thus the overall speed reduction is 3.34:1. Examining the drive you will see that this is correct and in accordance with Fig. 11.3.

CONSTRUCTION

The general arrangement drawings are given in Fig. 11.4 and the associated parts list in Table 13. Before you begin construction, it is advisable first to purchase the carding cloth and the gear/sprocket and chain drive. Suppliers for these items are given on p. 187. The carding cloth width is nominally 200mm (8in), but this varies a little depending on the source. This governs the frame width, hence the need to have it to hand before starting. Similarly differing sources for the gears/sprockets can affect the setting distances between the drums etc., so these need also to be acquired along with other items such as the drum shafts and bearings.

Frame The frame is constructed from 18mm ($\frac{3}{4}$in) thick birch faced multi-layer plywood. Although less easily obtainable than stoutheart, it is preferred because of its superior strength, and better resis-

Table 13: Drum Carder Parts List

Item	Description	No. off	Material	Dimensions
1	Side	2	Plywood	150 × 18 × 500 long (6 × $\frac{3}{4}$ × 20in long)
2	Crosspiece (1)	1	Plywood	150 × 18 × 260 long (6 × $\frac{3}{4}$ × 10$\frac{1}{4}$in long)
3	Crosspiece (2)	1	Plywood	85 × 15 × 260 long (3$\frac{3}{8}$ × $\frac{5}{8}$ × 10$\frac{1}{4}$in long)
4	Wool board	1	Plywood	240 × 15 × 200 long (9$\frac{1}{2}$ × $\frac{5}{8}$ × 8in long)
5	Carding Drum	1	Blockboard	190 sq. × 19 thick (11 off) (7$\frac{1}{2}$in sq. × $\frac{3}{4}$in thick)
6	Feeder drum	1	Blockboard	80 sq. × 210 long (3$\frac{1}{4}$in sq. × 8$\frac{1}{4}$in long)
7	Drum axle	2	Steel	12.7 dia. × 300 long ($\frac{1}{2}$in dia. × 12in long)
8	Bearing	2	'Lubronze'™	16 O.D. × 12.6 I.D. × 32 long ($\frac{5}{8}$in O.D. × $\frac{1}{2}$in I.D. × 1$\frac{1}{4}$in long)
9	Bearing cover	2	Alum. Al. angle	25 × 25 × 3 thick (1 × 1 × $\frac{1}{8}$in thick)
10	Carding cloth	1	Wire/cloth	205 nom. width × 840 long (8in nom. width × 33in lg)
11	Cover strip	2	Alum. Al. half rd.	13 × 3 × 210 long ($\frac{1}{2}$ × $\frac{1}{8}$ × 8$\frac{1}{4}$in long)
12	Flange	1	Steel plate	60 dia. × 5 thick (2$\frac{3}{8}$in dia. × $\frac{3}{16}$in thick)
13	Collar	1	Steel 'Picador'™	12.7 I.D. × 25 O.D. × 12.7 thick ($\frac{1}{2}$in I.D. × 1in O.D. × $\frac{1}{2}$in thick)
14	Crank arm	1	Steel plate	25 × 6 × 160 long (1 × $\frac{1}{4}$ × 6$\frac{1}{2}$in long)
15	Handle	1	Hardwood	28 sq. × 110 long (1$\frac{1}{8}$in sq. × 4$\frac{1}{2}$in long)
16	Rod	1	Steel	6 dia. × 150 long total ($\frac{1}{4}$in dia. × 6in long)
17	Spring cap	1	Steel	To fit item 16
18	Fulcrum arm	2	Steel	32 × 6 × 160 long (1$\frac{1}{4}$ × $\frac{1}{4}$ × 6$\frac{1}{2}$in long)
19	Spacer bar	1	Hardwood	60 × 32 × 228 long (2$\frac{3}{8}$ × 1$\frac{1}{4}$ × 9in long)
20	Pivot bar	1	Steel	19 dia. × 50 long ($\frac{3}{4}$in dia. × 2in long)
21	Knob	1	Hardwood	38 dia. (1$\frac{1}{2}$in dia.)
22	Screw rod/nuts	–	Steel	M8 Isometric ($\frac{5}{16}$in Whit.)
23	Sprocket (1) 12 tooth	1	Steel	Bond's 0 Euston Fig C208 (see p. 187 for details)
24	Sprocket (2) 24 tooth	1	Steel	Bond's 0 Euston Fig C212 (see p. 187 for details)
25	Chain/connector	–	Steel	Fig. C217 × 500(20in) long Fig. C218 (see notes)
26	Gear (1)	1	Steel	Fig C111 14 DP × 38 (1$\frac{1}{2}$in) PCD (See notes)

27	Gear (2)	1	Steel	Fig C113 14 DP × 63.5 (2½in) PCD (See notes)
28	Sleeve	1	Steel	12.7 O.D. × 24 long (½in O.D. × 15⁄16in long)
29	Cam	1	Steel	Hex. 12.7 (½in) A/F and 2 (1⁄16in) thick plate
30	Spacers/ washers	–	Steel	To suit detail
31	Bolt/nut	1	Steel	M6 Iso. × 50 long (¼in Whit. × 2in long)

tance to tearing when cross cut. You may have to search to obtain this, but it makes an altogether cleaner job. If 18mm (¾in) thickness is unobtainable, an alternative is to purchase some 12mm (¾in) and 6mm (¼in) thick plywood and glue these together. You can also use 12mm (½in) thick plywood for the wool board, so this approach is a good compromise.

The frame sides (1) are joined to the cross pieces (2) and (3) using a housing joint (*Fig. 11.5*). Make the cross pieces initially slightly longer than required; they can then be trimmed later to suit the final drum width, which is primarily governed by the smaller drum and its fulcrum arrangement. Also at this stage complete the various holes and cut-outs whilst the pieces are still separate. A preliminary assembly can then be carried out, but at this point it is not glued.

plastic tube respectively, again fixing in end boards. If you have no wood turning facilities, this is quite a good alternative, but the source of the tubes is often a problem. The small drum could be a piece of drain pipe, but finding a 200mm (8in) diameter pipe for the larger cylinder, although not insurmountable, can present difficulties.

A third method, which is very easy and the one used in this design for the larger drum, is simply to glue 11 slabs of blockboard together (*Fig. 11.4 section AA*). To reduce cost you could consider replacing the centre slabs with chipboard, and use plywood facing boards at each end to preserve appearance. The resulting drum is by nature heavy, but it does help to stop the carder sliding about on the table, especially if no G-cramps are to hand to clamp it down.

The next step is to make the drum axle from 12.7mm (½in) diameter bright steel bar. Drill an accurately positioned centre hole in one end of the bar. This is required for wood turning purposes later. It may be necessary to resort to a metalwork lathe to do this. A flange (12) also needs cutting out and welding to the shaft. For the flange details see Fig. 11.6.

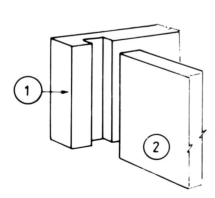

Fig. 11.5 Frame joint detail

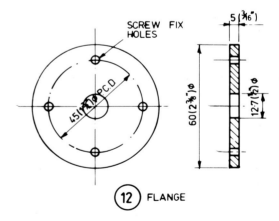

Fig. 11.6 Flange dimensions

Carding drums There are several ways of making drums. One possibility is to glue a series of circumferential segments together, and fix these to two end boards. This is a rather fiddly method of making them, requiring accurately cut segments. Another solution is to make the drums from a large and small

Sprockets The spacer (30) and sprocket (23) are now added, the latter being tack welded to the shaft. Sprockets (23) and (24) obtained from the suppliers list are drilled 6.3mm (¼in) bore, so these need opening out to 12.7mm (½in) diameter. Sprocket (24) has a knockout centre boss leaving a hole exactly

12.7mm ($\frac{1}{2}$in) diameter as required. The smaller sprocket (23) has to be drilled out accurately and preferably reamed true. Drilling and reaming of holes in metal is discussed later in this chapter under the fulcrum construction.

Assuming the shaft is now complete, it is fitted into a matching hole drilled through the wooden drum. The flange is recessed into the drum end, and secured in place by screw fixing.

Drum machining The drum is machined to 180mm ($7\frac{1}{16}$in) diameter on a woodturning lathe. The mounting arrangement is shown in Fig. 11.7. A jacobs chuck is used to drive the shaft at the headstock end. The opposite end is mounted in the tailstock centre, using the previously machined shaft centre hole. Ideally a revolving tailstock is preferred but not essential. The drum is trued up using gouges and scrapers. When complete, the Lubronze™ bearing bushes are slipped over each shaft end, and the drum should drop neatly into the prepared cutouts in the sides of the frame assembly.

Wool feeder drum The construction of the wool feeder drum generally follows the same principles as the carding drum, though with one or two differences.

Firstly, being smaller, a built-up construction is unnecessary, and it can be machined from a solid piece of 80mm ($3\frac{1}{8}$in) square section wood. Hardwood such as beech, or alternatively softwood, is suggested. For the arrangement see Fig. 11.4, section BB.

The axle is the same size as for the carding drum, i.e. 12.7mm ($\frac{1}{2}$in) diameter, but has a spur gear (27) tack welded to it instead of a sprocket. This assembly is inserted through a matching hole in the feeder drum and secured by radial steel pins. This method of fixing is used because the size of the spur gear (27) effectively prevents the screw fixing of a flange arrangement as for the larger drum.

The drum diameter is 70mm ($2\frac{3}{4}$in), and machined up using the same arrangement as for the carding drum. Make sure the radial pins are driven well in to allow you to do the wood turning. Also note the gap between the spur gear and the drum needs to be accurately gauged, so that the sprocket (24) and the chain drive (25) will pass freely between without snagging.

Carding cloth Before proceeding with the fulcrum details, this is an opportune point to mount the carding cloth on both drums. The cloth base is secured using an impact glue, and a half round aluminium alloy strip (11) is pin fixed across the fabric joint. Make sure you get the carding cloth on the right way round. Once on it is not so easy to get off!

Fulcrum arrangement The fulcrum arrangement supports the feeder drum, and the swing arms (18) are cut from 32 × 6mm ($1\frac{1}{4} × \frac{1}{4}$in) bright steel bar to the dimensions as in Fig. 11.8. They screw fix onto the ends of the spacer bar (19). The latter should be of hardwood such as beech, not softwood, and have a 19mm ($\frac{3}{4}$in) hole drilled right through it. A steel pivot bar (20) slides into this. Referring to fig. 11.4, section CC, this pivot bar is used as a means of moving the small drum position about the fulcrum point by means of the adjusting screw (22) and knob (21).

Drilling holes in metal Before fixing the fulcrum arms, the drum axle and pivot point holes require drilling. These are 12.7mm ($\frac{1}{2}$in) diameter, with the exception of one hole which is 6.3mm ($\frac{1}{4}$in) diameter.

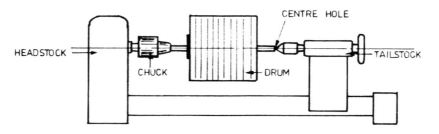

Fig. 11.7 Lathe set up for drum machining

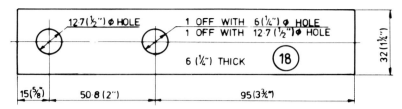

Fig. 11.8 Fulcrum detail

It is essential that these holes are accurately marked and bored out, otherwise the spur gears (26) and (27) will not mesh smoothly together. This applies particularly to the 12.7mm (½in) holes which should be reamed out. To those who are engineers the reasons for this should be self evident, but for the benefit of others it is worth clarifying, as follows.

In general a twist drill when cutting through metal produces an oversize hole. One drilled 12.7mm (½in) N.B. may be larger by say 0.25mm (0.010in). In fact the precision of a twist drill hole size is governed by the accuracy of the drill tip concentricity. This initially guides the drill through the hole, and any slight deviation in the concentricity say of 0.1mm (0.004in) can produce double this error in the hole size. Thus it may be larger by this amount. In the meshing of spur gears (26) and (27) this sort of inaccuracy is not acceptable, causing either a sloppy or a rough movement.

To drill accurately sized holes in metal, therefore, you first machine a hole with an undersize twist drill, and then follow this through with a precision reamer. In the case of a 12.7mm (½in) hole the initial twist drill size might be 12mm (15⁄32in) N.B. If you cannot obtain or borrow a suitable reamer, then the only other way of getting a hole of reasonable precision is to machine out progressively with larger twist drills. In this way the sides of the drill rather than the tip guide the drill through the hole. However even this does not work absolutely, since it depends to some degree on the accuracy of the drill tip and the rake angles. All this may confound the reader into thinking the job is impossible. It is not. Given a little care and attention a perfect result will be achieved.

Gear/sprocket sub-assembly Fig 11.9 gives the gear/sprocket sub-assembly details (24, 25 and 30) together with the sleeve (28). In screwing the gear and sprocket together make sure it spins freely on

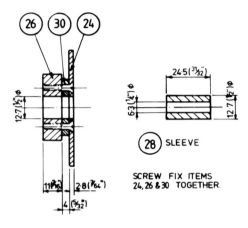

Fig. 11.9 Gear and sprocket sub assembly

the sleeve when bolted in position through the fulcrum arm.

ASSEMBLY

The preliminary assembly carried out earlier can now be continued and the fulcrum arrangement complete with feeder drum added. Note the pivot holes for the fulcrum arm require positioning accurately both vertically and horizontally (reference the starred dimensions in Fig. 11.4). This is so that the 8mm (5⁄16in) pitch chain will fit properly over the sprockets.

As previously mentioned, the cross pieces (2) and (3) should still be slightly overlength. These are now trimmed back until the fulcrum arrangement fits snugly between the frame sides, and swings freely. Having accurately gauged the internal width, which should be about 240mm (9 7⁄16in), the woolboard (4) can then be made to fit tightly in between. This item needs local cut-outs so that it will fit round the fulcrum arms. The frame can then be finally glued

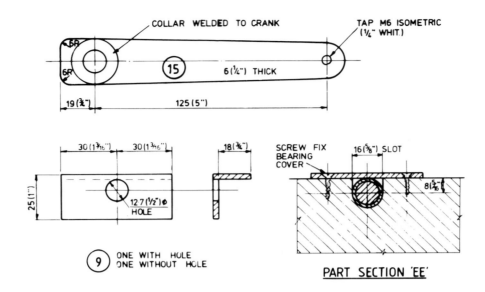

Fig. 11.10 Crank and bearing cover details

up, after temporary removal of the drums etc.

Handle/bearing covers/chain cam The dimensions of the bearing covers and method of fixing are given in Fig. 11.10 along with the crank details. The crank requires a collar (13) tack welded to it. For the handle details refer to Fig. 11.4, section AA. A spring cap (17) holds the handle grip in place. The carding drum should now rotate smoothly, and to complete the drive it only remains to add the chain cam. Details of this are in Fig. 11.11.

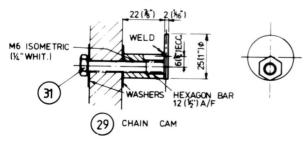

Fig. 11.11 Chain cam eccentric

Adjusting screw The last items to add are the adjusting screw (22) and knob (21). You can either buy the knob or, if you want a challenge, woodturn it. The assembly is held in position with locknuts. The adjusting screw should move the feeder drum

smoothly back and forth. The drum carder completed, it only remains to give it a suitable finish to stop dirt penetrating the wood. A coat of sanding sealer followed by a clear semi-matt cellulose lacquer is suggested. The machine can then be put to the test.

USING THE DRUM CARDER

First secure the drum carder to the table with G-clamps fitted into the side slots so it will not slide about. Then wash and tease the wool you wish to card. Place some wool fibres on the feeder board and turn the drums to draw them in and card them onto the larger drum. Continue entering wool so that it is evenly spread across the drum face. Finally, peel the *lap* off the drum. This operation can be difficult. To overcome this, before carding is commenced, a strip of close-mesh plastic pea-netting, or equivalent, is usually tamped down over the drum carding cloth wires, the ends meeting at the aluminium cover strip (11). After carding the lap is lifted at this joint, using a pointed steel rod (e.g. skewer), and the netting is then used to ease the wool off the drum. The lap is then either split across into say three pieces for making rolags for woollen spinning. Alternatively the lap can be split lengthwise into strips for semi-worsted spinning.

IMPROVEMENTS

A useful addition is to make a small guard to protect the gears and the chain drive and stop the wool from getting trapped in these items. This can be made from steel or aluminium sheet, and screw fixed to the top edge of the side frame. Experience also suggests that it is advantageous to fit tapered guides to the wool board fixed to the side frames. This directs the wool onto the drum wires, and stops it coming off the edge of the drums, particularly on the gear wheel side.

BELT DRIVE ALTERNATIVE

Mention was made earlier of an alternative belt/pulley drive arrangement. In this design (Fig. 11.12) it is the carding drum rather than the feeder drum which moves. It is quite a cunning movement employing two idlers, and because of this a vee section belt cannot be used. Usually the belt is either of round or flat section so that it can drive on both sides. Examining Fig. 11.12 you will note that the speed reduction is fixed by the ratio of pulleys A and B. The same ratio of 3 or 4:1 as for the gear/sprocket system is used. The carding drum movement is adjusted by a screw/wingnut and this moves the idler in tandem. If you study the movement you will see that any extension in the belt length X is compensated for by a reduction in belt length Y, thus keeping the tension sensibly constant.

If you want to adopt this drive method some redesign will be necessary. One of the problems with this arrangement is belt tension. This has to be quite high to stop drum judder, otherwise the carder will not work properly. It is not such a tidy and compact arrangement as the gear/sprocket model, and although the latter may cost more to build it is generally worth it.

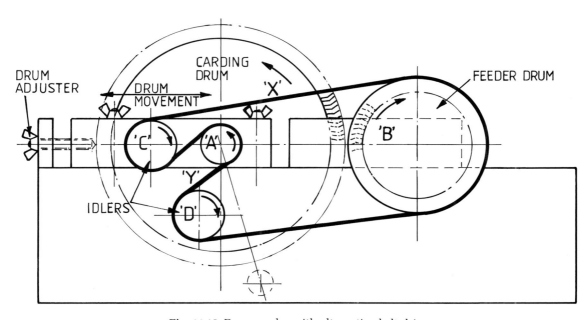

Fig. 11.12 Drum carder with alternative belt drive

12
WEAVING PROLOGUE

INTRODUCTION

A book of this nature would not be complete without presenting a collection of designs for weaving equipment to complement those for spindles and spinning wheels etc., given in the earlier chapters. The second half of this book is therefore devoted to a selection of loom designs and weaving accessories. These vary from looms suited to weaving narrow braids, right up to a foot power loom capable of weaving material 1070mm (42in) wide.

In the spinning section the designs were introduced historically, and it was proposed to treat weaving equipment in the same manner. With the earliest looms this is possible, but as we move on to even simple designs, and particularly the more complicated types, the mechanical differences become much more important. Accordingly the discussion switches to an emphasis on technical rather than historical development. The first design in the next chapter is for a tabby loom, and to trace its roots in history, let us reflect for a moment on loom development through the ages.

EARLY LOOMS

Archaeological records suggest that weaving was being practised many thousands of years ago, and there are several arguments which can be put forward as to how it evolved. It may have been man's interest in other things, for example watching spiders make a web, birds build a nest, or the way vines twist and cling to trees, which first gave him the idea. Another plausible argument, perhaps in combination with these is that, as an alternative to living in caves, he experimented with building a shelter, putting together a framework of sticks, overlaying these with rushes, reeds or grasses to keep out the elements. By interleaving these he found he could make them stay on the structure. His bedding was no doubt also rather primitive, but the knowledge of building a shelter probably inspired him to make simple mats, again by interleaving rushes and reeds. Thus, in a rather crude way, he had perhaps unknowingly invented the process of weaving, which in simplicity is the alternate interleaving of one group of fibres at right angles to another, such that when released they hold firmly together as a composite structure, or as it came to be known, a piece of *woven* material.

Prehistoric man must also have attempted to keep himself warm by making clothing, perhaps from the skins of the animals he had killed for food. His early explorations with spinning fibres from the hairs on these skins, e.g. wool, using the spinning spindle, would have encouraged him also to try weaving with these, to make a coat, as an alternative to using the animal skin. Eventually he devised an independent structure to help him weave, and this aid became known as a *loom*.

Fig. 12.1 Ancient tree loom

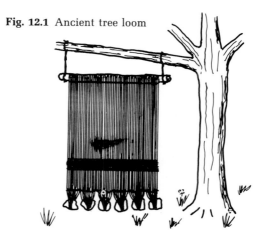

The first looms must have been rather clumsy affairs, an arrangement consisting of a horizontal pole, maybe tied to a tree, from which was suspended a number of weighted vertical roughly-spun fibres. These were interwoven by similar coarse threads in the horizontal direction, as shown in Fig. 12.1. In time the vertical fibres became known as the *warp*, and the horizontal fibres the *weft*. A development of this vertical loom was to rearrange the warp so that it lay parallel to the ground. Again it was tied to a tree or stump, but at the other end it was secured to the weaver's waist. This became known as a *backstrap* loom. A further adaptation to stiffen up the arrangement was to add a pair of side sticks, and the result was a rather inelegant *frame* loom as shown in fig. 12.2.

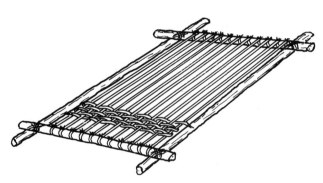

Fig. 12.2 Early frame loom

SHED FORMATION

In parallel with the development of these early looms were improved techniques in the method of weaving. One of the obvious difficulties, for example, with the frame loom in Fig. 12.2, is the somewhat fiddly process of threading the weft alternately over and under the warp when weaving. A significant aid would be to separate groups of warp threads apart, and open up a space between them, so that the weft could then be passed through much more easily. A means of switching these warp thread groups over was also needed. The method of achieving this is shown in fig. 12.3 and 12.4. In Fig 12.3 the warp is stretched across the loom frame, and a pole known as a shed stick is inserted, separating alternate warp threads, e.g. 1, 3, 5, 7, over

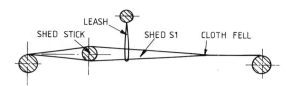

Fig. 12.3 Frame loom with shed stick and leashes

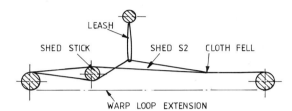

Fig. 12.4 Second shed formation on the frame loom

and 2, 4, 6, 8 under etc. This produces a shed at S1, through which a shuttle of weft may easily pass. To make the second shed a set of leashes is secured to the lower warp threads, raised, as shown in Fig. 12.4, to give a shed (S2) above the warp line. This system was well established in Roman times and perhaps very much earlier. It was used in the backstrap loom and indeed still is today in tapestry looms.

INCREASING WARP LENGTH

The length of material that can be woven on a frame loom is clearly limited, but it can be extended by mounting the warp as a complete loop as shown in dot dash in Fig. 12.4. As material is progressively woven the warp is moved along a bit to expose new yarn. The warp length can be increased still further by arranging the crossbars at either end of the warp as rollers. Fig 12.5 shows a simple frame loom with rollers, and, as material is woven, the warp is progressively transferred from one to the other. This arrangement with its shed stick and leash pole for alternately lifting and lowering half of the warp will produce a plain weave known as tabby. Tabby forms the basis of all weaving, and this is a convenient point to move forward now to the design of a simple modern loom on which to do this.

Fig. 12.5 Frame loom with rollers

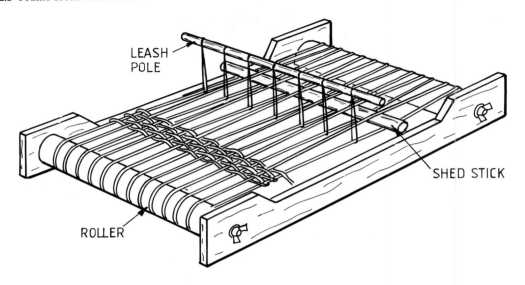

13
TABBY LOOM

INTRODUCTION

The first weaving design is for a simple tabby loom as shown in Fig. 13.2. It is an ideal subject for a beginner because it introduces the foundations of weaving, heddles, sheds, and warping up, etc., an understanding of which is necessary before progressing to the larger and more complicated looms.

In the weaving prologue the frame loom with rollers was mentioned briefly (*Fig. 12.5*), and the tabby loom can be looked upon as a very simple adaptation of this, but with a fixed heddle rather than a leash pole arrangement for lifting the threads, and which dispenses with the need for a shed stick. Another modification is the introduction of a breast and back beam above the end rollers, as shown in Fig. 13.1. These are a common feature of all looms which use a controlled heddle movement, thus requiring a uniform warp line. An arrangement where the warp is connected directly between a pair of rollers (e.g. Fig. 12.5) would not give this, as the warp line would vary as yarn is transferred from one to the other.

DESIGN

The general arrangement drawings are given in Fig. 13.3 and the associated parts list in Table 14. The

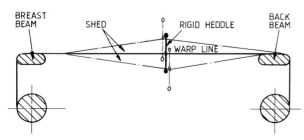

Fig. 13.1 Shed formation

loom consists of two side frames (1) joined by cross bars (2) and (3). Fitted through each end is a warp/cloth beam (4). The warp is connected between these passing up and over the breast and back beams (2). Fitted in the middle is a rigid heddle (7) supported in a crossbar (10). The latter rests in one of three pairs of slots 'X', 'Y' or 'Z' in the side frames (see *Fig. 13.4 section AA*).

Weaving tabby, half the warp threads (i.e. alternate ones) pass through the heddle eyes, while the remainder pass straight through between the front and back beams. Thus moving the heddle support bar (10) to slot 'X' will lift half the warp threads, forming a shed above the warp line. Conversely, lowering this to slot 'Z' will form a shed below this. Weaving is accomplished by alternately switching the shed above and below the warp line, and passing a shuttle loaded with weft through the shed each time. The rigid heddle also serves conveniently as a beater. The warp tension is maintained by a ratchet and pawl fitted to each roller. The latter are also each equipped with an apron cloth arrangement. This is a standard means by which a warp is connected to the rollers, and is discussed later.

CONSTRUCTION

Before you start, first purchase the rigid heddle. This is nominally 380mm (15in) wide, but can vary a little, and may thus marginally affect the width dimensions given. They can be purchased in other widths, if required, and the loom width altered to suit. Sources of rigid pattern heddles are given in the list of suppliers (p. 187).

The side frames are made from 12mm ($\frac{1}{2}$in) thick plywood, preferably birch faced multiply, rather than stoutheart to make a better job. It should be possible to cut out both from a piece of plywood

Fig. 13.2 Tabby loom

500 × 370mm (20 × 15in) with careful sawing. Note that the design is based on an overall heddle height of 72mm (2$\frac{3}{16}$in). If this is different some changes to the starred dimensions will be required. In cutting out the side frames take the opportunity to machine the 38mm (1$\frac{1}{2}$in) diameter roller holes as well as the slots 'X', 'Y' and 'Z', before doing any assembly work.

Breast/back beams The breast and back beams (2), and the crossbars (3) are all from 45 × 19mm (1$\frac{3}{4}$ × $\frac{3}{4}$in) section softwood. In the case of the breast and back beams the edges are rounded over to provide a smooth passage for the warp. They should all be the same length, square at the ends, and are screwed/glue fixed to the sides. Use long screws as they are being fixed into end grain.

Rollers The rollers (4) are woodturned, and are nominally 38mm (1$\frac{1}{2}$in) diameter × 515mm (20$\frac{1}{4}$in) long. Again the actual heddle width may marginally

affect the roller length. Machine the rollers to be snug, but freely rotating in the side frame holes. If woodturning facilities are not available this can probably be overcome by trimming a square bar carefully round. First plane it octagonal, then cut the corners down, finally sanding these round. A 10mm ($\frac{3}{8}$in) diameter handle (5) is then fitted in a transversely drilled hole through one end of each roller. The latter can then be offered to the frame and held in position by two retaining pins (6) made from 3mm ($\frac{1}{8}$in) diameter stainless steel or aluminium rod.

Ratchets and pawls Ratchets and pawls (7) and (8) are always the most difficult items to make, a problem compounded by the fact that there are few if any commercial sources. To ease construction these have been made as large as practically possible and of wood rather than metal, since some may find the latter tedious to cut out. The dimensional details and fixing are given in Fig. 13.5. Use 12mm ($\frac{1}{2}$in) birch faced plywood, as for the sides. To

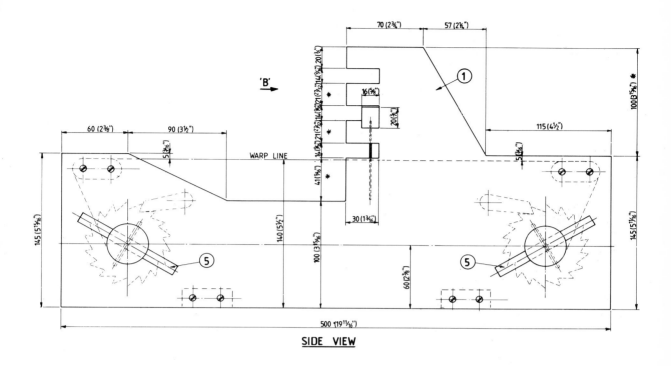

SIDE VIEW

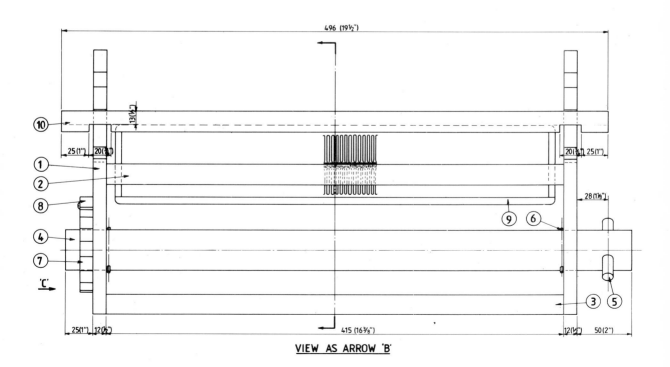

VIEW AS ARROW 'B'

Fig. 13.3 General arrangement of tabby loom

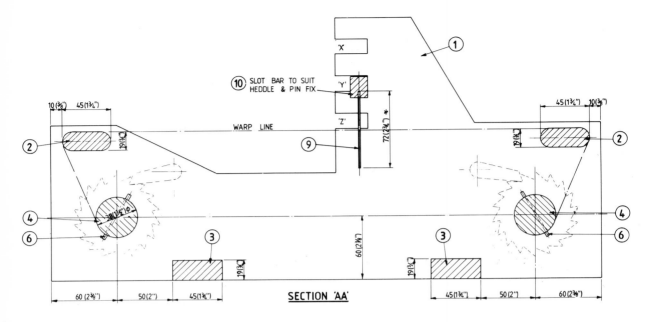

Fig. 13.4 Sectional arrangement of tabby loom

Table 14: Tabby Loom Parts List

Item	Description	No. off	Material	Dimensions
1	Side frame	2	Plywood	500 × 370 × 12 thk. total (20 × 15 × ½in thick)
2	Breast/back beam	2	Softwood	45 × 19 × 415 long (1¾ × ¾ × 16⅜in long)
3	Crossbar	2	Softwood	45 × 19 × 415 long (1¾ × ¾ × 16in long)
4	Warp/cloth beam	2	Softwood	42 sq. × 530 long (1⅝in sq. × 21in)
5	Handle	2	Hardwood dowel	10 dia. × 100 long (⅜in dia. × 4in long)
6	Retaining pin	4	Stainless steel	3 dia. × 50 long (⅛in dia. × 2in long)
7	Ratchet	2	Plywood	85 sq. × 12 thick (3⅜in sq. × ½in thick)
8	Pawl	2	Plywood	50 × 16 × 12 thick (2 × ⅝ × ½in thick)
9	Heddle	1	Steel or plastic	See p. 187 for details
10	Heddle support bar	1	Softwood	20 × 16 × 496 long (¾ × ⅝ × 19½in long)
11	Apron cloth	1	Canvas	380 sq. (15in sq.)
12	Apron rod	1	Hardwood	19 × 4 × 400 long (¾ × ⁵⁄₃₂ × 15¾in long)
13	Shuttle	1	Hardwood	40 × 7 × 350 long (1⁹⁄₁₆ × ¼ × 13¾in long)

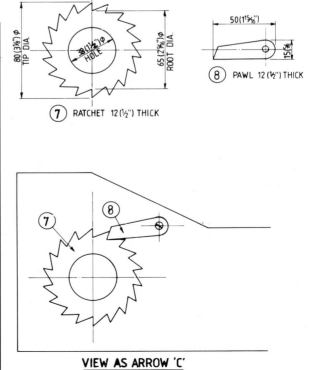

Fig. 13.5 Ratchet and pawl dimensions

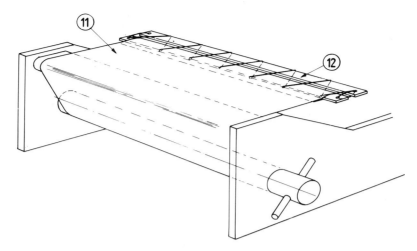

Fig. 13.6 Apron cloth and rod arrangements

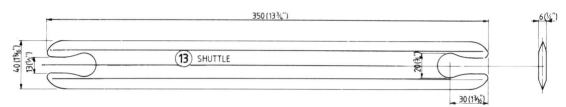

Fig. 13.7 Shuttle dimensions

make a good job they should be accurately marked out and cut. The hole in the centre should be almost a tight fit on the roller ends. You may find one of the adjustable tip type wood twist bits ideal for this. Experiment first on a piece of scrap plywood until you feel the hole size is correct. The ratchets are glue fixed onto the roller ends, but it might be worth considering pinning them transversely as well. Predrill the pin hole so the plywood does not split.

Heddle The rigid heddle is fitted in a 20×16mm ($\frac{3}{4} \times \frac{5}{8}$in) section support bar (10), and is pin fixed in a groove in this item. The length of the support bar may be affected by the choice of heddle, as previously discussed.

Apron cloth rods The last items to fit to the loom are an apron cloth and rod arrangement as shown in Fig. 13.6. Each apron cloth (11) is made from a piece of 380mm (15in) square strong canvas, calico or equivalent material. This is sewn over at one end to make a sleeve to fit an $18 \times 4 \times 400$mm ($\frac{3}{4} \times \frac{5}{32} \times 15\frac{3}{4}$in)

long apron rod. At the opposite end the apron cloth is doubled over and tacked squarely to the roller. Four apron rods are required. Finally you need to make a shuttle to the details in Fig. 13.7.

TABBY LOOM WEAVING

Weaving on the tabby loom, indeed on any loom, is not as simple as it first might seem. The actual process of weaving is the easy part, and fairly straightforward. However, the key to success lies to a large degree in correctly mounting the warp onto the loom at the start. This warping up procedure, or method of beaming on say 150–200 threads in a controlled manner without tangle, securing it to the apron rods, and evenly tensioning out, is a skill in itself. It requires the use of another essential piece of weaving equipment called the warping frame, or alternatively warping posts. The design of this is the subject of the next chapter, and so the details of warping up the tabby loom ready for weaving are discussed later at the conclusion of this next chapter.

14
WARPING POSTS AND FRAME

INTRODUCTION

Before mounting a warp onto a loom you have to prepare anything from 50–500 threads all cut to the same length. You could crudely use the backs of two chairs set the requisite distance apart, and wind the yarn round and round these a number of times, equal to the number of warp threads required. However, this is not a very satisfactory arrangement. For one thing the chairs tend to move as the tension builds up, making the warp lengths irregular, and for another, when the warp is removed, the struggle to separate and disentangle the threads is not an easy task, indeed sometimes impossible.

It becomes apparent, therefore, that some sort of weaving accessory for preparing the warp in a controlled manner without tangle for easy mounting onto a loom is just as important as the loom itself. Warping posts are the simplest equipment for doing this, and for longer warps a warping frame is used.

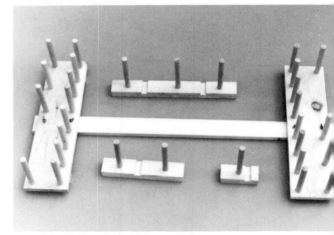

Fig. 14.1 Warping posts and warping frame

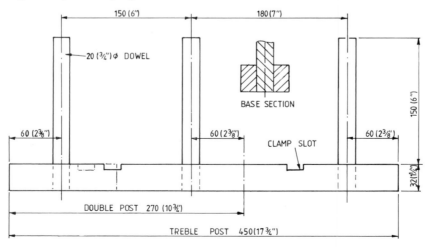

Fig. 14.2 Warping post dimensions

These are shown in Fig. 14.1. They may seem rather insignificant accessories, but they are inseparable from the loom, and you cannot weave without them. The design of this equipment is now described, along with some notes on its use, and the chapter concludes by discussing the warping up of the tabby loom.

WARPING POSTS

Short warps can be prepared using a simple *warping post* arrangement. Traditionally these are of single or double post form, but there are advantages in having a treble post set as well, as will become apparent later in this book (*see* p. 153). They are very easy to make, and the dimensional details are given in Fig. 14.2. The base consists of 57 × 32mm (2¼ × 1¼in) section softwood, or alternatively a hardwood such as beech.

Holes are drilled in this base to take the 20mm (¾in) diameter ramin dowel posts, which are glue fixed. The treble post set is the full length, as illustrated, the double post set 270mm (10¾in), and the single post 125mm (5in) long. Each base has a cut-out along the top edge which serves as a slot for a G-cramp to secure the warping post to a table (*Fig. 14.3*). Initially for warping up the tabby loom only a single and double post set are required.

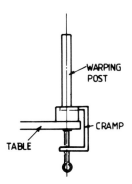

Fig. 14.3 Warping post clamp detail

Using warping posts In use the double post is set up at one end of the table, and some distance away a single post is similarly secured. The distance between these is the warp length. To prepare a warp, referring to fig. 14.4, start by tying yarn from a bobbin to post (1). Now lead this forward, under post (2), across round post (3), back cross and over post (2), and then to post (1) again. This is two warp

Fig. 14.4 Porrey cross formation

lengths, and the point where the second warp thread crosses the first between posts (2) and (3) is known as the *porrey cross*. This cross is the most important feature of the warp preparation, and serves as a means of separating alternate warp threads so that they cannot tangle. This will become clearer as further yarn is run back and forth between the posts (1), (2) and (3) as just described, until the required number of warp threads are added. The porrey cross is then secured by tying a piece of string round the middle. A string loop is also tied at each end of the warp, i.e. at posts (1) and (3). The warp can then be gently eased off the posts ready for mounting on a loom, and the porrey cross tie will keep the alternate threads separate, so that they can be picked off one by one. The procedure for beaming the warp onto a loom is concluded later in this chapter, when threading up the tabby loom is discussed, but first we will take a look at the design of the alternative to warping posts, the warping frame.

WARPING FRAME

If you need a longer warp, it will be apparent that a pair of warping posts clamped to a work surface is somewhat limiting. You could clamp extra posts to the table, and lead the yarn back and forth round these to extend the warp length; however, a more practical solution is to incorporate these into an accessory called *a warping frame*. This has perhaps 10 or 20 vertical posts set into a board arrangement, to enable varying warp lengths to be prepared. A set of triple posts either end, B, C, D and F, G, H, enable the porrey/portée crosses to be formed.

Design The warping frame design here is suitable for the smaller loom such as the tabby or 610mm (24in) table loom, to produce a warp up to 12 metres (13 yards) long. The dimensional information is given in fig. 14.5. It consists of two identical end boards 150 × 20 × 560mm (6 × ¾ × 22in), each having a number of 19mm (¾in) diameter warping posts set into them at the pitching shown, and glue fixed.

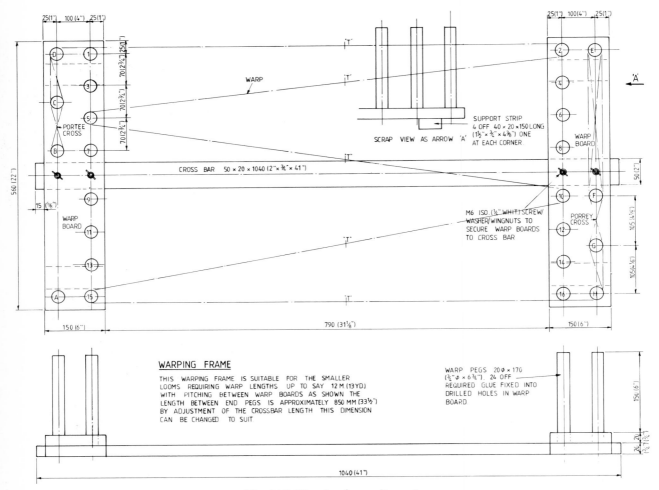

Fig. 14.5 Warping frame dimensions

These end boards are connected by a cross bar 50 × 20 × 1040mm (2 × ¾ × 41in), long using screw/wingnut fixtures. So that the warping frame does not rock when laid on a table, support strips are screw fixed to the underside of each end board.

The pitching between the end posts is approximately 850mm (33½in), and warp lengths can thus be made up in multiples of this. If required, the separation can be varied by altering the spacer bar length, or by providing a selection of screw holes in this strip. For portability the end boards are simply unscrewed. Sometimes it is convenient to prepare the warp with the frame hung on a wall, rather than laid on a table. If you wish to do this, fix a couple of strong screw eyes into the 150mm (6in) end of the peg boards to facilitate this. Alternatively drill a couple of small holes in these, so that it can be strung up on the wall. The wood for construction is

not too important. Softwood will suffice for the end boards and the cross bar, with ramin for the warping posts, but if you prefer, beech or ash could be used for these items.

Using the warping frame The use of the warping frame is similar to that of the posts described earlier, except that the warp length is extended as required by winding it back and forth over a preselected number of posts. Let us assume, for example, that you wish to make a 4.25m (4½ yd) warp for mounting on the tabby loom in Chapter 13. Referring to Fig. 14.5, this length will require the yarn to be carried back and forth round posts 1, 2, 5, 10, 15 and 16. We do not need to form the portée cross, which is only necessary for more advanced looms, e.g. the four shaft table loom. Accordingly we do not need to use post B, C or E, and the warp can be started at post D and returned round post F.

When the required number of warp threads have been added, the warp is then secured with string ties as described previously, i.e. at the porrey cross and the warp ends. In addition further ties are made at intermediate positions (T) along the warp length. These serve to hold the warp together in a long snake, so that when it is lifted off the frame it does not dangle loosely.

MOUNTING THE WARP ON THE TABBY LOOM

The final operation in warp preparation is to transfer this from the frame to the tabby loom, and the following is a brief step by step description of the procedure for doing this. It assumes that each warp yarn is composed of a single thread, as opposed to a double commonly used, and therefore produces an open or loose weave.

Step 1 The warp securely tied at the porrey cross and ends is lifted off the warping frame and looped into a chain, as shown in Fig. 14.6. In this the warp is effectively formed into a rather large crochet chain using your hand as a gigantic crochet hook. This reduces the warp length, and makes it more manageable to handle. Start from the loop end of the warp (i.e. post D) so that the warp will naturally unwind from the porrey cross.

Step 2 Lay the chained warp on a table and insert a pair of lease sticks through the porrey cross (one on either side). Tie the ends of the lease sticks together so that the warp cannot slip off. When this is done the string tie through the porrey cross may be released. The loop ends now need moving away from the lease sticks to provide a working length in between. Hook your finger in the loop end and ease back the cross, holding the chain while you do this so it does not undo. You can place the chain over a single warping post clamped to the table to assist, if necessary. Fig. 14.7 shows the situation now reached.

Step 3 The warp now has to be spread out ready for beaming on. On a larger loom (e.g. four shaft table) you would normally use a raddle (c.f. Chapter 18 for its design), but on the tabby loom we can make use of the rigid heddle for this purpose. To hold the heddle during this operation it is useful to clamp it

Fig. 14.6 Step 1: chaining a warp to reduce its length

Fig. 14.7 Step 2: inserting lease sticks in the porrey cross

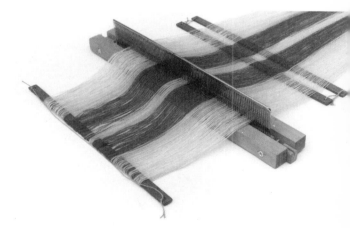
Fig. 14.8 Step 3: spreading warp and threading through heddle

Fig. 14.9 Step 4: securing warp to apron rod

Fig. 14.10 Step 5: beaming on

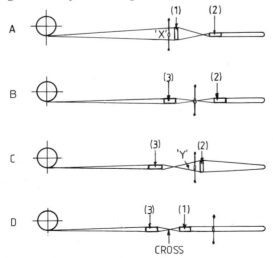

Fig. 14.11 Step 6: transferring the cross

vertically between two horizontal wood strips, which are in turn secured to the table. The heddle should be clamped in upside down for reasons which later become apparent. Now undo the warp end ties and thread each looped pair of warp threads through consecutive heddle slits. In this operation we ignore the heddle eyes. Do not cut the loop ends. Continue until the whole of the warp is threaded through the heddle in this way, as shown in Fig. 14.8.

Step 4 You are now nearly ready for beaming on. Bring the tabby loom up to the end of the warp, and release the apron rod end ties from the apron cloth on the warp beam. Thread this apron rod through the row of warp end loops which have been previously threaded through the heddle slits, and then resecure it back onto the apron cloth with the end ties. You are now in a position where the warp is fixed to the warp beam and cannot slip back through the rigid heddle. The latter is also serving to spread the warp evenly apart, and the lease sticks are maintaining the cross so the threads cannot tangle. The position now reached is shown in Fig. 14.9.

Step 5 Before beaming on the warp, first clamp the tabby loom to the table, and have 10 or 20 warp sticks ready to hand. Release the chain, and hold the warp firmly with your hand, letting this move up to the loom as you wrap. Do not let the warp slip through the hand. Having wrapped on so much, enter a warp stick between the warp and the roller. Change the position of the hand holding the warp, and wind on some more warp. Insert warp sticks about one a wrap. Undo the warp ties as they come out of the chain. Continue until you come to the loop end of the warp, and make sure that it is evenly and centrally wound onto the roller, especially if the warp is narrower than the heddle. Beaming on is shown in fig. 14.10.

Step 6 At this point you will have realised that the thread cross is on the wrong side of the rigid heddle, and before proceeding further this has to be transferred to the other side. A spare lease stick (3) is needed to assist this. Referring to Fig. 14.11 (A), turn the lease stick (1) nearest the rigid heddle vertical to open up a shed at 'X'. Insert the spare lease stick (3) through the warp at this position, and release the lease stick (1). The thread cross is now through the heddle, as at Fig. 14.11 (B). Now turn the lease stick (2) vertical and move the rigid heddle close up to it to expose a shed 'Y' on the opposite side (*Fig. 14.11 (C)*). Insert the now spare lease stick (1) through this shed, and then remove the lease stick (2). The position is now as in fig. 14.11 (D), and the thread cross has been transferred to the opposite side of the heddle.

Step 7 The next operation is *drawing in*, that is threading the warp alternately through the slits and eyes of the heddle. This can be done with the heddle in place on the loom, but it is rather easier to complete this while the heddle is still between clamp strips fixed to the table. From the previous beaming on operation you will have discovered that the warp end loops will be butting up to the heddles, each one straddling across from one slit to the next. Thus half the drawing on process has been completed already, and all you have to do is cut each warp loop and thread the second end through the heddle eye. So that the warp does not slip back through the heddle, the threads should be tied in groups every 25mm (1in) with a slip knot, as shown in Fig. 14.12.

Step 8 The next step is to transfer the rigid heddle complete with warp threads onto the loom. You will now realise why the heddle was threaded with it upside down, because when you reverse it over the loom it will fit in the support slots 'Y' correctly. The last operation is to secure the warp ends to the apron rod on the cloth beam. The warp is split into small groups of say 15–25 threads. Each group passes over and under the apron rod. As it comes back up it divides into two and is tied back on top with a reef knot, as shown in Fig. 14.13. Continue this process across the loom until all the warp threads are secured and evenly tensioned.

Step 9 The loom is now virtually ready for weaving, and it only remains to wind on the warp so that the cloth beam apron rods are past the breast beam. The warp is then stretched a little using the ratchets and pawls to provide a nice firm surface, and with shuttle in hand you can now weave away (*Fig. 14.14*).

Fig. 14.12 Step 7: drawing in

Fig. 14.13 Step 8: securing warp to cloth beam

Fig. 14.14 Step 9: tabby loom ready for weaving

15
TABLET LOOM

INTRODUCTION

Tablet loom weaving is a rather unusual method of making braids, ties, belts, etc. It is quite unique in that it does not use a conventional heddle arrangement to produce a warp shed. Instead it uses small cardboard or plastic cards to do this. For this reason it is sometimes known as card weaving. It works on a system of card rotation which switches threads up and down, thus changing the warp and the tablets are in fact a disguised form of a rigid heddle.

It is a form of weaving in which the warp plays the dominant role in appearance, and the weft serves only to bind the weave together, and is lost amongst the warp threads. Historically it can be shown to have been practised as long ago as 3000 years, but quite how anybody stumbled on the idea of using little cards to switch the warp is a mystery.

Tablet weaving can be and still is practised with the warp suspended between a wall or chair back and the weaver's waist. Indeed some may prefer still to do it this way. However, a frame such as that in Fig. 15.1 has the advantage of freeing the weaver from restraint. It also assists in stopping the warp from getting twisted up, especially when the cards are being continually turned in one direction.

DESIGN

The general arrangement of the tablet loom is given in Fig. 15.1, and the associated parts list in Table 15. It has a form rather like a bedstead, having two end boards, a warp and cloth end (1), (3), set apart 760mm (30in), and supported by a spacer board. The warp is mounted across these two ends passing through a series of tablets in between. At the cloth end the warp is secured with a clamp bar (5), and at the warp end the threads separate and pass between a series of steel pins. Finally they are attached to a number of lead weights which serve to keep the

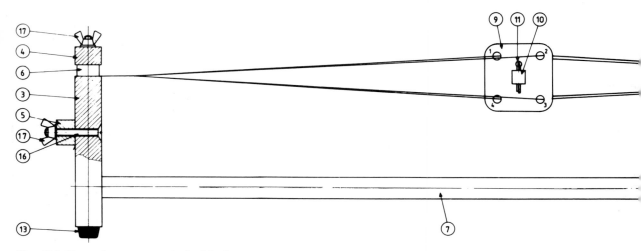

Fig. 15.1 General arrangement of tablet loom

warp taut and maintain an even tension.

Each tablet is warped up with four threads, one to each corner hole, and this group passes between a pair of warp end pins (14), and attached to one lead weight. The pin separation allows up to 24 tablets each of four threads to be accommodated, although by doubling up it is possible to mount 48 tablets. The loom will weave braids typically up to 50mm (2in) wide.

WEAVING PRINCIPLE

To understand the weaving principle refer to Fig. 15.1 and study the tablet threading. Note that one thread passes through each numbered corner hole. On either side of the tablets the warp forms a wedge shaped gap: this is the shed through which a shuttle is passed loaded with weft. Consider now rotation of a card group a quarter turn clockwise. A thread which was in the up position (2) moves down, and one which was down (4) moves up. A further quarter turn will transpose all the threads which were up to the down position, and vice versa. Thus the warp is changed and weft may be passed through to bind the weave. If you continue this procedure alternately rotating the cards a quarter or half turn, and passing weft thread through each time, a woven strip of fabric will be formed. It is a fascinating method of weaving, and later in this chapter, after construction, some easy patterns are given for the beginner.

FRAME CONSTRUCTION

The dimensions of the frame components are given in Fig. 15.2. The cloth end consists of a board $140 \times 22 \times 133$mm ($5\frac{1}{2} \times \frac{7}{8} \times 5\frac{1}{4}$in) long, to which is fitted screw studs (15), distance pieces (6), a cloth end cover (4) and a clamp bar (5) as per the measurements given. The warp end (1) is a larger board $133 \times 22 \times 245$mm ($5\frac{1}{4} \times \frac{7}{8} \times 9$in) long. This has a row of 23 stainless steel 3mm ($\frac{1}{8}$in) diameter steel pins (14) fixed into drilled holes in the top edge. Screw studs (15), distance pieces (6) and a cover (2) are added, as to the cloth end. Note that when the warp end cover (2) is fitted, the pins (14) project

Table 15: Tablet Loom Parts List

Item	Description	No. off	Material	Dimensions
1	Warp end	1	Hardwood	$133 \times 22 \times 245$ long ($5\frac{1}{4} \times \frac{7}{8} \times 9\frac{3}{4}$in long)
2	Warp end cover	1	Hardwood	$22 \times 16 \times 245$ long ($\frac{7}{8} \times \frac{5}{8} \times 9\frac{3}{4}$in long)
3	Cloth end	1	Hardwood	$133 \times 22 \times 140$ long ($5\frac{1}{4} \times \frac{7}{8} \times 5\frac{1}{2}$in long)
4	Cloth end cover	1	Hardwood	$22 \times 16 \times 140$ long ($\frac{7}{8} \times \frac{5}{8} \times 5\frac{1}{2}$in long)
5	Clamp bar	1	Hardwood	$22 \times 16 \times 140$ long ($\frac{7}{8} \times \frac{5}{8} \times 5\frac{1}{2}$in long)
6	Distance piece	4	Hardwood	19 dia. $\times 10$ thick ($\frac{3}{4}$in dia. $\times \frac{3}{8}$in thick)
7	Spacer board	1	Hardwood	$94 \times 19 \times 760$ long ($3\frac{3}{4} \times \frac{3}{4} \times 30$in long)
8	Spacer tube	2	Aluminium or steel	19 dia. $\times 760$ long ($\frac{3}{4}$in dia. $\times 30$in long)
9	Tablet	24	Plastic sheet	60 sq. $\times 0.8/1.6$ thick ($2\frac{3}{8}$in sq. $\times \frac{1}{32}/\frac{1}{16}$in thick)
10	Tablet bar	1	Hardwood	12 sq. $\times 150$ long ($\frac{1}{2}$in sq. $\times 6$in long)
11	Split pin	1	Steel	
12	Lead weight	24	Lead	110g (4oz)
13	Rubber stop	4	Rubber	
14	Pin	23	Stainless steel	3 dia. $\times 600$ long total ($\frac{1}{8}$in dia. $\times 24$in long)
15	Screw studding	—	Steel	M6 Iso. $\times 360$ long total ($\frac{1}{4}$in Whit. $\times 15$in long)
16	Screw	2	Steel	M6 Iso. $\times 50$ long ($\frac{1}{4}$in Whit. $\times 2$in long)
17	Wingnuts/ washers	6	Steel	M6 Iso size ($\frac{1}{4}$in Whit. size)
18	Shuttle	1	Plywood	$22 \times 3 \times 150$ long ($\frac{7}{8} \times \frac{1}{8} \times 6$in long)

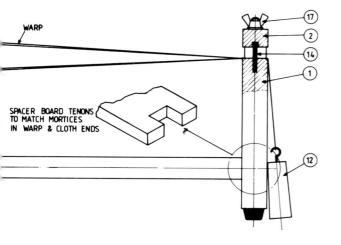

WARP

SPACER BOARD TENONS
TO MATCH MORTICES
IN WARP & CLOTH ENDS

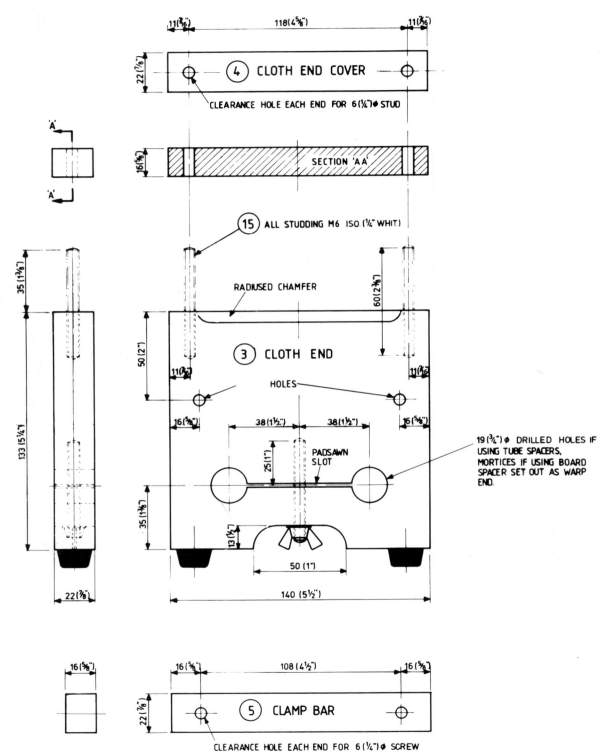

Fig. 15.2 Warp and cloth end details

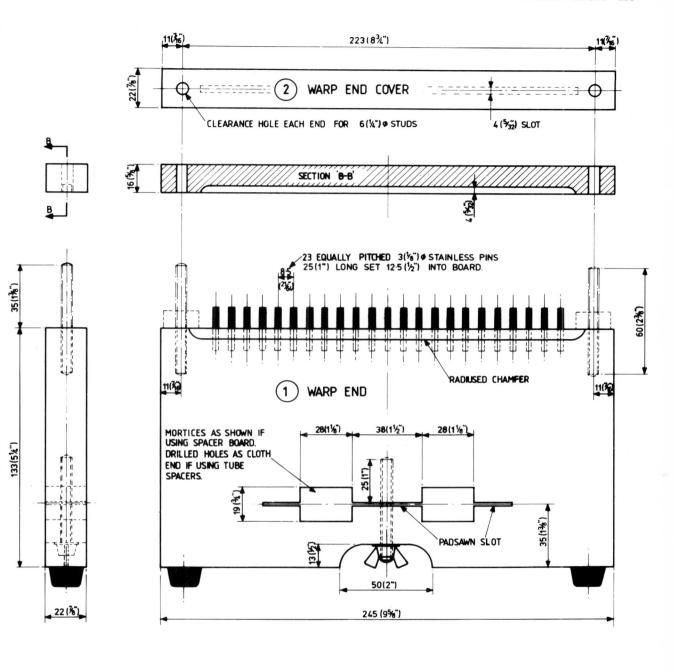

11 (7/16")   223 (8 3/4")   11 (7/16")

22 (7/8")   (2) WARP END COVER

CLEARANCE HOLE EACH END FOR 6 (1/4") φ STUDS   4 (5/32") SLOT

16 (5/8")   SECTION 'B-B'   4 (5/32")

35 (1 3/8")   23 EQUALLY PITCHED 3 (1/8") φ STAINLESS PINS
25 (1") LONG SET 12.5 (1/2") INTO BOARD.
8.5 (21/64")   60 (2 3/8")

133 (5 1/4")   (1) WARP END   RADIUSED CHAMFER

11 (3/8")   11 (3/8")

MORTICES AS SHOWN IF
USING SPACER BOARD.
DRILLED HOLES AS CLOTH
END IF USING TUBE
SPACERS.   28 (1 1/8")   38 (1 1/2")   28 (1 1/8")

25 (1")

19 (3/4")   35 (1 3/8")

PADSAWN SLOT

13 (1/2")

50 (2")

22 (7/8")   245 (9 5/8")

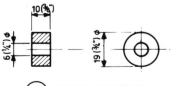

10 (3/8")

6 (1/4") φ   19 (3/4") φ

(6) DISTANCE PIECE

slightly into a slot in this item. This prevents the warp threads accidentally jumping a pin space.

The warp and cloth ends are separated by a horizontal board (7) 94 × 19 × 760mm ($3\frac{3}{4}$ × $\frac{3}{4}$ × 30in) long. Alternatively, two 19mm ($\frac{3}{4}$in) diameter galvanised steel or brass tubes can be used. The differing slot arrangements are given in Fig. 15.2. Which method is used is left to personal choice. Both use a similar stud/wingnut clamping system. Studding will self tap into a core diameter hole in wood, but the latter should be clamped on either side when tapping to prevent splitting the timber. The frame can be made in softwood, but a utilitarian hardwood such as beech is preferred. The suggested finish is two coats of sanding sealer to keep out the dirt. Four rubber stops (13) will help prevent the loom sliding about when in use.

Tablets The tablets (9) are preferably made from 0.8/1.6mm ($\frac{1}{32}$/$\frac{1}{16}$in) thick plastic. These are nominally 60mm ($2\frac{3}{8}$in) square made to the details in Fig. 15.2. Note the square hole in the centre; this serves to take the tablet bar (10), which locks the tablet bunch together when the loom is not in use. The tablets have 6mm ($\frac{1}{4}$in) holes drilled in each corner and are marked 1 to 4 in clockwise rotation. A useful jig for making these is shown in Fig. 15.6. This consists of two steel plates cut to the tablet shape. A dozen or so tablets can be cut at a time using this. Finish off the tablet edges smoothly to prevent warp abrasion. An alternative is to purchase ready-made tablets. These are usually of card, but sometimes do not have the locking hole in the centre. A source of ready-made tablets is given in the list of suppliers.

Fig. 15.4 Jig for making tablets

Warp tension weights The lead weights are nominally 280 grams ($\frac{1}{4}$lb) to the details in Fig. 15.5. If you make them yourself you might consider machining a tapered steel mould to assist this. After the lead has been poured and solidified, they can then be easily knocked out. Do, however, take proper precautions in handling this hazardous material. As an alternative you could consider

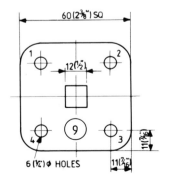

Fig. 15.3 Tablet dimensions

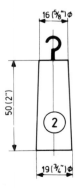

Fig. 15.5 Dimensions of lead weights

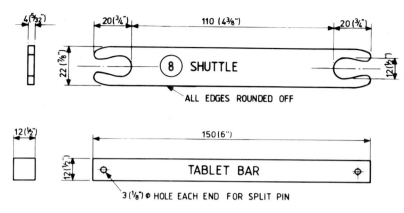

Fig. 15.6 Shuttle and table bar details

machined steel weights or perhaps some smart brass ones.

Shuttle and tablet bar The dimensions of the final items to make, the shuttle (8) and tablet bar (10), are given in Fig. 15.6. The tablet bar should fit closely through the tablet centre holes.

SETTING UP A WEAVE

The loom can now be put to use, placing it on a table with the warp end to one edge, so that the weights hang down over the side. The process of setting up a weave is not complex, but it must be done rigorously to order for it to be successful. It is best illustrated by an example such as that commonly known as two way weaving. In this the tablets are threaded in a manner where a band can be woven with one colour on one side and another colour on the other. Let us assume that you are making a braid about 25mm (1in) wide and accordingly this requires 12 tablets warped up. At four threads per tablet, 48 threads in total will be required cut to a desired length, say 2.5m (8ft), and without tangle so they can then be picked off individually. A warping board will assist but it is not absolutely essential. Half of these threads will be required in one colour, say red, and the other half in another, say yellow, and are threaded as follows.

Take tablet number one and, laying this on a table with the corner hole 1 in the top left position, thread holes 1 and 2 with red yarn from the left front to the right back. Similarly, thread holes 3 and 4 but with yellow yarn. Thread all 12 cards in this manner and firmly knot each tablet group of four threads at the cloth end. Stack all 12 cards on top of each other in the same orientation.

The next step is to transfer these cards onto the loom; to prevent inadvertent tablet rotation during this operation, the tablet bar should be inserted through the card stack. Tie the ends of this bar together with string so that it does not fall out. Alternatively, and perhaps rather better, split pins may be inserted through the tablet bar ends. Now remove both the warp and cloth end covers, and lay the warp roughly in position across the loom. At the cloth end tie all 12 sets of tablet threads together as one, and firmly secure these here under the clamp bar. At the warp end divide out the warp across 12 consecutive pin slots and tie on a lead weight to each tablet thread group (i.e. four threads) when the warp will then tension out. Finally, screw back on the warp and cloth end covers to secure the warp in place, load up a shuttle of weft (say yellow), remove the tablet bar and you are ready to commence weaving.

Pattern 1 (Fig 15.7A and B**)** With the tablets aligned as warped up, with the number one hole in the top left position pass the weft through the shed on the cloth side. Rotate the tablets one quarter turn anti-clockwise and pass the weft again, followed by two quarter turns clockwise, similarly passing the weft at each quarter turn. The weave is continued alternating two quarter turns anti-clockwise, two quarter turns clockwise, etc. (i.e. 1, 2, 1, 4, 1, 2, 1, 4, etc). A band of red will be formed on one side (top) and yellow on the underside (Fig. 15.7A). These colours can be interchanged by first rotating all the

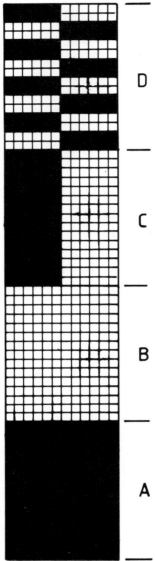

Fig. 15.7 Weaving patterns 1 and 2

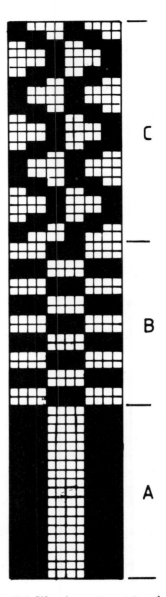

Fig. 15.8 Weaving patterns 3 and 4

cards two quarter turns anti-clockwise (i.e. number 3 hole in top left position), and recommencing the two turns forwards and backwards from here (i.e. 3, 4, 3, 2, 3, 4, 3, 2, etc., *Fig. 15.7B*).

Pattern 2 (*Fig 15.7C and D***)** Leave tablets 1 to 6 as originally warped up with hole 1 in the top left position, but turn round tablets 6 to 12 initially two quarter turns anti-clockwise (hole 3 in top left

position). Recommence weaving as before for pattern 1, alternating two quarter turns anti-clockwise and then clockwise etc. This will produce a band each of red and yellow on top and these colours will be opposite on the underside (*Fig. 15.7C*). If instead the cards are turned continuously in one direction, a check pattern will be obtained, with alternating red and yellow (*Fig. 15.7D*).

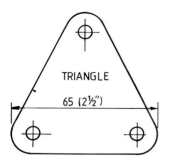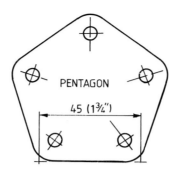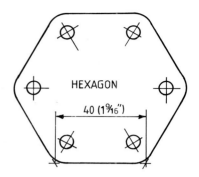

Fig. 15.9 Alternative tablet shapes

Pattern 3 (*Fig 15.8A and B*) Leave tablets 1 to 4 and 9 to 12 as in the original warped up position, but turn round tablets 5 to 8 initially two quarter turns anti-clockwise. Recommence weaving as for pattern 1. This will produce a triple band of red/yellow/red on top, and yellow/red/yellow underneath (*Fig. 15.8A*). Alternatively, rotating the cards continuously in one direction will change this banding into a three row check (*Fig. 15.8B*).

Pattern 4 (*Fig. 15.8C*) Set up cards 1, 2, 7 and 8 in their original position, cards 3, 4, 9 and 10 one quarter turn anti-clockwise, and cards 5, 6, 11 and 12 two quarter turns anti-clockwise. Weave, alternating with four quarter turns anti-clockwise, four quarter turns clockwise etc. (i.e. 1, 2, 3, 4, 3, 2, 1, 4, etc.). This will produce the pattern as in fig. 15.8C.

More complex patterns The above considers tablet threading only from the left front to the right back, but one can, of course, thread in reverse from the right front to the left back. Cards alternately threaded in this manner from the left to right will form a plait-like weave, and the tablets will be in zigzag formation when viewed on edge in plan. Further pattern development can include variations in this threading, choice of up to four different yarn colours per tablet, and card rotation forwards or backwards, depending upon the weave. An example of the latter is that to form a good braid edge the border cards are sometimes rotated continuously in one direction during the weave, whilst the middle cards are turned back and forth according to the requirements of the pattern proper.

OTHER TABLET SHAPES

In the weaving process described above we have considered square tablets threaded with yarn through each corner (i.e. four threads). However, you can weave with the warp passing through only two opposing corner holes. It is also possible to use other tablet shapes, with three, five or six holes, as in Fig. 15.9. Warps using tablets with higher numbers of holes are thicker and stronger than those using two or three holes. The five and six hole tablets increase the pattern scope, but they can be a little more difficult to weave with. Depending on the position of the tablets you can produce more than one shed, and this is not as wide as that produced by a four hole tablet. Hence it is less easy to pass the shuttle through the warp.

16
INKLE LOOMS

INTRODUCTION

The inkle loom, like the tablet loom, is another somewhat unconventional piece of weaving equipment, and used similarly for making braids, belts and ties, etc. Some authorities suggest that it is of Scottish origin but this is difficult to trace. It is one of the easiest forms of weaving to grasp, particularly as it does not need the use of warping equipment to warp it up. Because of this, beginners are often introduced to inkles before moving on to other looms, and a child of any reasonable intelligence is both able to warp it up and weave on it quite quickly. Two designs are offered, a table model and a floor-standing inkle loom.

Although it might not seem so at first, the inkle loom has similarities to the frame loom in Chapter 12 (*Fig. 12.4*). The warp on the latter takes the form of a continuous loop, and on the inkle loom shown in Fig. 16.4 the same principle is used. The only difference is that the warp has been expanded to make a longer usable length. This is achieved by introducing a series of extra pegs, and the result is a vertical loom structure rather than a horizontal frame. The warp length may be varied according to the pegs selected.

SHED FORMATION

Where the inkle differs most significantly from other looms is in the method of shed formation. This is done by hand and not by any mechanical device such as a tablet, heddle or even leashes, although the latter are used but only as a means of setting up the warp. To understand the shed formation you need to appreciate first how the loom is warped up. The following description makes reference to Figs. 16.4 and 16.1.

The warp consists of a number of individual yarn

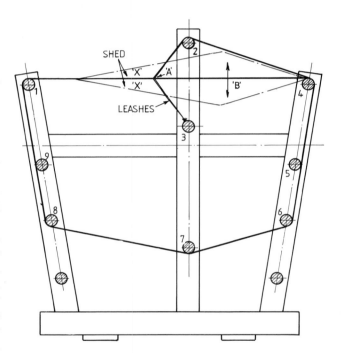

Fig. 16.1 Shed formation on the inkle loom

lengths secured round a series of posts. The first warp thread starts at peg 1, passes between pegs 2 and 3, then follows round pegs 4, 5, 6, 7, 8 and 9, then back to peg 1 where the two ends are knotted. The second warp thread again starts at peg 1, but follows a slightly different route. This passes up over peg 2, down to peg 4, then round pegs 5, 6, 7, 8 and 9, then back to peg 1 where the ends are knotted together, the same as for the first warp thread. Between pegs 1 and 2 a leash loop is attached to the second warp thread, and this is tied back to peg 3, to pull this yarn down to warp line level between peg 1 and point 'A'. The third warp thread is then mounted as the first, the fourth as the second, and so on alternately, until the required number of warp threads have been added. Peg 7, which is movable, is then adjusted to tighten up the warp.

If you place your hand under the warp at position 'B' and lift, this half of the warp will rise above the rest, and a shed will be formed at 'X' above the warp line. Similarly, if you lower the warp at 'B' by pushing down, a shed will be formed at 'X' below the warp line. In effect your hand is acting as a rigid heddle does on the tabby loom, and each time the warp is raised or lowered, weft is passed through to bind the threads. This in simplicity is the principle of weaving on the inkle loom. Let us now move forward to the designs which incorporate this.

Table 16: Table Inkle Loom Parts List

Item	Description	No. off	Material	Dimensions
1	Basebar	1	Hardwood	40 sq. × 760 long (1$\frac{9}{16}$in sq. × 30in long)
2	Foot stand	2	Hardwood	60 × 20 × 200 long (2$\frac{3}{8}$ × $\frac{3}{4}$ × 8in long)
3	Upright	2	Hardwood	40 sq. × 260 long (1$\frac{9}{16}$in sq. × 10$\frac{1}{4}$in long)
4	Fixed peg	6	Hardwood	22 dia. × 190 long ($\frac{7}{8}$dia. × 7$\frac{1}{2}$in long)
5	Warp tension peg	1	Hardwood	25 dia. × 150 long (1in dia. × 6in long)
6	Screw stud/ washer/ wingnut	1	Steel	M6 Isometric ($\frac{1}{4}$in Whitworth)

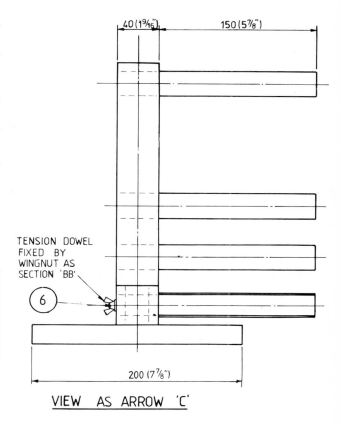

VIEW   AS   ARROW   'C'

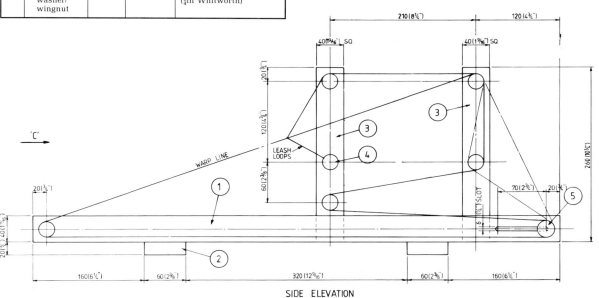

SIDE   ELEVATION

Fig. 16.2 General arrangement of inkle loom (table loom)

TABLE INKLE LOOM

The table version of the inkle loom is shown in Fig. 16.2. It can accommodate a warp length of up to 2m ($2\frac{1}{4}$yd), and a braid width of between 100–125mm (4–5in). The dimensional details are given in Fig. 16.2, and the associated parts list in Table 16. It consists of a compact frame arrangement fitted out with a number of horizontal posts or pegs on which the warp is mounted.

Begin construction with the base bar (1), and the two uprights (3). These are formed from 40mm ($1\frac{9}{16}$in) square section material, and a hardwood such as beech is suggested. The uprights are morticed and tenoned into the basebar. Make the connection square, so that there is no twist on the framework side face into which the dowel posts (4) fit. Machine the 22mm ($\frac{7}{8}$in) diameter dowel holes and the 6mm ($\frac{1}{4}$in) slot in the basebar before assembling and gluing up the frame.

While the frame is setting, the fixed dowel posts (4), which are 22mm ($\frac{7}{8}$in) diameter × 190mm ($7\frac{1}{2}$in) long can be prepared. Glue these squarely into the frame. Lastly add the warp tension peg (5). This is 25mm (1in) diameter × 150 mm (6in) long and is fixed with an M6 Isometric ($\frac{1}{4}$in Whitworth) stud/wingnut arrangement. See Fig. 16.3 for typical detail. Finally screw on two 60 × 20mm ($2\frac{3}{8} × \frac{3}{4}$in) section foot stands to the basebar underside to make the arrangement freestanding.

FLOOR-STANDING INKLE LOOM

The floor-standing inkle loom is illustrated in Fig.

Table 17: Floor Standing Inkle Loom Parts List

Item	Description	No. off	Material	Dimensions
1	Basebar	1	Hardwood	60 × 50 × 660 long ($2\frac{3}{8} × 2 × 26$in long)
2	Foot stand	2	Hardwood	90 × 20 × 230 long ($3\frac{1}{2} × \frac{3}{4} × 9$in long)
3	Upright	3	Hardwood	60 × 32 × 800 long ($2\frac{3}{8} × 1\frac{1}{4} × 31\frac{1}{2}$in long)
4	Crossbar	1	Hardwood	60 × 22 × 750 long ($2\frac{3}{8} × \frac{7}{8} × 30$in long)
5	Fixed peg	10	Hardwood	25 dia. × 182 long (1in dia. × $7\frac{1}{4}$in long)
6	Warp tension peg	1	Hardwood	25 dia. × 150 long (1in dia. × 6in long)
7	Screw stud/ washer/ wingnut	1	Steel	M6 Isometric ($\frac{1}{4}$in Whitworth)

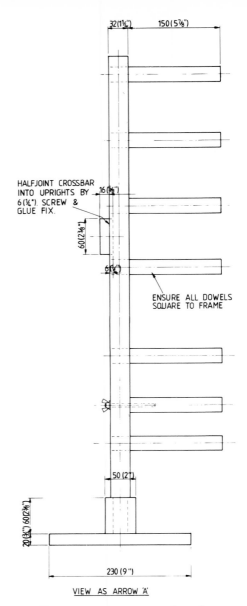

VIEW AS ARROW 'A'

16.3. It will accommodate a warp length up to 2.58m ($8\frac{1}{4}$ft), and weave widths similar to the table model. With a slight modification it also has a useful feature in being able to double up as a warping frame, as described later. The general arrangement drawing is given in fig. 16.4, and for the parts list see Table 17.

Construction is along the lines of the table model, beginning with the 60 × 50mm ($2\frac{3}{8} × 2$in) section basebar (1). Into this is morticed and tenoned three uprights (3), the outer two being at a slight angle. The crossbar (4) is made from 60 × 22mm ($2\frac{3}{8} × \frac{7}{8}$in) section timber, and is let into the uprights with shallow 6mm ($\frac{1}{4}$in) half joints (*Fig. 16.4 view 'A'*). As

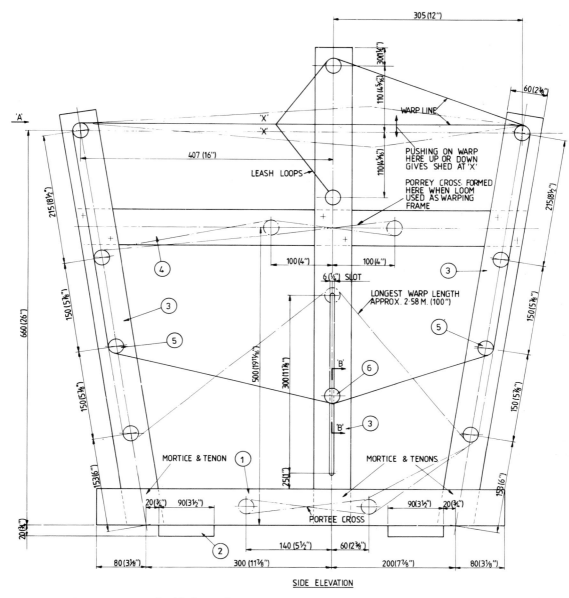

305 (12")
300(11¾")
60(2⅜")
110 (4⅝")
WARP LINE
110(4⅝")
PUSHING ON WARP
HERE UP OR DOWN
GIVES SHED AT 'X'
'A'
'X'
'X'
407 (16")
LEASH LOOPS
PORREY CROSS FORMED
HERE WHEN LOOM
USED AS WARPING
FRAME
215(8½")
215(8½")
④
100(4")
100(4")
③
150(5⅞")
6 (¼") SLOT
LONGEST WARP LENGTH
APPROX. 2·58 M. (100")
③
150(5⅞")
660 (26")
⑤
500(19¹¹⁄₁₆")
300(11⅞")
⑤
'B'
⑥
150(5⅞")
150(5⅞")
'B'
③
25(1")
MORTICE & TENON
①
MORTICE & TENONS
153(6")
153(6")
20(¾")
90(3½")
90(3½")
20(¾")
20(¾")
PORTEE CROSS
②
140 (5½")
60(2⅜")
80(3⅛")
300 (11⅞")
200(7⅞")
80(3⅛")

SIDE ELEVATION

Fig. 16.3 General arrangement of inkle loom (floor-standing)

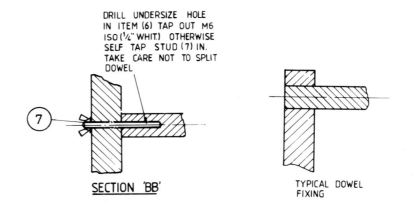

DRILL UNDERSIZE HOLE
IN ITEM (6) TAP OUT M6
ISO (¼" WHIT) OTHERWISE
SELF TAP STUD (7) IN.
TAKE CARE NOT TO SPLIT
DOWEL

⑦

Fig. 16.4 Peg fixing details

SECTION 'BB'

TYPICAL DOWEL
FIXING

for the table model, none of the joints is glued yet, until all the dowel holes and slots have been formed. This loom is fitted out with 25mm (1in) diameter warp posts: ten fixed posts and one adjustable one; for fixing details see Fig. 16.4. The last items to add are the two footstands (2) which are from 90 × 20mm ($3\frac{1}{2} \times \frac{3}{4}$in) section hardwood, and are screw fixed to the basebar.

USING INKLE LOOMS

The method of warping up the inkle loom, the shed formation and the weaving principle have been described earlier. Assuming you have warped up say 40–50 threads, and then tensioned these with the adjustable peg, you may, however, still find odd individual threads a little slack. The warp will, therefore, have to be released temporarily while these are corrected. Weaving then proceeds alternately lifting and lowering the warp by hand, and

passing a shuttle loaded with weft through the shed each time. The weft is beaten to straighten it out and compact it each time. When a length of braid has been woven, and there is no more room to weave, the warp is slackened off, and gently eased along a bit round the pegs to expose new warp. The loop is then re-tensioned, and weaving proceeds again as before.

USE AS A WARPING FRAME

The floor-standing inkle loom is not dissimilar to the warping frame design in Chapter 14, if you imagine this simply to be a board of pegs turned vertical. By introducing extra pegs it can be adapted for warp preparation besides weaving. Four additional pegs are required to do this, and are used to make the porrey and portée crosses. Their position is shown chain dotted in Fig. 16.3. A warp length up to 4m ($4\frac{1}{2}$ft) can be prepared, and although this is somewhat limiting, it is nevertheless a useful feature.

17
FOUR SHAFT TABLE LOOM

INTRODUCTION

The tabby loom design in Chapter 13 has limitations, in that it can only produce a plain weave or subtle variations on this theme. The serious weaver will no doubt wish to progress into patterned weaving, and the 610mm (24in) four shaft table loom, as shown in Fig. 17.1, forms an ideal project for this. Before discussing the detail construction, however, let us look at the differences between the two looms as a background to the development.

A tabby loom with a fixed heddle can only raise or lower a set group of warp threads, usually alternate ones. Thus the pattern is a regular one such as plain linen sheet. The colours can be varied making, say, alternate bands of warp or weft stripes, but you are not in the true sense able to weave patterns. The tabby loom can be thought of as a two shaft loom, as in Fig. 17.2, where half the warp threads pass through the heddles of one shaft, and the remainder through the second. Lifting each shaft gives the

Fig. 17.1 610mm (24in) four shaft table loom

same effect as alternately raising and lowering the fixed tabby heddle, and a two shaft loom is thus no real improvement or aid to weaving patterns. The

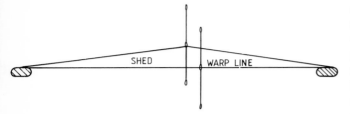

Fig. 17.2 Two shaft heddle arrangement

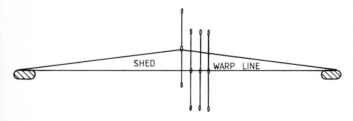

Fig. 17.3 Four shaft heddle arrangement

logical progression is to double up and make the loom with four shafts, as in Fig. 17.3. This modification makes it possible to weave a wide variety of patterns, because you can now be more selective on which warp threads are to be lifted to form a shed. Indeed you can add even more shafts, say eight or 12, to improve the choice still further. Four shafts thus represent the minimum on which to start weaving patterns such as twill, diamond, rosepath and many others.

Another point of difference between the two looms is the method of beating the weft. In the tabby loom the rigid heddle, besides being a shaft, also acts as a beater. Of course, this is impractical in a four shaft loom where the heddle movement is individually operated by levers, cords, or some combination thereof. A separate beater/reed is hence fitted in front of the shafts.

To summarise, the loom is designed to weave material up to 610mm (24in), this being about the greatest practical width in a table model. Its four shaft rising shed harness enables a variety of patterns to be woven, and incorporates string or wire heddles to personal choice.

STRUCTURE

The general arrangement of the loom is given in Figs. 17.5 and 17.6, and the associated parts list is in Table 18. One basic feature of loom construction always to keep in mind is the importance of strength. If you consider for a moment the loom warped up to 610mm (24in) width, using a ten dent per 25mm (1in) reed, then there will be about 240 threads stretched between the breast and back beams, and together with the shaft lift to form a shed this must represent a significant tension. It is therefore essential the loom structure is well built and strong.

The frame consists of a centre box section, side rails, crossbars and corner posts. Start by building the box section, comprising the two centre posts (2) connected by a top and bottom crossbar (1), (3). The centre posts (2) each have a number of heddle frame grooves/slots cut into them in accordance with Fig. 17.4. These can either be routed or alternatively cut using a circular saw. When completed the box section can be screwed and glued together, no jointing being necessary.

While the box section is setting, work can proceed with the two side frames, items (4) and (5). These are plain stripwood components. Before assembly drill out the roller holes in the corner posts (4). Again a screwed and glued fixing is used. Make sure the side frames are identical, i.e. to keep the breast and back beam equally spaced apart. When completed these may then be screw fixed to the sides of the centre box section, but not glued yet as the rollers (8) have still to be fitted. The opportunity can also be taken to make the breast/back beams (7) and the stretchers (6). These are all the same section except the formers have a rounded edge where the warp passes over them. These are similarly screw fixed with no glue application at this stage. At this point review the assembly, and make a dimensional check on the structure.

Rollers, ratchets and pawls The dimensions of the warp and cloth beams (8) are given in Fig. 17.7 together with the ratchet (10) and pawl (11) details. The rollers are woodturned from 57mm (2¼in) square section hardwood. Turn the roller length 669mm (26⅜in) slightly oversize at this stage, and leave the end centres in, so that this can be trimmed back later to fit accurately within the frame. Also,

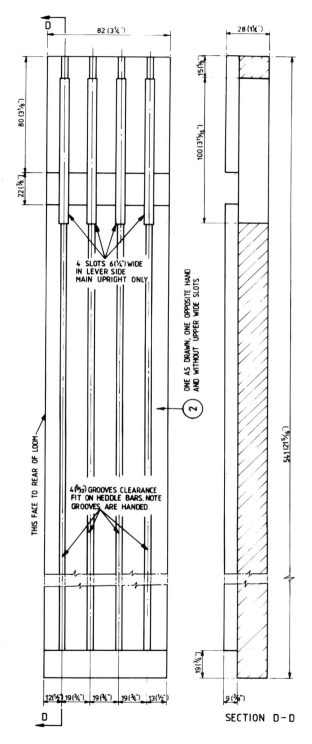

Fig. 17.4 Dimensional details of centre post

drill the transverse holes for the handles (9), but do not insert these yet, else the rollers cannot be fitted through the corner post holes.

The ratchets and pawls are rather fiddly to make, and as mentioned previously there are few if any commercial sources. The ratchets are cut from 2mm ($\frac{1}{16}$in) thick steel plate, and to make a good job these need to be accurately marked, sawn out and the teeth carefully filed to shape. A little patience and persistence here will win the day. They are then slipped over the roller ends and screw fixed. The pawls are similarly cut out and filed to shape. They look good in a matt black finish.

Now check each roller length including the ratchet to see if it fits correctly between the corner posts. They may need trimming back on the lathe a bit until they are a clearance fit, as previously mentioned.

ASSEMBLY

With the rollers complete these are now offered to the loom structure, by taking off one of the side frames temporarily and rescrewing. Assuming the rollers run smoothly, then finally glue the side frames to place, also the breast/back beams (7) and the stretchers (6). Lastly add the roller handles (9).

Shafts

Details of the four shafts are given in Fig. 17.8. Each heddle frame consists of two steel strips (17) joined by guide strips (18) at either end with screw connections. The nominal heddle height is 215mm (8½in) and the frames are designed to take wire or string heddles to personal choice. Wire heddles give a more positive shed, but some say they tend to chafe the warp. With both string and wire heddles, if when warping up you accidentally miss a warp thread, you can tie another string one in. A source for wire heddles and heddle string is given in the appendix. If in difficulty with 215mm (8½in) wire heddles, the loom could probably safely accommodate these in 228mm (9in) height as an alternative. The heddle frames are fitted to the loom running in the guide slots of the centre posts (2). You may need to unscrew items (17) and (18) temporarily to facilitate this. For a heddle tying jig see Fig. 17.9.

Shaft lifting mechanism The shaft movement is lever operated (*Fig. 17.6, section CC*). A chain link

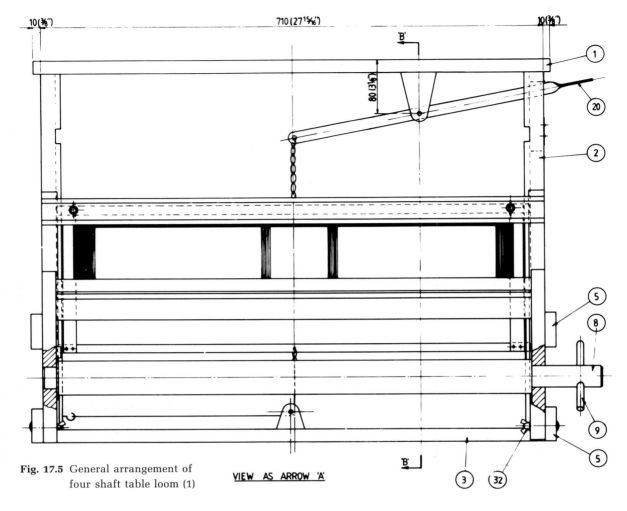

10(⅜")   710(27¹⁵⁄₁₆")   10(⅜")

80(3⅛")

'B'

Fig. 17.5 General arrangement of
four shaft table loom (1)

VIEW AS ARROW 'A'

B

Table 18: 610mm Four Shaft Table Loom Parts List

Item	Description	No. off	Material	Dimensions
1	Crossbar (top)	1	Hardwood	$82 \times 19 \times 730$ long ($3\frac{1}{4} \times \frac{3}{4} \times 28\frac{3}{4}$in long)
2	Centre post	2	Hardwood	$82 \times 28 \times 541$ long ($3\frac{1}{4} \times 1\frac{1}{8} \times 21\frac{1}{2}$in long)
3	Crossbar (bottom)	1	Hardwood	$82 \times 19 \times 672$ long ($3\frac{1}{4} \times \frac{3}{4} \times 26\frac{1}{2}$in long)
4	Corner post	4	Hardwood	$82 \times 19 \times 252$ long ($3\frac{1}{4} \times \frac{3}{4} \times 10$in long)
5	Side rail	4	Hardwood	$50 \times 16 \times 710$ long ($2 \times \frac{5}{8} \times 28$in long)
6	Stretcher	2	Hardwood	$50 \times 19 \times 710$ long ($2 \times \frac{3}{4} \times 28$in long)
7	Breast/back beam	2	Hardwood	$50 \times 19 \times 672$ long ($2 \times \frac{3}{4} \times 26\frac{1}{2}$in long)
8	Warp/cloth beam	2	Hardwood	50 sq. $\times 820$ long (2in sq. $\times 32\frac{1}{4}$in long)
9	Handle	2	Hardwood dowel	10 dia. $\times 115$ long ($\frac{3}{8}$in dia. $\times 4\frac{1}{2}$in long)
10	Ratchet	2	Steel	70 sq. $\times 2$ thick ($2\frac{3}{4}$in sq. $\times \frac{1}{16}$in thick)
11	Pawl	2	Steel	$12 \times 35 \times 6$ thick ($\frac{1}{2} \times 1 \times \frac{1}{4}$in thick)
12	Beater upright	2	Hardwood	$22 \times 38 \times 370$ long ($\frac{7}{8} \times 1\frac{1}{2} \times 14\frac{3}{4}$in long)
13	Beater cover bar	1	Hardwood	$35 \times 38 \times 710$ long ($1\frac{3}{8} \times 1\frac{1}{2} \times 28$in long)
14	Beater support bar	1	Hardwood	$35 \times 38 \times 710$ long ($1\frac{3}{8} \times 1\frac{1}{2} \times 28$in long)
15	Reed	1	Stainless	127 high $\times 610$ long (5in high $\times 24$in long)
16	Stop	2	Rubber	
17	Heddle bar	8	Steel	$12 \times 3 \times 670$ long ($\frac{1}{2} \times \frac{1}{8} \times 26$in long)

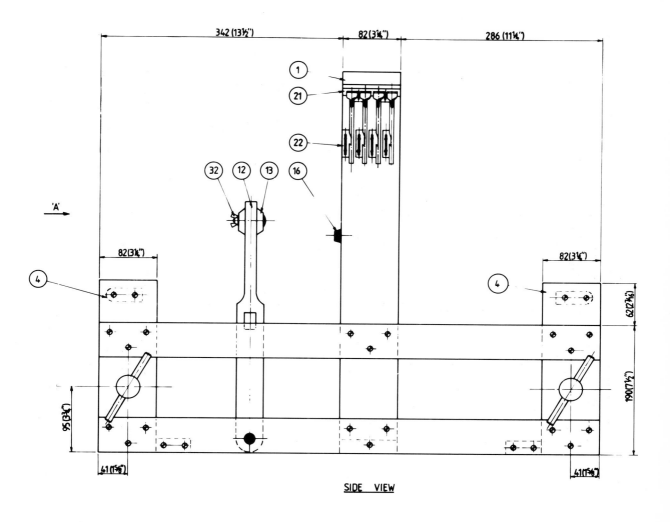

SIDE VIEW

18	Heddle frame guide	8	Steel strip	19 × 3 × 215 long ($\frac{3}{4} \times \frac{1}{8} \times 8\frac{1}{2}$in long)
19	Heddle	500	Wire	See notes
20	Operating lever	4	Steel strip	16 × 3 × 440 long ($\frac{5}{8} \times \frac{1}{8} \times 17\frac{1}{2}$in long)
21	Adjusting plate (top)	1	Steel strip	20 × 82 × 2 thick $\frac{3}{4} \times 3\frac{1}{4} \times \frac{1}{16}$in thick
22	Lever latch plate	4	Steel strip	13 × 40 × 2 thick ($\frac{1}{2} \times 1\frac{9}{16} \times \frac{1}{16}$in thick)
23	Lever pivot block	1	Hardwood	50 × 82 × 73 long (2 × 3$\frac{1}{4}$ × 3in long)
24	Rod	1	Steel	5 dia. × 170 long ($\frac{3}{16}$in dia. × 6$\frac{3}{4}$in long)
25	Tension block	1	Hardwood	40 × 38 × 82 long ($1\frac{9}{16} \times 1\frac{1}{2} \times 3\frac{1}{4}$in long)

26	Roller	4	Steel or plastic	To fit item 24
27	Chain link		Steel	Length to suit
28	Apron cloth	2	Calico	380 × 600 wide (15in × 24in wide)
29	Screw/spring washer/nut	32	Steel	M3 Isometric (0 B.A.)
30	Apron rod	4	Hardwood	20 × 7 × 650 long ($\frac{3}{4} \times \frac{1}{4} \times 26$in long)
31	Lease stick	2	Hardwood	32 × 8 × 750 long ($1\frac{1}{4} \times \frac{5}{16} \times 30$in long)
32	Bolt/washer/ wingnut	4	Steel	M6 Isometric ($\frac{1}{4}$in Whit.)
33	Woodscrew	–	Steel	Miscellaneous

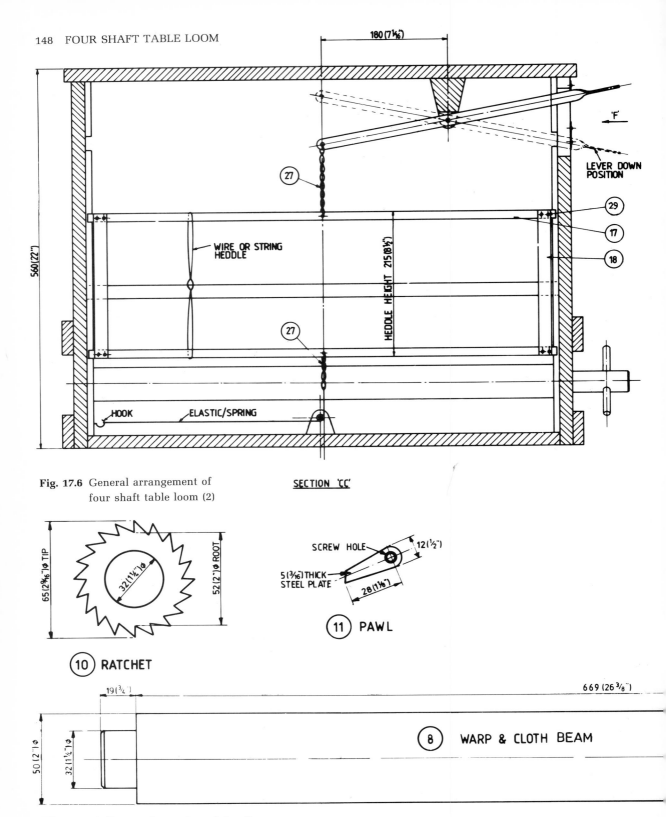

Fig. 17.6 General arrangement of four shaft table loom (2)

SECTION 'CC'

Fig. 17.7 Roller, ratchet and pawl details

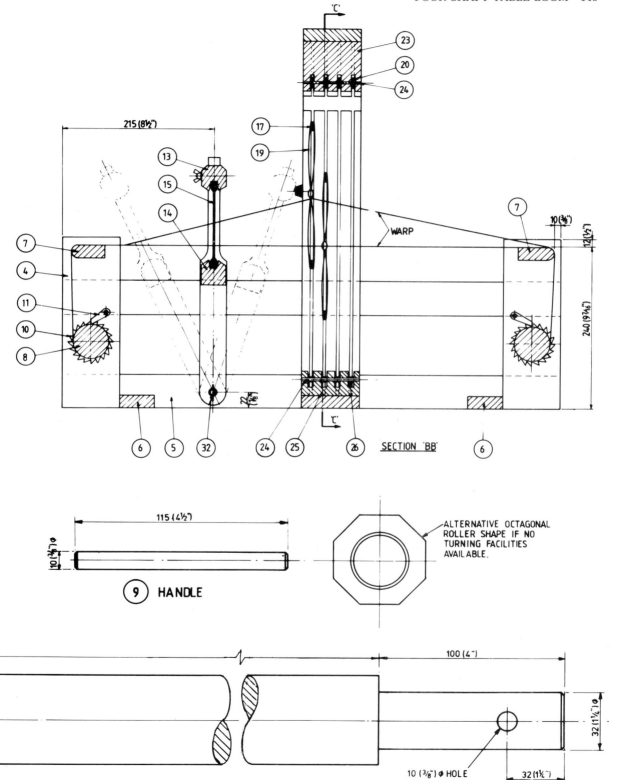

'C'

23
20
24

17
19

13
15
14

7

7

7

4

11
10
8

WARP

10 (³⁄₈")
12 (½")

240 (9⁹⁄₁₆")

215 (8½")

22 (⅞")

6
5
32
24
25
26

'C'

SECTION 'BB'

6

115 (4½")

10 (³⁄₈") ⌀

9 HANDLE

ALTERNATIVE OCTAGONAL
ROLLER SHAPE IF NO
TURNING FACILITIES
AVAILABLE.

100 (4")

32 (1¼") ⌀

10 (³⁄₈") ⌀ HOLE

32 (1½")

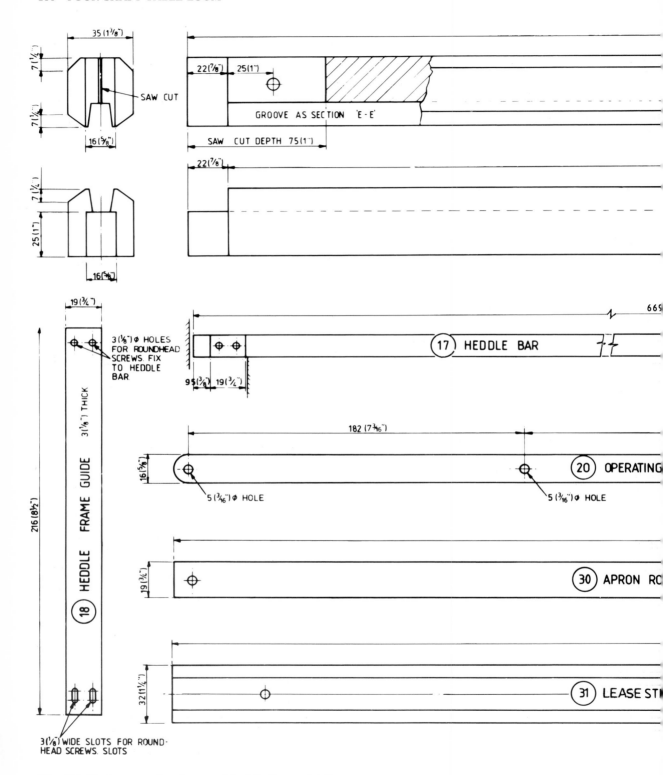

Fig. 17.8 Beater, operating lever and heddle frame details

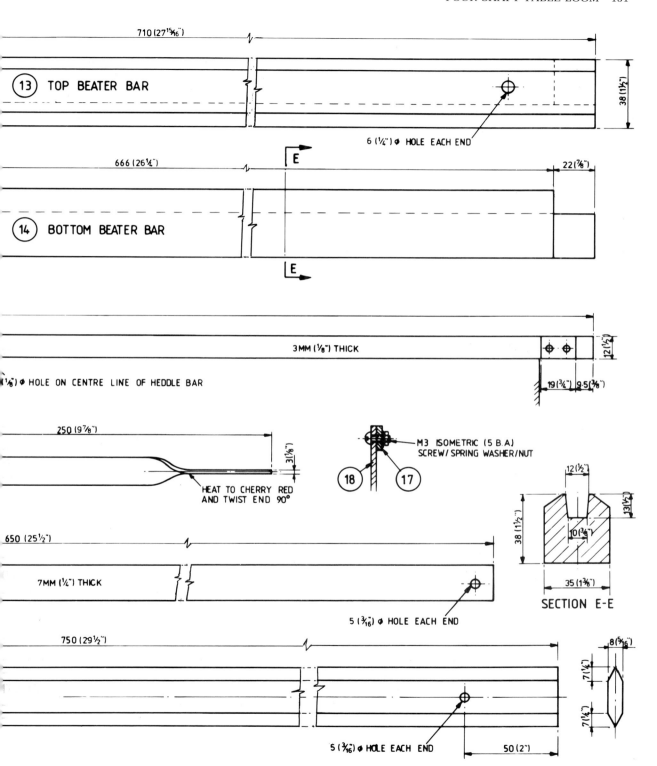

710 (27¹⁵/₁₆")

(13) TOP BEATER BAR

38 (1½")

6 (¼") Φ HOLE EACH END

666 (26¼")

(14) BOTTOM BEATER BAR

E

22 (⅞")

3MM (⅛") THICK

12 (½")

1/₈") Φ HOLE ON CENTRE LINE OF HEDDLE BAR

19 (¾") 9.5 (⅜")

250 (9⅞")

3 (⅛")

HEAT TO CHERRY RED
AND TWIST END 90°

M3 ISOMETRIC (5 B.A.)
SCREW/SPRING WASHER/NUT

(18)   (17)

12 (½")

38 (1½")   13 (½")

10 (¾")

35 (1⅜")

SECTION E-E

650 (25½")

7MM (¼") THICK

5 (³/₁₆") Φ HOLE EACH END

750 (29½")

8 (⁵/₁₆")

7 (¼")

7 (¼")

5 (³/₁₆") Φ HOLE EACH END

50 (2")

HEDDLE TYING JIG
4 PINS SET REQUISITE DISTANCE APART IN BLOCK OF WOOD.

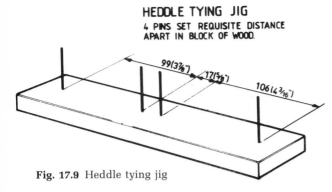

Fig. 17.9 Heddle tying jig

(27) connecting the operating lever (20) and the heddle frames ensures a uniform lift, and thus a clear shed for shuttle passage. The degree of lift is governed by a set of lever latch plates (22). The shaft release is assisted by an elastic/spring return, the final level being regulated by an adjusting plate (21) at warp height. For details of the lever pivot block (23), latch and guide plates (21), (22) etc. see Fig. 17.10. The operating lever dimensions are given in Fig. 17.8.

Reed and beater The beater frame consists of two uprights (12), joined by a top and bottom beater bar (13), (14). Details of these items are given in Figs. 17.8 and 17.11. The lower bar (14) tenons into the uprights (12), and in fact this is the only woodwork jointing used on the loom. The upper bar (13) is held in place by a screw/wingnut fixture, and is thus removable so that reeds can be interchanged. The beater pivots from the bottom side rail (5), as in Fig 17.6, section BB, and two rubber stops (16) buffer it against damaging the centre post.

The nominal reed height is 127mm (5in), and it fits in the longitudinal grooves in items (13) and (14). Reeds can be obtained in various dentages, and it is suggested that one of say eight or ten dents per 25mm (1in) length is initially purchased. It is normal practice to enter two ends per dent, and on occasions more. For an open weave, however, it is essential to enter only one end per dent. Reeds can be either ordinary steel or stainless steel, the latter being more expensive. A source is given in the list of suppliers.

Fig. 17.10 Lever pivot block, latch and guide plate details

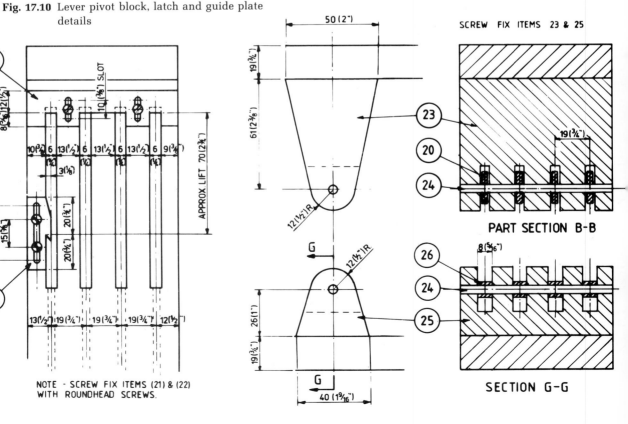

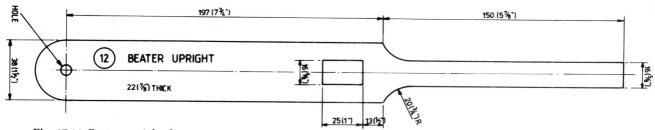

Fig. 17.11 Beater upright dimensions

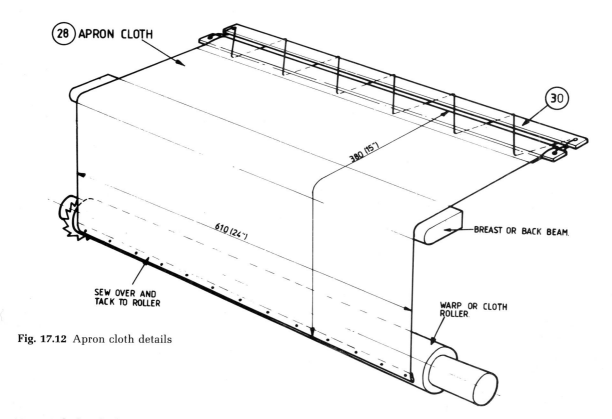

Fig. 17.12 Apron cloth details

Apron cloth The last item to add to the loom is the apron cloth arrangement, items (28) and (29). Details are given in Fig. 17.12, and are basically enlarged versions of those fitted to the tabby loom. The description of these was covered in Chapter 13 so does not need repeating here. An apron cloth should be fitted to each roller.

Warp preparation Warp preparation, insofar as it applies to the tabby loom, has been described earlier in Chapter 13. The same basic principles apply to the warping up of the four shaft table loom, though there are some differences in the procedure, and these are amplified as follows.

Porrey and portée crosses In preparing a longer length warp, and especially for a loom which does not use a rigid heddle, it is necessary to make a thread cross (porrey and portée) at either end of the warp, for reasons which will become apparent. The warping frame design (*Fig 14.5*) is provided with facilities to do this, but to show the method of preparing the warp let us step back for a moment to the use of simple warping posts, but using a double and treble post set as in Fig. 17.13.

Rather than warp up with a single thread, it is common practice to carry at least two yarns at a time. These are tied to post (1), passed together up over post (2), and carried to post (3), passing either

Fig. 17.13 Double and treble warping posts

PORTÉE CROSS · PORREY CROSS
DOUBLE POST · TREBLE POST

Fig. 17.14 Porrey and portée cross formation

side of this. Between posts (3) and (4) they are fingered to form a thread cross, and come together again round post (5). On the return warp length the yarns divide again on either side of post (4) so that a cross can be made between this and post (3). The two threads are then carried to post (2), passing under and across round post (1) as shown in Fig. 17.14. The double thread cross between posts (1) and (2) is called the *portée*, and the single thread cross between posts (3) and (4) the *porrey*.

Moving now onto the warping frame (*Fig. 14.5*), you will see that the portée and porrey crosses are formed between posts B/C and F/G respectively, with post E being equivalent to post 5 in Fig. 17.14. When using the warping frame and carrying two threads, it is essential to keep your forefinger in between, to separate them as you go round the posts from end to end. Failure to observe this simple rule will result in thread tangle. The warp should now be secured with string ties at both crosses, the warp end loops, plus intermediate ties as necessary.

Chaining The warp, having been lifted off the frame, now has to be chained, but this has to be started from the porrey cross end (unlike the tabby warp), with the portée leading out and naturally unwinding.

Raddling/beaming on The portée cross is secured with leases in the same way the porrey was on the tabby loom warp (*Fig. 14.7*). Instead of the rigid heddle a raddle is used to spread the warp prior to beaming on. The warp is secured to the warp end apron rod similar to Fig. 14.9. The warp is then beamed on in the manner previously described. Some may, however, prefer to wind onto the warp beam over the back beam from the front of the loom (i.e. above the breast beam). This alternative necessitates temporary removal of the shafts/heddles. In this case the raddle sits on the loom frame side stretchers in front of the back beam. The beaming on process will, of course, loose the portée cross, but remember the thread separation is still recorded at the porrey cross at the opposite end of the warp.

Drawing in With the warp now wound onto the back beam, the porrey cross is then secured with a pair of lease sticks as the portée was. The string ties can then be released, and the warp spread out ready for the next operation, which is *drawing in*. The warp is threaded through the heddles on the four shafts in accordance with the pattern draft. Some simple examples of pattern draft are given below. The significance of the extra space between the warping frame posts E and F will now be apparent. This ensures that the warp ends as they are cut for threading through the heddles do not fall back accidentally through the porrey cross. Finally the warp is secured to the cloth beam apron rod in a similar manner to the tabby loom (*Fig. 14.13*). When weaving on the four shaft table loom and others larger, it is not really practical to use an open shuttle as for the tabby loom (*Fig. 13.6*), as the weft catches on the warp and will not pass through the shed easily. You should therefore change to a boat shuttle such as that shown in Fig. 17.15. In this the weft is wound onto a spool which neatly fits within the thickness of the wooden shuttle, and it thus slides through the warp smoothly. It is probably easier to buy this item rather than make it.

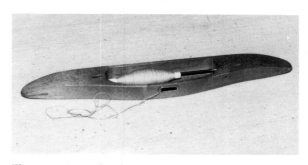

Fig. 17.15 Boat shuttle

PATTERNS

The principal advantage of the four shaft loom is, of course, to weave patterns, and there are a multitude to choose from. Patterns are best planned out on squared paper to establish the *threading draft* and the order of shaft movement. The draft and shaft movement order for two patterns, twill and herringbone, are given in Fig. 17.16. As confidence is gained the weaver can experiment with more complicated patterns such as honeycombe, gooseye and butternut etc. However, these are outside the scope of this book, but some useful references are given in the bibliography should the reader wish to follow this up.

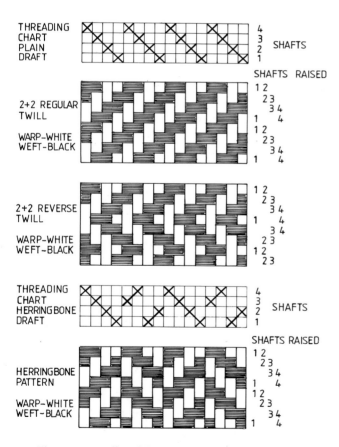

Fig. 17.16 Twill and herringbone patterns

ALTERNATIVE SHAFT MOVEMENT

Some readers may find the fabrication of the operating levers (20), requiring twisting at the end possibly a little difficult. As an alternative which is easier to construct, the shaft movement in Fig. 17.17 could be considered. In this the same basic mechanism is used, but the levers are split two to each side to give more space between them. They can be made of wood or steel. To accomodate, the crossbar (1) is replaced by two side cross pieces butting onto the front and back edges of the centre post (2). The operating levers are pivoted on two pins fixed between these cross pieces.

INCREASING NUMBER OF SHAFTS

At the beginning of this chapter it was mentioned that looms can have more than four shafts, and this increases the pattern scope.

The 610mm (24in) loom could be expanded to eight shafts, say, by widening the centre post (2) to take the extra heddle frames. If you do this it is suggested that the distance between the beater and the centre posts should remain unchanged, so that the reed functions correctly without fouling the warp, i.e. the extra thickness should be put on the back side of the centre post. Keep the shafts as close together as practically possible without catching. The reason here is because the increased distance from the front cloth beam (7) and the shaft furthest from the beater tends to reduce the shed space for a shuttle to pass through. The distance between the wider centre post and the back beam should be

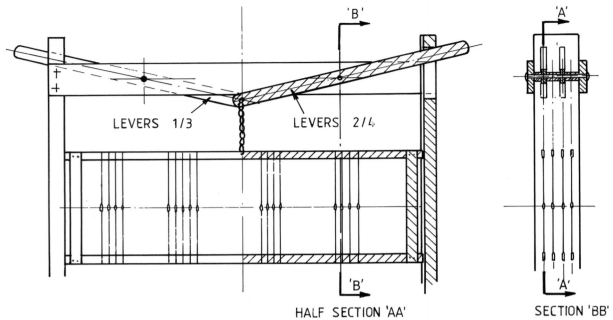

LEVERS 1/3

LEVERS 2/4

HALF SECTION 'AA'

SECTION 'BB'

Fig. 17.17 Modified shaft lift arrangement

maintained at least equal to the original design, and
may need increasing to give more space for the lease
sticks. An additional warp beam is sometimes also
fitted and this will require extra space.

18
WEAVING ACCESSORIES

INTRODUCTION

In foregoing chapters the design of four different types of loom have been discussed, and the essential weaving aid, the warping frame. There are other useful accessories, and this is a good point to stop now and review some of these. They include the raddle, doubling stand, bobbin rack, and single and double rice.

RADDLES

The raddle shown in Fig. 18.1 is an accessory used for spreading a warp being mounted on a loom. The main application is on larger looms of say 610mm (24in) width or greater. It is basically a long wooden strip, set with a row of closely spaced pins or dowels.

The dimensional details are given in Fig. 18.1. The base section is 60×25mm ($2\frac{3}{8} \times 1$in), and the length

is dependent upon the loom width. It has to be long enough to fit comfortably over the weaving width, and if the loom side frame members are at a convenient height relative to the warp, it can rest on these. For the 610mm (24in) table loom a base length of 780mm ($30\frac{3}{4}$in) is suggested, and for the 1070mm (42in) foot power loom in the next chapter a length of 1370mm (54in) is probably about right.

Set into the base are a row of 3mm ($\frac{1}{8}$in) diameter stainless steel, or alternatively aluminium alloy, pins. The suggested pitching is four per 25mm (1in), but this is not mandatory, and can be varied to suit

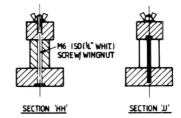

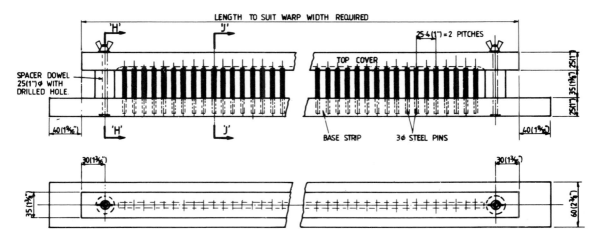

Fig. 18.1 Raddle dimensions

the warp or the selected reed dentage. As an alternative to metal pins, you could use wood dowels, but as the smallest commonly available size is 6mm ($\frac{1}{4}$in) diameter, the pitching would need to be proportionately greater. Make a neat job by drilling the pin/dowel holes in the base accurately and nicely in line. At each end of the raddle is fitted a screw/wingnut arrangement, with a 25mm (1in) diameter spacer dowel for the cover strip to bed down onto. The latter is of 35 × 25mm ($1\frac{3}{8}$ × 1in) section, and has a longitudinal groove in the underside. When the cover is fitted, the row of pins recess slightly into this, so that the warp thread cannot accidentally jump over to an adjoining pin space. You may find hardwood rather than softwood more appropriate for this item.

Use In use the raddle is temporarily fitted at the back of the loom, between the heddles and the pair of lease sticks (for the porrey cross) during the warping up process. As the warp is drawn through the lease sticks, it is separated and spread out across the raddle prior to beaming on over the back beam. When warping up is completed the raddle is removed. In the case of the foot power loom you may find it necessary to clamp some support blocks to the frame to lift the raddle up to warp level.

DOUBLING STAND
The doubling stand is illustrated in Fig. 18.2, and should not be confused with the lazy kate discussed in the earlier chapters on spinning. Both are devices for doubling up thread, but whereas the lazy kate can only accommodate small bobbins for plying on the spinning wheel, the doubling stand can handle much larger cops, and is ideal for multiplying a lightly twisted weft yarn.

The dimensional details of the doubling stand are given in Fig. 18.2. Construction should begin with the base, which consists of a small platform 170 × 240mm ($6\frac{3}{4}$ × $9\frac{1}{2}$in) long, supported on short wood strips. In a cut-out at the back of this is fitted a 50 × 20mm (2 × $\frac{3}{4}$in) section vertical post. This screw fixes into the side of the basebar (see plan view). To locate the cops on the platform, two 12mm ($\frac{1}{2}$in) diameter dowels are fixed in the base.

Half way up the vertical post is fitted an upper platform. This is cut to the dimensions given, and fits round the post being screw fixed from the back.

This platform also has a short post to locate the cop on this, but it is in the form of a tube to allow thread from the lower cops to pass through. Finally at the top of the post is fixed a threading wire bent into a small spiral loop at the end.

Use Doubling threads is quite straightforward. Cops are placed on each platform, and thread drawn from the lower one up through the tube/cop on the upper platform. From here it joins with the thread from the upper cop up to the spiral loop. As the two (or more) threads are drawn off together, they will loosely twist around each other.

BOBBIN RACK
Another useful accessory is the bobbin rack. They come in various shapes and sizes, and this one stands about 800mm ($31\frac{1}{2}$in) high × 520mm ($20\frac{1}{2}$in) wide, as shown in Fig. 18.3. It is fitted with four spool rods, and these will accommodate about 12 bobbins. In addition the base also has a small platform on which cops can be mounted. A row of screw eyes along the top crossbar serves as thread guides when drawing off yarn.

Construction Construction is very simple, and should begin with the two bobbin side posts, the top crossbar and the basebar, which are from 60 × 32mm ($2\frac{3}{8}$ × $1\frac{1}{4}$in) section material. Also make the two 80 × 32 × 280mm ($3\frac{1}{8}$ × $1\frac{1}{4}$ × 11in) long footbars. The bobbin posts and the footbars are mortice and tenon jointed, and the top crossbar ends are half jointed. The base is provided with a plywood pattern 280 × 520mm (11 × $20\frac{1}{2}$in) long, and has local cut-outs in it to fit round the bobbin posts. Carry out a preliminary assembly to check the components fit together correctly, but apply no glue yet, while the bobbin axle rods have still to be fitted.

The bobbins are mounted on 6mm ($\frac{1}{4}$in) diameter steel rod, and two methods of fitting these into the bobbin posts are given. The first is as shown in Fig. 18.3, section GG, where the steel rods slide into angled slots, cut in the inside face of the uprights. With this arrangement the axle length must be a close fit between the uprights, with little or no side play so that they cannot drop out. The distance between the bobbin posts should be accurately gauged from top to bottom.

The second method is less critical to make, and

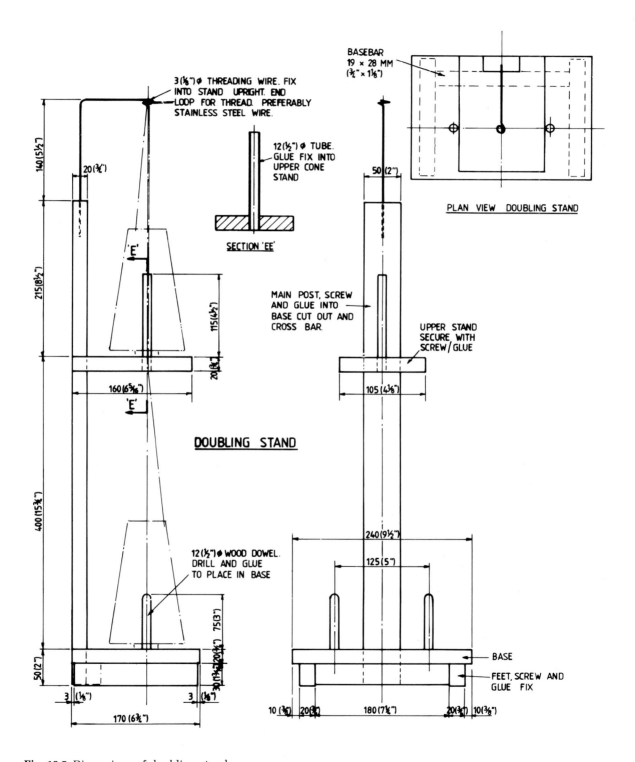

Fig. 18.2 Dimensions of doubling stand

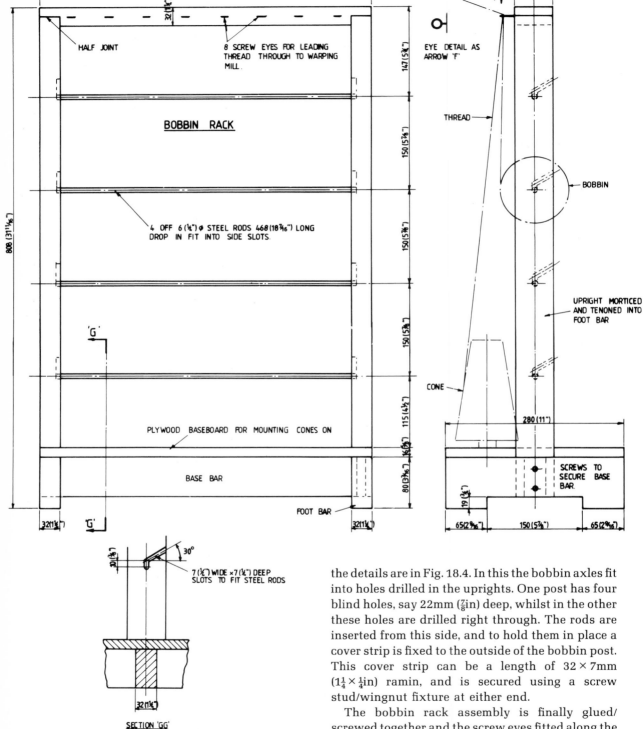

Fig. 18.3 Bobbin rack dimensions

the details are in Fig. 18.4. In this the bobbin axles fit into holes drilled in the uprights. One post has four blind holes, say 22mm ($\frac{7}{8}$in) deep, whilst in the other these holes are drilled right through. The rods are inserted from this side, and to hold them in place a cover strip is fixed to the outside of the bobbin post. This cover strip can be a length of 32×7mm ($1\frac{1}{4} \times \frac{1}{4}$in) ramin, and is secured using a screw stud/wingnut fixture at either end.

The bobbin rack assembly is finally glued/screwed together and the screw eyes fitted along the edge of the top crossbar.

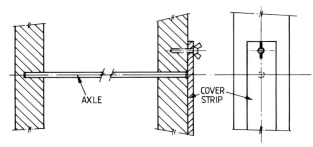

Fig. 18.4 Alternative shaft fitting detail

SINGLE AND DOUBLE RICE

The last weaving accessory discussed is the single and double rice, which is a device for holding skeins of wool, as shown in Fig. 18.7. The design consists of a stand, on which are mounted two single spools, or alternatively pairs of spools, which can be set at varying distances apart to accommodate different skein lengths.

Stand The stand construction is rather similar to that of the doubling stand, with some variations in the dimensions. The base is $225 \times 25 \times 300$mm ($8\frac{7}{8} \times 1 \times 11\frac{3}{4}$in) long, and supported on two side strips. A longitudinal basebar is fitted between the latter. A slotted vertical post $75 \times 25 \times 1060$mm ($3 \times 1 \times 41\frac{3}{4}$in) long is fitted into a mortice in the platform and screw fixed to the basebar underneath, as shown in Fig. 18.5. The post is also reinforced by a support block.

Skein spools The skein spools are of skeleton design. Each one consists of six 10mm ($\frac{3}{8}$in) diameter $\times$ 170mm ($6\frac{11}{16}$in) long dowels set into 125mm (5in) diameter $\times$ 18mm ($\frac{11}{16}$in) thick plywood disc blanks at either end. The spools run on 10mm ($\frac{3}{8}$in) diameter steel rod. In the case of the single rice design only two spools, type 'Y', are required. To fix these the axle is threaded M10 Isometric ($\frac{3}{8}$in Whitworth) for a short length, where it passes through the vertical post, and is secured by a wingnut/washer behind. The double rice design requires two pairs of spools type 'X', and the alternative fixing details for these are given in Fig. 18.6. The ends of the spools are held on by spring caps.

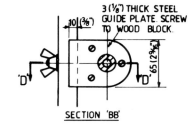

SECTION 'BB'

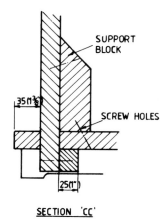

SECTION 'CC'

Fig. 18.5 Stand base detail

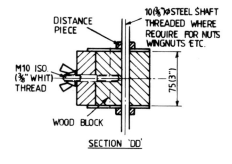

SECTION 'DD'

Fig. 18.6 Double spool fixing detail

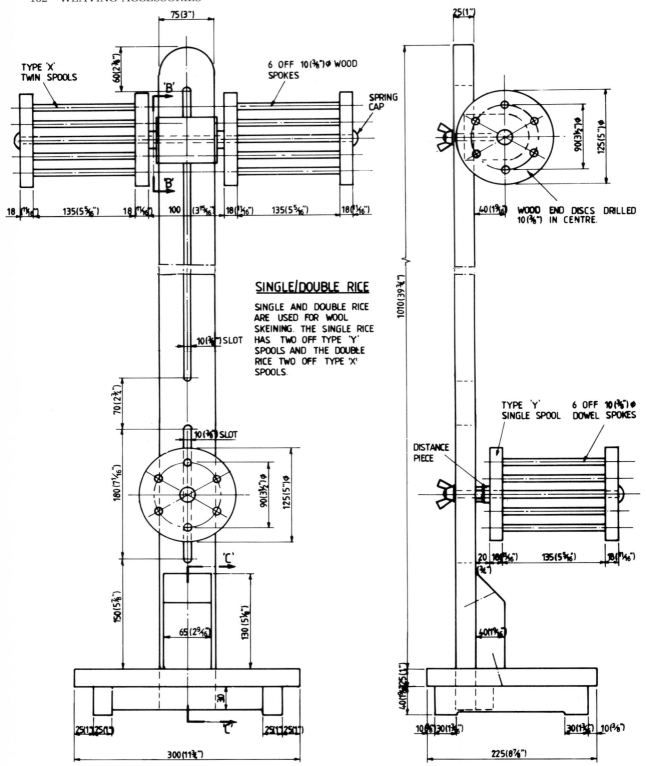

TYPE 'X' TWIN SPOOLS

6 OFF 10(3/8")⌀ WOOD SPOKES

SPRING CAP

75(3")

60(2⅜")

'B'

'B'

18(¹¹/₁₆") 135(5⁵/₁₆") 18(¹¹/₁₆") 100 (3¹⁵/₁₆") 18(¹¹/₁₆") 135(5⁵/₁₆") 18(¹¹/₁₆")

25(1")

90(3½")⌀

125(5")⌀

40(1⁹/₁₆") WOOD END DISCS DRILLED 10(3/8") IN CENTRE.

1010(39¾")

SINGLE/DOUBLE RICE

SINGLE AND DOUBLE RICE ARE USED FOR WOOL SKEINING. THE SINGLE RICE HAS TWO OFF TYPE 'Y' SPOOLS AND THE DOUBLE RICE TWO OFF TYPE 'X' SPOOLS.

10(3/8")SLOT

70(2¾")

10(3/8") SLOT

180(7¹/₁₆")

90(3½")⌀

125(5")⌀

'C'

150(5⅞")

130(5⅛")

65(2⁹/₁₆")

'C'

DISTANCE PIECE

TYPE 'Y' SINGLE SPOOL

6 OFF 10(3/8")⌀ DOWEL SPOKES

20(¾") 18(¹¹/₁₆") 135(5⁵/₁₆") 18(¹¹/₁₆")

40(1⁹/₁₆")

40(1⁹/₁₆") 25(1")

25(1") 25(1") 25(1") 25(1")

30

10(3/8") 30(1³/₁₆") 30(1³/₁₆") 10(3/8")

300(11¾")

225(8⅞")

Fig. 18.7 Single and double rice arrangement

19
FOOT POWER LOOM

INTRODUCTION

This chapter considers a design for a 1070mm (42in) counterbalance foot power loom, as shown in Fig. 19.4. It has the same four shaft configuration as the table loom design in Chapter 17, but this is where the similarity ends, there being major differences in the shed harness, operation and, of course, frame size. As an insight to its construction let us examine the design aspects of foot power looms, in contrast to the table loom.

In general terms the widest table looms are commonly for warps of about 600mm (24in). Occasionally they are made with greater widths, but they tend to become unwieldy, difficult to lift about, and need a fixed table to rest on. A natural development, therefore, is to incorporate the table as part of the loom structure, and make this free-standing from the floor. This in turn, leads to other changes.

FOOT PEDALS

Firstly, instead of raising the shafts by hand levers, or other similar devices positioned above the warp, this is modified to foot power operation. Looms with larger warp widths need greater forces to open the shed, and a foot pedal gives far more leverage than hand-operated levers can ever do. In addition, pedals can be conveniently positioned directly beneath the weaver's foot, whereas hand levers, or the equivalent on larger looms, tend to be less accessible. This is because of the increased frame size and greater reach required.

Shaft movement by foot pedals also frees the hands to focus attention on the weaving. The weaver no longer has to operate both the shaft movement and the shuttle/beater alternately by hand. This is now a coordinated action between hands and feet, and the operation is generally smoother and faster.

COUNTERBALANCE HARNESS

The second area in which a foot power loom differs markedly from a table loom is in the shaft movement, indeed by comparison there is a wide variety of harnesses to choose from on a foot power loom.

You will recall that on the table loom each heddle is individually raised by a lever. By suitable design foot pedals can be arranged to provide a similar movement. Many patterns, however, require two shafts to be lifted at a time, and hence two pedal operations. A very useful harness arrangement, which permits any pair of shafts to be raised or lowered, but needs only one pedal operation, is the *counterbalance harness*. This is the system used in the design here, and the movement is shown in Fig. 19.1. It consists of a treble roller heddle support together with four lamms interposed below the shafts, and a complement of six pedals.

Starting from the top, the four shafts are mounted on two rollers, the latter being supported by a third larger roller suspended from a frame cross member. Beneath the shafts are set four lamms pivoting from the side of the frame. The latter are individually tied one to each shaft, the connection being in the centre, so that any movement of a lamm will pull the associated shaft down evenly. The lamms in turn are connected to the pedals by various tie ups. In the four shaft counterbalance harness there are a possible six combinations of rise and fall of pairs of heddles. The tie up between the lamms and pedals which gives one pedal operation for each of these is as follows.

Lamms/shafts		to pedal	
Lamms/shafts	2 and 3	to pedal	1
Lamms/shafts	1 and 4	to pedal	2
Lamms/shafts	1 and 3	to pedal	3
Lamms/shafts	2 and 4	to pedal	4
Lamms/shafts	1 and 2	to pedal	5
Lamms/shafts	3 and 4	to pedal	6

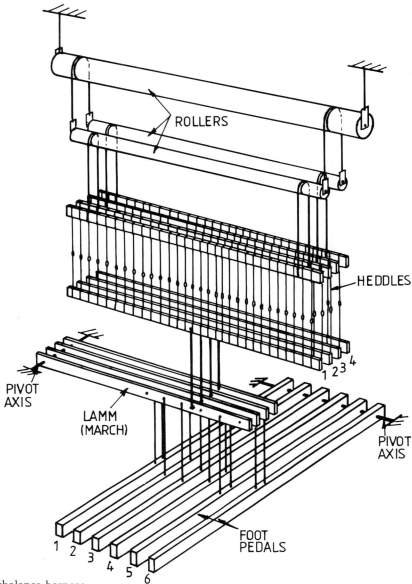

ROLLERS

HEDDLES

PIVOT
AXIS

LAMM
(MARCH)

PIVOT
AXIS

FOOT
PEDALS

Fig. 19.1 Counterbalance harness

This tie up will give the following combinations of shaft movement as in Fig. 19.4, using pedals 1, 2 and 3. Operating pedals 2, 4 and 6 will reverse these shaft movements, and thus give a total of six possible sheds.

A big advantage of the rise and fall shed compared to a rising only movement is that the strain on the warp is much less because the deflection from the warp line is reduced by a half. As with all harnesses the counterbalance arrangement does

have its drawbacks. These are discussed at the end of the chapter. The system is, however, a good general purpose movement.

STRUCTURE

The general arrangement of the loom is given in Figs. 19.4 and 19.5. For the associated parts list see Table 19. The importance of strength and robustness in loom design has been stressed earlier in this

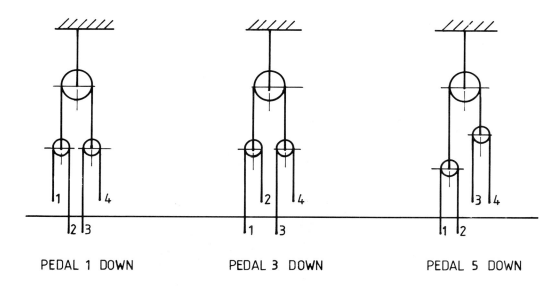

Fig. 19.2 Shaft movement on the counterbalance loom

book. This is particularly so in the foot power loom with its continual pounding and beating during operation. Thus the structure consists in principle of two rugged side frames, joined together by a number of strong cross members. The frames comprise a centre post (1), and two corner posts (2), joined together by stretchers (3) and (4). A vertical roller support (7) is fitted between the front stretchers (3).

The centre post (1) has a beater support arrangement, items (5) and (6), fitted at the top end. All these items are mortice and tenon jointed, and use standard planed softwood section readily available from the local timber yard. Note that the roller support (7) must be fitted to stretchers (3) before the latter can be offered to the centre/corner post mortice slots.

At this point, while the parts are unglued and loose, take the opportunity to cut out the various slots etc. Similarly make the bearing covers (12) to the details as in Fig. 19.3. Leave the drilling of the 50mm (2in) diameter holes for the roller ends until after the covers have been bolted to the roller supports (7). Having completed all the detail work on the side frame components, these can then be assembled, glued and cramped together.

While the side frames are setting, work can progress with making the three cross members (8),

and the breast and back beams (9). These again are standard wood sections, and the fixing details are given in Fig. 19.6. The cross members fix through slots in the frame and are held by pegs (39). The breast and back beams are morticed at the ends, and drop onto tenons on the ends of the corner posts. These items are thus removable, which is useful during the warping up process. The frame structure is now basically complete and ready for the addition of the warp and the shaft arrangement.

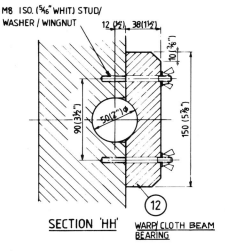

Fig. 19.3 Bearing cover detail

Fig. 19.4 General arrangement of foot power loom (1)

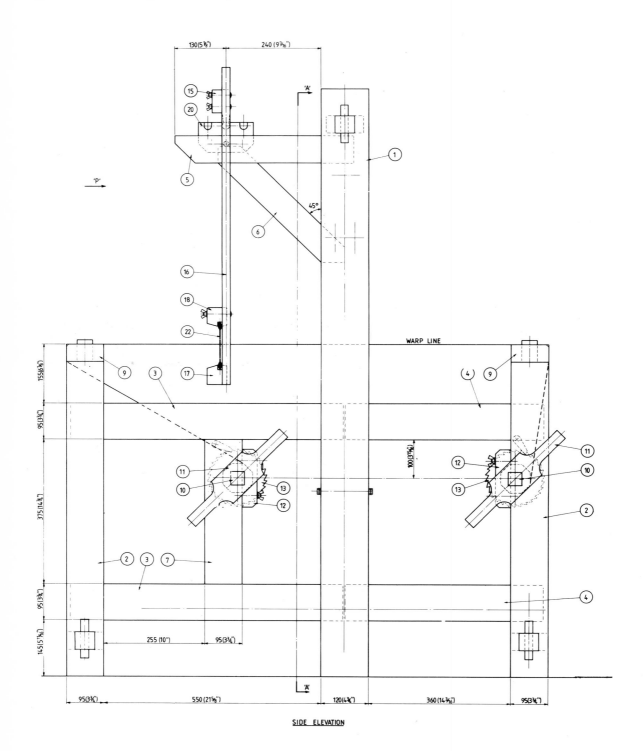

SIDE ELEVATION

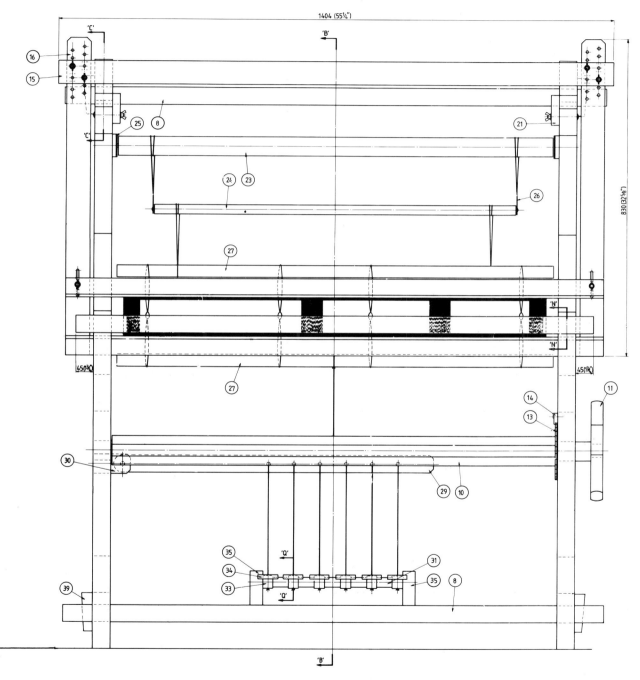

VIEW AS ARROW 'P'

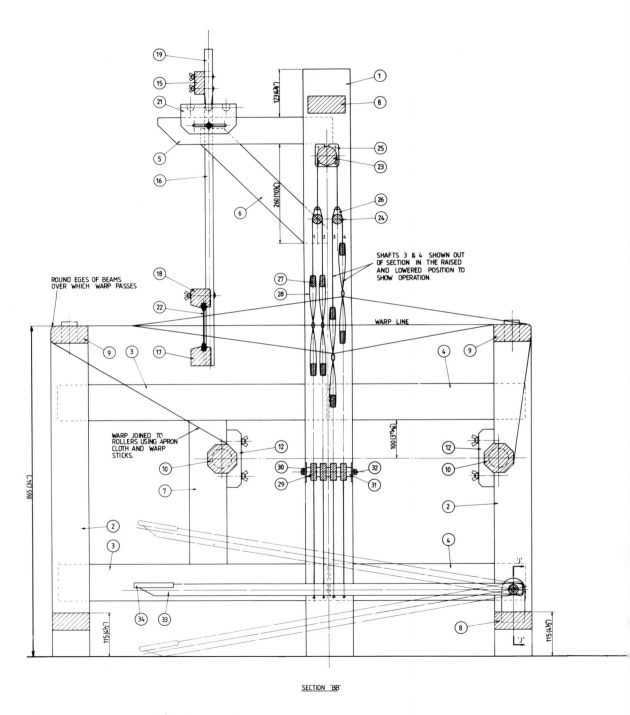

Fig. 19.5 General arrangement of foot power loom (2)

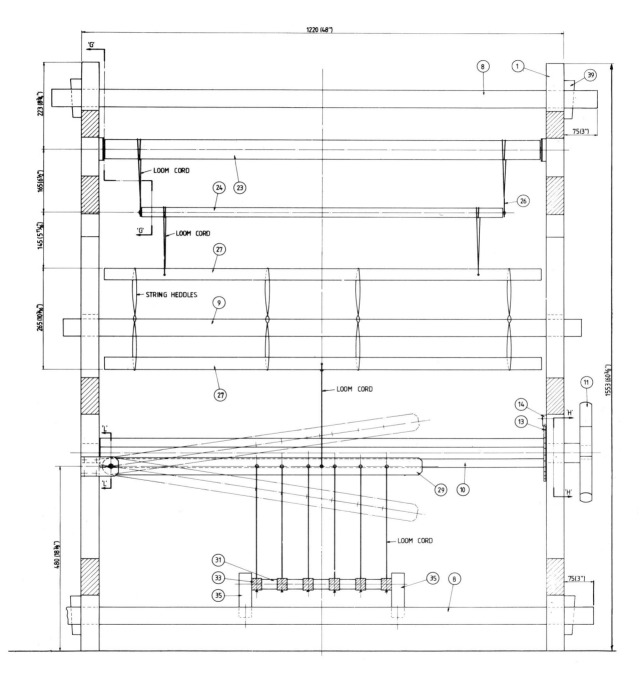

1220 (48")

'G'

8   1

39

223 (8¾")

75(3")

LOOM CORD

165(6½")

24   23

26

'G'

145 (5¹¹⁄₁₆")

LOOM CORD

27

STRING HEDDLES

265(10⅜")

9

27

LOOM CORD

11

14

'H'

13

'L'

'L'

29   10

'H'

LOOM CORD

480 (18⅞")

31

33

35

35   8

75(3")

1553 (60¾")

SECTION 'AA'

Table 19: Foot Power Loom Parts List

Item	Description	No. off	Material	Dimensions
1	Centre post	2	Softwood	120 × 45 × 1533 long ($4\frac{3}{4} × 1\frac{3}{4} × 60\frac{1}{2}$in long)
2	Corner post	4	Softwood	95 × 45 × 865 long ($3\frac{3}{4} × 1\frac{3}{4} × 34$in long)
3	Side stretcher (1)	4	Softwood	95 × 45 × 700 long ($3\frac{3}{4} × 1\frac{3}{4} × 27\frac{3}{4}$in long)
4	Side stretcher (2)	4	Softwood	95 × 45 × 510 long ($3\frac{3}{4} × 1\frac{3}{4} × 20\frac{1}{2}$in long)
5	Support arm	2	Softwood	95 × 45 × 450 long ($3\frac{3}{4} × 1\frac{3}{4} × 17\frac{3}{4}$in long)
6	Support stay	2	Softwood	70 × 45 × 520 long ($2\frac{3}{4} × 1\frac{3}{4} × 20\frac{1}{2}$in long)
7	Roller support	2	Softwood	95 × 45 × 550 long ($3\frac{3}{4} × 1\frac{3}{4} × 21\frac{3}{4}$in long)
8	Frame cross member	3	Softwood	95 × 45 × 1370 long ($3\frac{3}{4} × 1\frac{3}{4} × 54$in long)
9	Breast/back beam	2	Softwood	95 × 45 × 1310 long ($3\frac{3}{4} × 1\frac{3}{4} × 51\frac{3}{4}$in long)
10	Warp/cloth beam	2	Softwood	75 sq. × 1290 long (3in sq. × 51in long)
11	Handle	2	Softwood	80 × 30 × 330 long ($3\frac{1}{4} × 1\frac{1}{4} × 13$in long)
12	Bearing cover	4	Softwood	45 × 38 × 150 long ($1\frac{3}{4} × 1\frac{1}{2} × 6$in long)
13	Ratchet	2	Steel plate	150 sq. × 5 thick (6in sq. × $\frac{1}{4}$in thick)
14	Pawl	2	Steel plate	60 × 25 × 8 thick ($2\frac{1}{2} × 1 × \frac{5}{16}$in thick)
15	Sword support beam	1	Softwood	60 × 25 × 1404 long ($2\frac{1}{2} × 1 × 55\frac{1}{4}$in long)
16	Sword	2	Softwood	60 × 20 × 830 long ($2\frac{1}{2} × \frac{3}{4} × 32\frac{3}{4}$in long)
17	Batten	1	Softwood	50 sq. × 1360 long (2in sq. × $53\frac{3}{4}$in long)
18	Reed cover batten	1	Softwood	50 × 50 × 1360 long (2in sq. × $53\frac{3}{4}$in long)
19	Knuckle	2	Hardwood	45 × 20 × 105 long ($1\frac{3}{4} × \frac{3}{4} × 4\frac{1}{4}$in long)
20	Fulcrum	2	Hardwood	45 × 35 × 140 long ($1\frac{3}{4} × 1\frac{1}{2} × 5\frac{1}{2}$in long)
21	Fulcrum side plate	2	Plywood	80 × 20 × 140 long ($3\frac{1}{4} × \frac{3}{4} × 5\frac{1}{2}$in long)
22	Reed	1	Stainless Steel	See p. 000
23	Upper roller	1	Hardwood	50 dia. × 1098 long (2in dia. × $43\frac{1}{4}$in long)
24	Lower roller	2	Hardwood	25 dia. × 915 long (1in dia. × 36in long)
25	Roller endplate support	2	Steel/plywood	60 ($2\frac{1}{2}$in) sq. × thickness to suit
26	Roller support lug	4	Steel plate	45 × 25 × 3 thick ($1\frac{3}{4} × 1 × \frac{1}{8}$in thick)
27	Heddle bar (string)	8	Hardwood	38 × 12 × 1100 long ($1\frac{1}{2} × \frac{1}{2} × 43\frac{1}{4}$in long)
28	String heddle	–	Heddle string	See p. 000
29	Lamm	4	Hardwood	45 × 16 × 810 long ($1\frac{3}{4} × \frac{5}{8} × 32$in long)
30	Lamm support plate	2	Steel plate	95 × 50 × 6 thick ($3\frac{3}{4} × 2 × \frac{1}{4}$in thick)
31	Spacer piece	10	Hardwood	25 (1in) dia. × length to suit
32	Lamm support bolts/nuts	1	Steel	10 dia. × 150 long ($\frac{3}{8}$in dia. × 6in long)
33	Footpedal	6	Softwood	35 × 25 × 980 long ($1\frac{3}{8} × 1 × 38\frac{3}{4}$in long)
34	Foot piece	6	Plywood	50 × 12 × 100 long ($2 × \frac{1}{2} × 4$in long)
35	Foot pedal support block	2	Softwood	60 × 32 × 120 long ($2\frac{1}{2} × 1\frac{1}{4} × 4\frac{3}{4}$in long)
36	Foot pedal support rod	1	Steel rod	12 dia. × 400 long ($\frac{1}{2}$in dia. × $15\frac{3}{4}$in long)
37	Heddle frame (for wire heddles)	8	Hardwood	40 × 12 × 1090 long ($1\frac{1}{2} × \frac{1}{2} × 43$in long)
38	Heddle support strip	8	Steel	10 × 3 × 1110 long ($\frac{3}{8} × \frac{1}{8} × 43\frac{3}{4}$in long)
39	Peg	6	Hardwood	25 × 20 × 100 long ($1 × \frac{3}{4} × 4$in long)
40	Warp stick	40	Hardwood	25 × 6 × 1100 long ($1 × \frac{1}{4} × 43\frac{1}{4}$in long)
41	Bolts/wingnuts	–	Steel	Miscellaneous
42	Wire heddle	–	Steel wire	See p. 00
43	Heddle frame end strip	16	Steel strip	10 × 3 ($\frac{3}{8} × \frac{1}{8}$) × length to suit

Warp and cloth beam The warp and cloth beams are arranged in principle so that warp tension causes these to pull against the loom structure rather than against the bearing covers (12), as shown in Fig. 19.5, section BB. The cloth beam at the front is also tucked well in to allow the weaver suitable knee space when operating the loom. For the dimensional details of the rollers see Fig. 19.8. An octagonal roller shape has been selected, bearing in mind the length and the difficulty you may have in otherwise turning this span. Nevertheless, the cylindrical ends which fit through the bearing covers may present a problem, but with some careful marking out, trimming, and gentle easing into the bearing holes, a successful result should be achieved.

Each roller has a ratchet and pawl arrangement fixed to it. The details are given in Fig. 19.7. These are basically enlarged versions of those used on the table loom. The ratchets are screw fixed to the ends

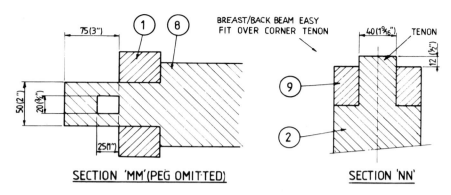

Fig. 19.6 Cross beam fixing details

of the rollers. If you find the metal sawing tedious there is an alternative warp weighting arrangement which can be applied to the back roller, which has advantages. It is described later in this chapter. This will relieve you of one ratchet and pawl, if required.

Finally, the handles (11) need making and fixing to the squared ends of the rollers. Make sure there is no free play or sloppiness in the square connection. The rollers, now complete, may then be offered into position in the loom frame and secured by the bearing covers. When assembled make a check for ease of rotation, adding a little candle grease to the bearings if necessary.

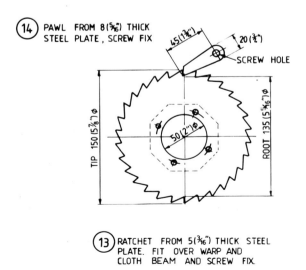

Fig. 19.7 Ratchet and pawl dimensions

Counterbalance rollers Details of the counterbalance rollers are given in Fig. 19.8. The two smaller rollers (24) are 25mm (1in) diameter, and dowel of this size should be readily available at your local sawmill. The larger roller (23) is 50mm (2in) diameter, and you may have to hunt a bit to procure this. Alternatively it could be woodturned, or, failing this, cut from square section timber, trimmed first octagonal, and then sanded to a round section. The roller sits in a support endplate (25) secured to the centre post. The smaller rollers are suspended from the larger one using support lugs (26) and loom cord. Note that the loom cord passes a loop and a half round the larger roller, so as to provide necessary grip to hold the shafts level during the rise and fall motion. There are alternatives to rollers and these are discussed at the end of this chapter.

Shafts The design can use either string or wire heddles, to personal choice. The nominal wire heddle height is 215mm (8½in) but if these cannot be obtained the design will accept longer heddle lengths than this. If you decide to use string heddles, there is, of course, rather more scope on heddle height. A source for wire heddles and heddle cord is given in the list of suppliers. Each shaft on a string heddle arrangement consists simply of a pair of 40 × 12mm (1$\frac{9}{16}$ × $\frac{1}{2}$in) section hardwood strips. A heddle tying jig is given in Fig. 17.9. The wire heddle arrangement, on the other hand, requires a more formal construction (Fig. 19.8) comprising items (37), (38) and (43). Note that the heddle support strip (38) requires tying back intermittently along its length to the frame (37). A 1070mm (42in) weaving

Fig. 19.8 Rollers, heddles and pedal details

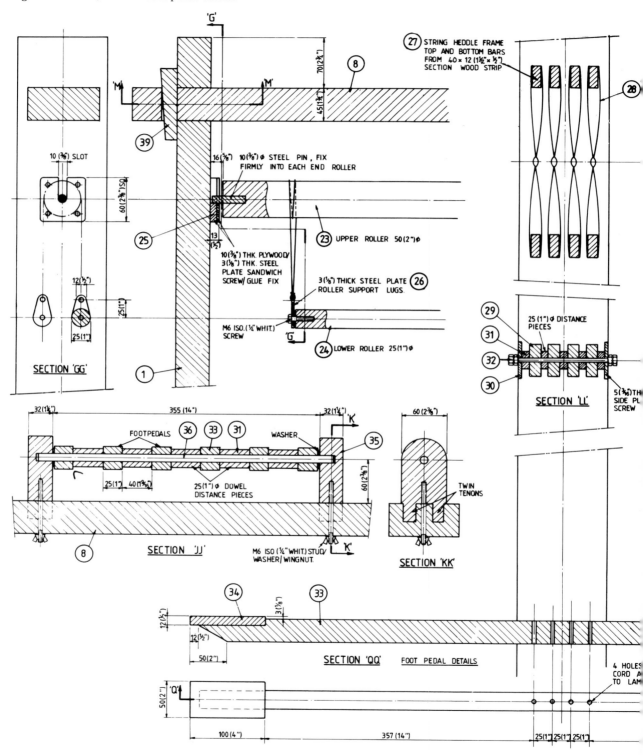

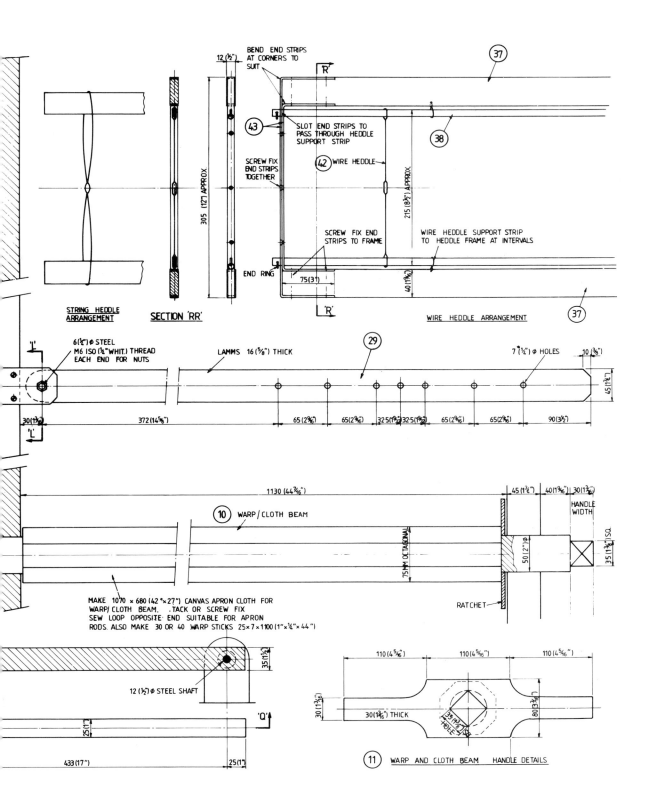

BEND END STRIPS
AT CORNERS TO
SUIT

12 (½")

'R'

37

SLOT END STRIPS TO
PASS THROUGH HEDDLE
SUPPORT STRIP

43

38

SCREW FIX
END STRIPS
TOGETHER

42 WIRE HEDDLE

305 (12") APPROX

215 (8½") APPROX

SCREW FIX END
STRIPS TO FRAME

WIRE HEDDLE SUPPORT STRIP
TO HEDDLE FRAME AT INTERVALS

END RING

75 (3")

40 (1½")

'R'

WIRE HEDDLE ARRANGEMENT

37

STRING HEDDLE
ARRANGEMENT

SECTION 'RR'

'I'

6 (¼") Ø STEEL
M6 ISO (¼" WHIT.) THREAD
EACH END FOR NUTS

LAMMS 16 (⅝") THICK

29

7 (¼") Ø HOLES

10 (⅜")

45 (1¾")

30 (1¼")

'L'

372 (14⅝")

65 (2⁹⁄₁₆") 65 (2⁹⁄₁₆") 32·5 (1⁹⁄₁₆") 32·5 (1⁹⁄₁₆") 65 (2⁹⁄₁₆") 65 (2⁹⁄₁₆") 90 (3½")

1130 (44³⁄₁₆")

45 (1¾") 40 (1⁹⁄₁₆") 30 (1³⁄₁₆")

HANDLE
WIDTH

10 WARP / CLOTH BEAM

75 MM OCTAGONAL

50 (2")Ø

35 (1³⁄₁₆") SQ.

RATCHET

MAKE 1070 × 680 (42" × 27") CANVAS APRON CLOTH FOR
WARP / CLOTH BEAM. TACK OR SCREW FIX
SEW LOOP OPPOSITE END SUITABLE FOR APRON
RODS. ALSO MAKE 30 OR 40 WARP STICKS 25 × 7 × 1100 (1" × ¼" × 44")

35 (1½")

12 (½") Ø STEEL SHAFT

25 (1")

'Q'

433 (17")

25 (1")

110 (4⁵⁄₁₆") 110 (4⁵⁄₁₆") 110 (4⁵⁄₁₆")

30 (1³⁄₁₆")

80 (3¼")

30 (1³⁄₁₆") THICK

35 (1⅜")
HOLE

11 WARP AND CLOTH BEAM   HANDLE DETAILS

width may need, say, 150 heddles per shaft, but the actual number depends on both the reed dentage selected and the pattern choice. The shafts are hung from the rollers (24) as in Figs. 19.5 and 19.8 using loom cord in a similar manner to the upper rollers (23).

Lamms and footpedals The lamm and footpedal details are given in Figs. 19.5 and 19.8. In particular the lamms (29) are supported from one of the centre posts beneath the shafts using side plates (30) etc. The six pedals are of 35×25mm ($1\frac{3}{8} \times 1$in) section, supported from the rear crossbar (8). The footpedals fit on a 12mm ($\frac{1}{2}$in) diameter shaft (36) between two support blocks (35), to the details in Fig. 19.8 sections JJ and KK. A shaft size smaller than this tends to be too flexible.

The connection of the lamm and pedals is as in Fig. 19.1, using loom cord. The tie up should be as per the details on p. 163. Some slight adjustments may be needed to level the heddle frames, and set the pedal movement correct, but otherwise the system should work satisfactorily.

Batten/beater The last major component to add to the loom is the batten/beater. This is an overslung arrangement (*Fig. 19.5, section BB*) generally preferred to one pivoted from the bottom of the loom as it is easier to remove this batten arrangement for access during warping up of the heddles. Its great advantage is that it can incorporate several pivot positions, enabling the batten to be moved at will during weaving. This will allow a longer piece to be woven before the cloth must be wound on. Dimensional information is given in fig. 19.9. The upper part of the assembly consists of two swords (16) attached to crossbeam (15), the latter being supported in a knuckle and fulcrum arrangement resting on the support arm (5). At the bottom end of the swords are fitted a batten and cover beam (17) and (18). The reed fits between these in a pair of transverse grooves. The cover beam (18) is adjustable to permit reeds to be interchanged. The reed nominal height is 125mm (5in). Stainless or plain steel reeds can be used, and a dentage of eight or ten per 25mm (1in) is suggested. A source for reeds is given in the list of suppliers.

To enable the reed to be positioned correctly relative to the warp, and allow the batten to swing properly for the beating action, there is provision for height adjustment in the mounting. To accommodate this the swords (16) are provided with a series of 6mm ($\frac{1}{4}$in) diameter holes at the top end. These match with corresponding holes in the crossbeam (15). Having selected the required height, screws/wingnuts are used to clamp these items together. Sometimes this is done by small wooden pegs instead, but a means of holding the parts together is also necessary. The front to back location of the batten can also be adjusted by changing the knuckle position in the fulcrum (20). Three positions are provided in addition to which the fulcrum is itself adjustable through a screw/wingnut slot fixture.

Apron cloth The loom is now virtually complete apart from adding the apron cloth arrangement to each roller (10). This is similar in principle to that used on the table loom (*Fig 17.12*). The suggested dimensions for the apron cloth are 1065mm (42in) wide × 1065mm (42in) long, but the back measurement could possibly be a little shorter. The apron rods need to be slightly more robust in section than those for the table loom, say 25×7mm ($1 \times \frac{1}{4}$in) section. Some lease sticks will also need making as for the table loom, but of course longer (*fig. 17.8*).

Counterbalance harness – further comments Although the three roller system tends to produce the most uniform counterbalance harness, there are other variations which achieve the same movement. For example, the upper roller (23) could be replaced with two pulleys, one at each side. The frame crossbar (8) makes a useful suspension point for these if this option is chosen. The lower rollers (24) can also be replaced by two more pairs of pulleys if required. As a source of pulleys, ships chandlers are very useful.

A third alternative is to replace the lower rollers with wooden *horses*. These are very easy to make. Fig. 19.10 shows a counterbalance loom using a combination of pulleys and horses. If you decide to use horses they should be correctly fitted to support the shafts evenly. Usually they are between 150–300mm (6–12in) long. If they are too short the shaft rise and fall may not be evenly split; conversely, if they are too long and the inboard shaft lift point is close or over the loom centre, the heddle may rise

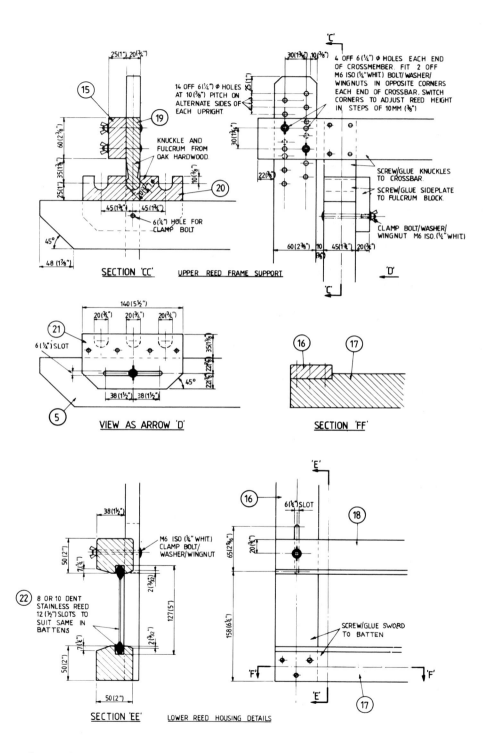

Fig. 19.9 Batten/beater details

Fig. 19.10 Counterbalance harness using pulleys and horses

and fall obliquely. Lastly, if you are interested in exploring other harnesses you will find that pulleys are more adaptable than rollers or horses.

Counterbalance harness – disadvantages The counterbalance harness permits pairs of shafts to be raised or lowered using one pedal operation. This gives a shed evenly split about the warp centreline. However, if you try an alternative tie up, for example to raise and lower only one of a pair of shafts, then a shed is produced which is low relative to the warp line, and the shuttle will not pass through (*Fig. 19.11*). This tendency can be corrected to a degree by adjusting the beater height slightly. Conversely, if you try a mixed shed, as in fig. 19.12, with three shafts lowered and one lifted, the shed is high. Thus the counterbalance motion will successfully weave patterns such as rosepath or twill which use an evenly balanced rise and fall shed, but if you try one which uses a mixed shed then you run into difficulties. If you wish to use a harness which gives a positive shed on all shaft movements then the countermarch could be considered as an alternative.

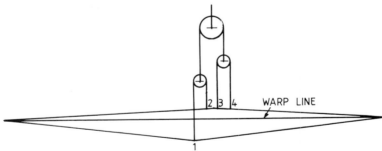

Fig. 19.11 Counterbalance motion – one shaft lowered

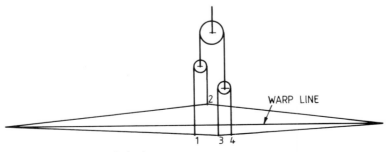

Fig. 19.12 Counterbalance motion – mixed shed

Countermarch harness The countermarch harness is shown in Fig. 19.13. In this arrangement each shaft is supported from a pair of coupers above the heddles by cord connections at the outer ends. Beneath the warp, in addition to the marches (lamms) and footpedals, there is also a set of countermarches. The inner end of each pair of coupers is connected through the warp to a marche, the latter then being connected to the footpedal. Each shaft is also linked directly to a countermarch beneath the warp.

If you consider the action for a moment without the countermarches, then depressing the first pedal will, via the marches/coupers, raise the first shaft. However, unless there is a steadying influence on the remaining three shafts, there will not be a clear shed for the shuttle to pass through. This is achieved by connecting the countermarches of shafts 2, 3 and 4 also to the first pedal. Thus when this pedal is now depressed, shaft 1 is lifted and 2, 3 and 4 will fall. The second, third and fourth shafts are connected in a similar way, e.g. shaft 2, via

Fig. 19.13 Countermarch harness

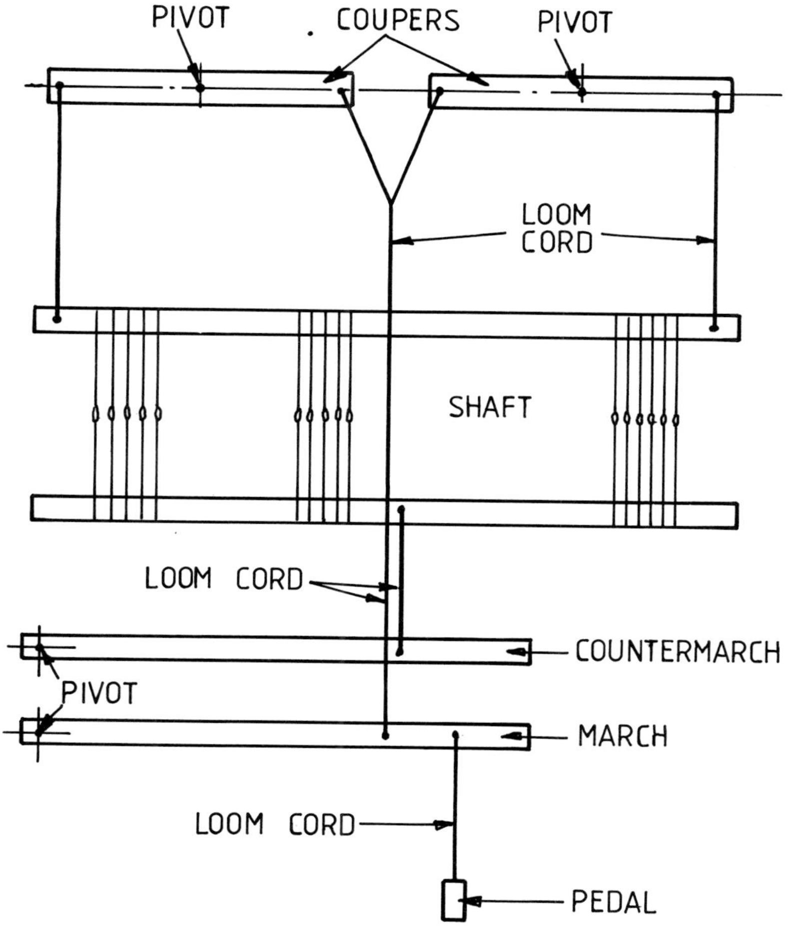

coupers/march, to second pedal, and shafts 1, 3 and 4, via the countermarches, also to this pedal, etc. Alternatively, if you wished to raise shafts 1 and 2, you would connect both these marches to one pedal, and the countermarches of shafts 3 and 4 also to this pedal.

In summary, the countermarch harness gives a rise and fall shed, but unlike the counterbalance movement, can lift any shaft combination, depending upon the tie up, giving a positive shed each time. It is a little more complex to connect up because every shaft has to be linked to every pedal via the marches/countermarches. However, its advantages often outweigh this difficulty.

If you wish to fit a countermarch harness to the foot power loom instead of the counterbalance arrangement, it is not difficult. First, the top crossmember (8) should be replaced with crossmembers on either side of the centre post, so that the coupers can be fitted in between. Secondly, a set of countermarches in addition to marches should be fitted below the heddles. If you incorporate these on a separate pivot shaft, the loom height will need increasing slightly to allow for their movement so that they do not clash with the heddles. Alternatively, they can be made thinner and fitted on the same axis as the marches.

WARP WEIGHTING

It was mentioned earlier that, as an alternative to using a ratchet and pawl on the back roller, a warp weighting system can be used which will dispense with these. Fig. 19.14 shows this method of tensioning the warp. It consists simply of a short length of rope secured to the loom structure at 'A', wound round the warp beam two turns, and with a heavy weight tied on the end. The rope coil and weight acts as a friction hold on the roller, and when the cloth beam ratchet is notched up a few teeth, applies a tension to the warp. The big advantage of this system over one which uses only ratchet and pawls is that it allows the warp to give a bit when the shafts are raised, thus maintaining a constant warp tension. This helps to produce a more even cloth. The foot power loom could be adapted for this method of warp tensioning by introducing cord and weights, as just described, to the warp beam (10). You can quite crudely use sand bags as weights, but it may be more practical to use large flat weights of say 20kg (40lb) to minimise the interference to the warp. A few extra centimetres on the loom width may be necessary to accommodate these weights.

WEAVING ON THE FOOT POWER LOOM

Since this is a book on equipment design, it is not

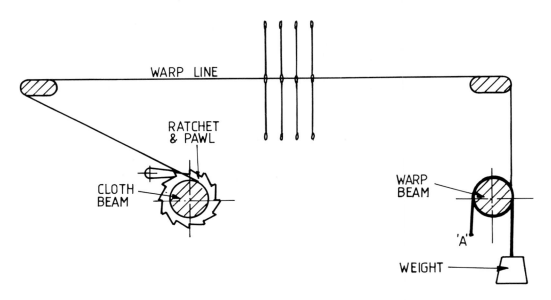

Fig. 19.14 Warp weighting alternative

intended to discuss in detail weaving techniques or pattern design, and these subjects are already admirably covered by others. However, it would not be right to leave the foot power loom design without giving just a little insight into its use, so by way of example two simple patterns and the tie up are included here. The first pattern is the rosepath, which uses an eight thread draft (*Fig. 19.15*). The second is the dog's tooth, which uses a plain four thread draft (*Fig. 19.16*). With a counterbalance harness only four pedal operation is necessary, and the suggested tie up is as follows.

Lamms/shafts	1 and 4	to pedal	1
Lamms/shafts	2 and 3	to pedal	2
Lamms/shafts	1 and 2	to pedal	3
Lamms/shafts	3 and 4	to pedal	4

This arrangement allows you to operate pedals 1 and 2 with the left foot, and pedals 3 and 4 with the right. Thus weaving will proceed with a regular foot movement, left, right, left, right, etc. For the dog's tooth pattern, sometimes called a reversible broken check, the warp and weft each alternate with four threads black, four threads white, etc., or whatever colour combination you have chosen. For the reader interested in weaving techniques and pattern design, some useful references are included in the bibliography.

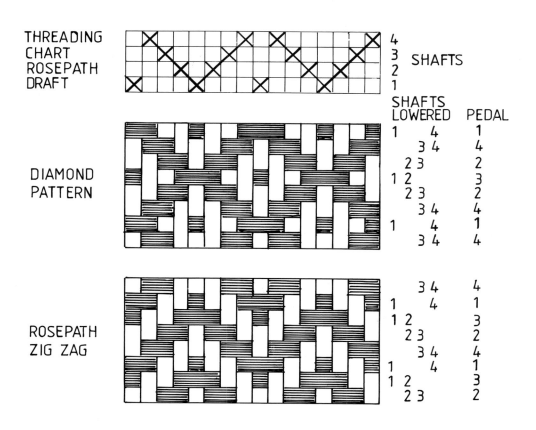

Fig. 19.15 Rosepath draft and patterns

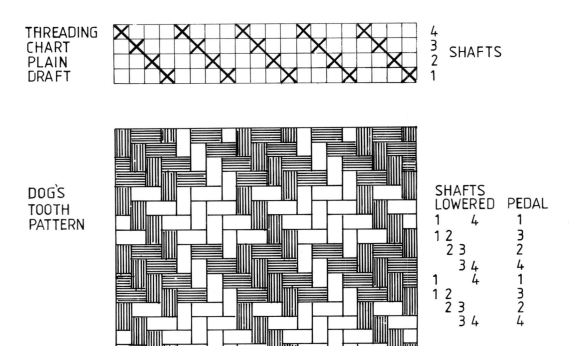

THREADING
CHART
PLAIN
DRAFT

4
3   SHAFTS
2
1

DOG'S
TOOTH
PATTERN

SHAFTS LOWERED		PEDAL
1	4	1
1 2		3
	2 3	2
	3 4	4
1	4	1
1 2		3
	2 3	2
	3 4	4

Fig. 19.16 Dog's tooth pattern

20
WARPING MILL

INTRODUCTION

The foot power loom design in the previous chapter in general uses warps which are longer than the tabby or four shaft table loom. Typically 15–20m (16½–22yd) is often required. The warping frame design in Chapter 14, of course, can only handle warps up to 12m (13yd) long, and to cope with a length greater than this something bigger is necessary. You could increase the distance between the warp end boards, but this tends to become a bit cumbersome and unwieldy. The solution adopted is to redesign the warping frame in the form of a rotating vertical drum. Fig. 20.1 illustrates a warping mill based on this arrangement, capable of winding warps up to 20m (22yd).

DESIGN

Warping mill drums are usually of the open frame pattern, comprising a number of vertical uprights connected by a crossbar arrangement. Often they have four uprights or, on occasions, eight. The design here is based on eight to make the drum more regular and stronger. The drum size is 820mm (32¼in) diameter × 1200mm (47¼in) long, and is supported on a stand arrangement at the base. The drum is free to rotate by hand on a vertical axis.

Fixed on the drum uprights are two sets of warping post/clamp bar assemblies. Each of these consists of a trio of posts, and the group is clamped between a pair of uprights, by a screw/wingnut arrangement (*Fig. 20.1, section AA*). The assembly can be fixed on any pair of drum uprights, and any position along their length, excepting locally where the crossbars fit. The drum circumference is 2m (2.2 yd), and thus by setting one warping post group at the top of the drum, and one at the bottom, a 20m (22yd) warp can be accommodated winding the yarn

ten times round the drum in between at an approximate pitch of 125mm (5in).

CONSTRUCTION

The general arrangement is given in fig. 20.1, and the associated parts list in Table 20. Commence construction by making the rotation drum assembly, beginning with the crossbars (2). Dimensions for these are given in Fig. 20.2 and eight are required. Each pair of crossbars are half jointed in the middle and glue fixed. The upper and lower crossbar assemblies each consist of two pairs of crossbars screwed together in an octagonal star formation. The lower crossbar assembly has a 32mm (1¼in) diameter hole drilled through the centre, to be a clearance fit on the shaft (3). Finally, the drum is assembled by screw fixing/gluing the 42 × 22 × 1200mm (1⅝ × ⅞ × 47¼in) long uprights (1), onto the crossbar ends at the pitching shown in Fig. 20.2. Note that for the warping frame to be successful it is important to set the distance between adjacent pairs of uprights the same, so that the warping post assemblies can be moved about without difficulty.

Stand The stand consists of two 75 × 50 × 600mm (3 × 2 × 24in) long footbars (4), which are half jointed/glued together at the centre. They are chamfered at the ends, as shown in Fig. 20.1. Four 75mm square × 10mm (3in square × ⅜in) thick footpads (5) are glued on the underside at the end of each footbar, and the arrangement stands on these.

Shaft and bearing The centre shaft on which the drum rotates is a length of 32mm (1¼in) diameter steel tube approximately 965mm (38in) long. A section of the shaft and the bearing details are given

Fig. 20.1 General arrangement of warping mill

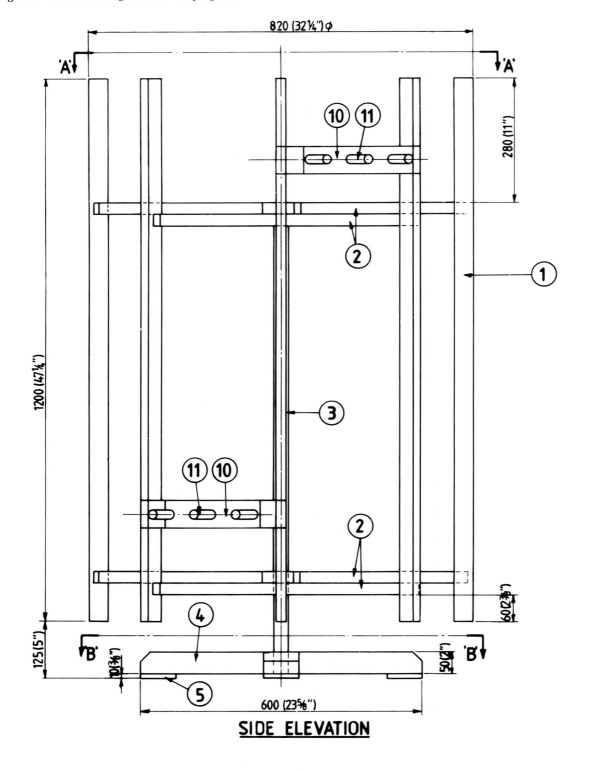

SIDE ELEVATION

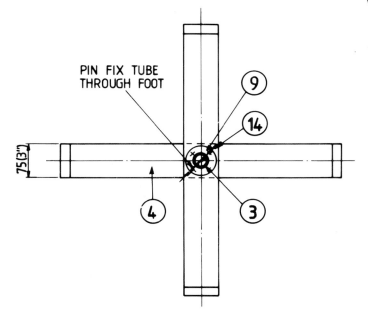

PIN FIX TUBE
THROUGH FOOT

⑨

⑭

75 (3")

④

③

SECTION 'BB'

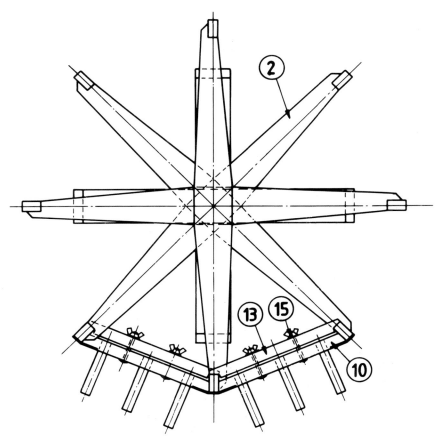

②

⑬ ⑮

⑩

SECTION 'AA'

Table 20: Warping Mill Parts Lists

Item	Description	No. off	Material	Dimensions
1	Drum upright	8	Softwood	42 × 22 × 1200 long ($1\frac{5}{8} \times \frac{7}{8} \times 47\frac{1}{4}$in long)
2	Crossbar	8	Softwood	82 × 25 × 820 long ($3\frac{1}{4} \times 1 \times 32\frac{1}{4}$in long)
3	Shaft	1	Galvanised steel tube	32 dia. × 1.2 thk. × 1000 lg. ($1\frac{1}{4}$in dia. × 18 s.w.g. × $39\frac{1}{2}$in lg.)
4	Footbar	2	Softwood	75 × 50 × 600 long (3 × 2 × 24in long)
5	Footpad	4	Softwood	75 sq × 10 thick (3in sq. × $\frac{3}{8}$in thick)
6	Thrust bearing	1	Steel	54 O.D. × 28 I.D. × 10 wide ($2\frac{1}{4}$in O.D. × $1\frac{1}{8}$ I.D. × $\frac{3}{8}$in wide)
7	Bearing cover	1	Hardwood	85 sq. × 20 thick (3in sq. × $\frac{3}{4}$in thick)
8	Spigot	1	Steel	38 dia. × 55 long ($1\frac{1}{2}$in dia. × $2\frac{1}{4}$in long)
9	Washer plate	2	Steel	70 dia. × 3 thick ($2\frac{3}{4}$in dia × $\frac{1}{8}$in thick)
10	Warp post bar	2	Softwood	60 × 25 × 300 long ($2\frac{3}{8} \times 1 \times 12$in long)
11	Warp post	6	Ramin dowel	20 dia. × 125 long ($\frac{3}{4}$in dia. × 5in long)
12	Holding plate	4	Steel	60 × 65 × 1.6 thick ($2\frac{3}{8} \times 2\frac{1}{2} \times \frac{1}{16}$in thick)
13	Clamp bar	2	Softwood	60 × 25 × 310 long ($2\frac{3}{8} \times 1 \times 12\frac{1}{4}$in long)
14	Pin	1	Steel	5 dia. × 100 long ($\frac{3}{16}$in dia. × 4in long)
15	Screw, washer, wingnut	4	Steel	M6 Isometric × 65 long ($\frac{1}{4}$in Whitworth × $2\frac{1}{2}$in long)

in Fig. 20.3. At the bottom end, the steel shaft is fitted in a hole drilled in the centre of the footbars. Additional support is provided by two washer plates (9). Dimensional information on these is given in Fig. 20.4. One acts as a support underneath the footbar so the shaft cannot slip down, but the arrangement is also pinned diagonally (item 14) across the half joint to stop the shaft from coming out (*Fig. 20.1, section BB*).

At the top end the rotating drum rests on a thrust bearing arrangement. A steel spigot (8) is machined to fit tightly in the end of the shaft tube, with a bearing fitted onto the end of this. The tolerance should be such that the bearing needs gently knocking on, and is not loose. A woodturned cover (7) fits on the outside of the bearing, and when screw fixed centrally to the upper crossbar assembly, the drum will be held on the stand.

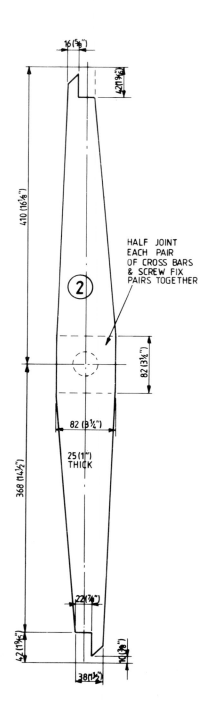

Fig. 20.2 Cross/bar dimensions

To make the bearing run smoothly, there must be a clearance between the side face of the inner bearing, and the underside of the crossbar assembly. The dimensions of the spigot (8), and the bearing cover (7) are given in Fig. 20.4. These are arranged for a nominal bearing size of 54mm (2$\frac{1}{4}$in) O.D. × 28mm (1$\frac{1}{8}$) I.D. × 10mm ($\frac{3}{8}$in) wide, but the dimensions can be amended to suit other sizes if required, depending upon what is available.

Warping posts/clamp bars Details of the warping posts and the clamp bars are given in Fig. 20.5. The warp post bar (10) is made from 60 × 25 × 300mm (2$\frac{3}{8}$ × 1 × 12in) long softwood, and has three 20mm ($\frac{3}{4}$in) diameter × 125mm (5in) long warp posts (11) glue fixed into these. The arrangement is also fitted with a pair of steel holding plates (12) which are screw fixed to the warp post bar. The clamp bar (13) is made from similar section wood to the warp post bar. These items are fixed to the drum uprights using M6 Isometric ($\frac{1}{4}$in Whitworth) clamp screws/wingnuts as described earlier.

USING THE WARPING MILL

A detailed description of using the individual warping posts and the warping frame was given in Chapter 14, and the method of using the warping mill is an extension of this, but in rotary form. There should, therefore, be no problems in using the warping mill, but if any do arise it is suggested that the instructions for the warping frame be restudied.

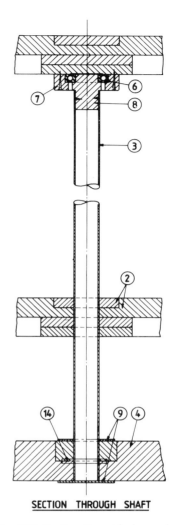

SECTION THROUGH SHAFT

Fig. 20.3 Section through drum shaft

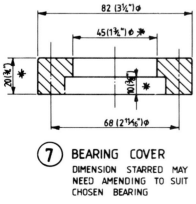

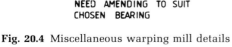

7 BEARING COVER
DIMENSION STARRED MAY NEED AMENDING TO SUIT CHOSEN BEARING

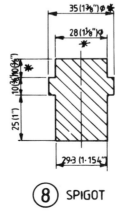

8 SPIGOT

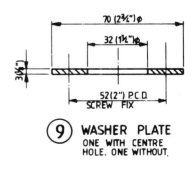

9 WASHER PLATE
ONE WITH CENTRE HOLE. ONE WITHOUT.

Fig. 20.4 Miscellaneous warping mill details

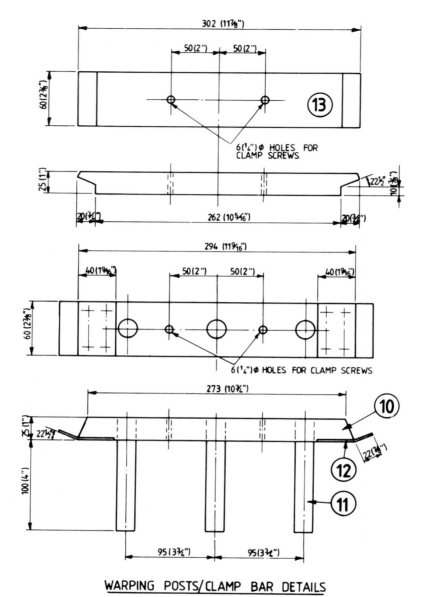

WARPING POSTS/CLAMP BAR DETAILS

Fig. 20.5 Warping post/clamp bar details

LIST OF SUPPLIERS

Exhibitions, information, slide collections

Crafts Council
12 Waterloo Place
London SW1Y 4AU
(01 930 4811)

Carding cloth

Critcheley, Sharp & Tetlow
Carclo House
Acre Street
Huddersfield HD3 3EB
(0484 654145)

Gears, sprockets and chain (Drum carder design)

Bond's 0 Euston Road Ltd
Arundel House
Rumbolds Hill
Midhurst
West Sussex GU29 9NE
(073081 3411/3424)

Heddles and reeds

Jones Textilities Ltd
Eclipse Mill
Eclipse Road
Feniscowles
Blackburn
Lancs BB2 5HA
(0254 22363)

T. Lund and Son Ltd
Argyll Mill
Bingley
Yorkshire BD16 4JW
(09766 2301)

Steel bar, tube and plate; 'Lubronze'^{TM} bearings, ball bearings and other miscellaneous metalwork

K.R. Whiston Ltd
New Mills
Stockport SK12 4PT
(0663 42028)

Spinning, weaving and textile courses

Styal Workshop
Quarry Bank Mill
Styal
Cheshire SK9 4LA
(0625 527468)

Woodturning and light woodwork machinery; also timber supply department including homegrown and imported hardwoods

Alan Holtham
The Old Stores Turnery
Wistaston Road
Willaston
Nantwich
Cheshire
(0270 67010)

Workshop plans; large A0 size working drawings of all designs in this book, also metalwork component packs for spinning wheels

David Bryant
4 Grassfield Way
Knutsford
Cheshire WA16 9AF
(0565 51681)

Spinning and weaving equipment; fleece, fibres and yarns; dyeing materials; books

Fibrecrafts
Style Cottage
Lower Eashing
Godalming
Surrey GU7 2QD
(04868 21853)

The Handweaver's Studio & Gallery Ltd
29 Haroldstone Road
London E17 7AN
(01 521 2281)

Frank Herring & Sons
27 High West Street
Dorchester
Dorset
(0305 64449)

Tynsell Handspinners
3 Chapel Brow
Tintwistle
Hyde
Cheshire SK14 7LB
(04574 5030)

BIBLIOGRAPHY

Spinning

Patricia Baines, *Spinning wheels: Spinners and Spinning*, Batsford

Eileen Chadwick, *The Craft of Hand Spinning*, Batsford

Elsie G. Davenport, *Your Handspinning*, Sylvan Press

Bette Hochberg, *Handspindles*, Bette & Bernard Hochberg

CIBA Review, Libraries only

British Sheep, The National Sheep Association

British Sheep Breeds, British Wool Marketing Board

Weaving

John Tovey, *Weavers and Pattern Drafting*, Batsford

Ann Sutton, Peter Collinwood & Geraldine St. Aubyne Hubbard, *The Craft of the Weaver*, BBC

Luther Hooper, *Handloom Weaving*, Pitman

Eric Broudy, *The Book of Looms*, Cassell

L.E. Simpson and M. Weir, *The Weaver's Craft*, Dryad Press

Ann Sutton and Pat Holtom, *Tablet Weaving*, Batsford

Dyeing

Hetty Wickens, *Natural Dyes for Spinners and Weavers*, Batsford

Jill Goodwin, *A Dyer's Manual*, Pelham

Elsie G. Davenport, *Your Yarn Dyeing*, Sylvan Press

Fibres

Marjorie A. Taylor, *Textile Properties*, Forbes Publications Ltd

Woodwork

Peter Child, *The Craftsman Woodturner*, G. Bell & Sons

W.C. Stevens & N. Turner, *Woodbending Handbook*, Forest Products Research Laboratory

R. Bruce Hoadley, *Understanding Wood*, Bell & Hyman

Dale Nish, *Creative Woodturning*, Stobart & Son Ltd

Ian Norbury, *Techniques of Creative Woodcarving*, Stobart & Son Ltd

C.H. Hayward, *The Complete book of Woodwork*

Journals

The Weavers Journal
Quarterly Journal of the Association of Guilds of Weavers, Spinners & Dyers
Federation of British Craft Societies
43 Earlham Street
London WC2H 9LD

Crafts
Crafts Advisory Committee
28 Haymarket
London SW1Y 45U

Practical Woodworking
IPC Magazines Ltd
King's Reach Tower
Stamford Street
London SE1 9LS

Shuttle, Spindle and Dyepot
998 Farmingham Avenue
West Hartford
CT.06107
USA

INDEX